Response to the Other

Response to the Other

Jews and Christians in an Age of Paganism
(The Greco–Roman World from 500 BCE–500 CE)

ROBERT P. VANDE KAPPELLE

WIPF & STOCK · Eugene, Oregon

RESPONSE TO THE OTHER
Jews and Christians in an Age of Paganism
(The Greco-Roman World from 500 BCE–500 CE)

Copyright © 2020 Robert P. Vande Kappelle. All rights reserved. Except for brief quotations in critical publications or reviews, no part of this book may be reproduced in any manner without prior written permission from the publisher. Write: Permissions, Wipf and Stock Publishers, 199 W. 8th Ave., Suite 3, Eugene, OR 97401.

Unless otherwise noted, Bible quotations are from the New Revised Standard Version of the Bible, copyright © 1989 by the Division of Christian Education of the National Council of the Churches of Christ in the United States of America. Used by permission.

Wipf & Stock
An Imprint of Wipf and Stock Publishers
199 W. 8th Ave., Suite 3
Eugene, OR 97401

www.wipfandstock.com

PAPERBACK ISBN: 978-1-7252-8574-3
HARDCOVER ISBN: 978-1-7252-8573-6
EBOOK ISBN: 978-1-7252-8575-0

Manufactured in the U.S.A. 10/16/20

All [is] changed, changed utterly:
A terrible beauty is born.
—William Butler Yeats

Contents

Preface   ix

PART I | THE PAGAN EXPERIENCE
Chapter 1   The Role of Religion in Antiquity   3
Chapter 2   The Role of Philosophy in Pagan Antiquity   13

PART II | THE JEWISH EXPERIENCE
Chapter 3   The Emergence of Monotheism   29
Chapter 4   Judaism in the Exilic Period   42
Chapter 5   Judaism in the Postexilic Period   54
Chapter 6   Judaism in the Hellenistic Period   72
Chapter 7   The Pagan-Jewish Debate   91

PART III | THE CHRISTIAN EXPERIENCE
Chapter 8   The Emergence of Christianity   111
Chapter 9   Early Christianities   127
Chapter 10   The Pagan-Christian Debate   145
Epilogue   161

Appendix: Chronological Timeline   169
Bibliography   173
Index   177

Preface

HUMAN BEINGS SEEK MEANING and purpose. To do so, we tell stories, stories about the past, which we call history, and stories about what will occur in the future, constructed from memory and imagination. History is not a subject we study, but one we live. History is our medium, as water is to fish and air to birds. Each of us acts today and hopes for tomorrow in light of experiences that have been woven into a life story. To be a self is to have a personal story. This is what defines one's uniqueness.

In large measure, this is also true of communities, especially those in which people are bound together primarily by shared experiences rather than by natural factors like blood and soil. National self-consciousness finds expression in the remembrance of events people have lived through that give them a sense of identity and destiny.

Until recent times, Western self-consciousness had been shaped by two great traditions, Greco-Roman tradition—primarily legal and cultural—and Judeo-Christian tradition—primarily religious and spiritual. Although Western civilization has compartmentalized and combined these traditions, the truth is that these traditions were once independent and all encompassing, equally cultural and political, legal and religious. In time, these separate streams mingled and merged, forming the single and ever-widening current that gave birth to modernity.

No period of antiquity is more informative and influential for current interreligious dialogue than the Greco-Roman period, the period from the time of Alexander the Great to the fall of the Roman empire in the fourth century CE. In this study, we expand those dates to include the period from the fall of Jerusalem in the sixth century BCE to the fall of Rome in the fifth century CE, essentially from 586 BCE to 476 CE. A story that begins with the literature attributed to the Hebrew prophet Isaiah and ends with the fall of the Roman empire is much too long to be covered in depth, whether historically, culturally, politically, or religiously. Our focus is on religion, particularly matters of identity shaped by cultural and theological interaction between Jews, Christians, and pagans.

While the timeframe for the Greco-Roman period begins with the pagan philosopher Plato and ends with Plotinus and Neoplatonism in the third and fourth centuries CE (see chapter 2), the focus for Judaism is on its interaction with pagan culture in the period roughly from the Babylonian Exile to the Fall of Jerusalem in the late first century CE (see chapters 3–7). The focus for Christianity is on its interaction with Judaism, its parent religion, as well as with Greek and Roman thought and culture, from the inception of Christianity in the first century until its cultural and political ascendency in the fourth century (see chapters 8–10). In these chapters we also examine the political treatment of Jews and Christians during the Hellenistic and Roman periods, concentrating on the interaction of pagan philosophers with Jewish and Christian groups and thinkers. The study opens with an essay on the role of religion in antiquity (see chapter 1) and concludes with an essay that contrasts the demise or decline of paganism and Judaism in antiquity with the ascendancy of Christianity (epilogue). The closing argument affirms that religious lives matter, not only in antiquity, but also in every age, and that Jewish, Christian, and pagan sensibilities must be appreciated, nurtured, and supported in our postmodern world, itself a revival of pagan sensibility.

Moving against the stream of religious exclusivism, this study does not seek to further the cause of one particular religious or non-religious movement, sect, or perspective, but rather to gain insight on how ancient pagans, Jews, and Christians interacted with one another. The results should help advance contemporary interreligious and intrareligious attempts at dialogue and cooperation, enabling people of differing and even opposing creeds and perspectives to set aside institutional, historical, cultural, and theological agendas in order to focus their energy on finding solutions to problems currently plaguing our planet, setting aside the suspicion, fault-finding, blaming, and condescension that blemish the postmodern sensibility.

Since our study involves paganism, it is important to define its meaning and usage, not in its common sense, as reference to one who is uncouth, counter-cultural, or simply non-Christian, but rather in its classical sense, as representing a polytheistic, nature-revering, religious perspective. In this respect, paganism is the ancestral religion of humanity. This ancient perspective, dominant in the Greco-Roman period, remains active in our world today, not only in its classical religious sense, but also in the pluralistic, permissive attitudes prevalent in contemporary anything-goes, popular mindsets characterizing postmodern Western culture. Most modern-day pagans, like their ancient counterparts, accept religious pluralism, while, unlike ancient pagans, themselves remaining agnostic or even atheistic.

The concept of paganism—together with labels such as heretic, apostate, and heathen—was created by proto-orthodox Christians[1] to define others, itself a process of self-definition. This sense of wariness of "the other" is also applicable to the term "Gentile," originally used disparagingly by Jews of non-Jews, but used more broadly today of outsiders to one's culture or religion.

As we think about the emergence and development of Judaism and Christianity in an alien world, we need to consider three topics: (1) the political changes that brought Jews under the power of a series of world empires; (2) the pressures on Jews to conform to the culture and customs of these dominant power; and (3) the efforts of Jews and their pagan and Christian contemporaries to find meaning in life and a sense of group identity in the midst of vast social and political changes.

As we consider the interaction between pagans, Jews, and Christians in the modern world, questions arise. For example, what does it mean to be pagan, Jewish, or Christian when pluralism receives social and political sanction, but when only certain types of particularism are accepted? Furthermore, what does it mean today to be Jewish and Christian in light of each tradition's belief that members belong to communities claiming a special relationship to God? Such factors influenced pagans, Jews, and Christians, not only in antiquity, but also in all times and places since.

Response to the Other is useful for individual or group study. Each chapter concludes with questions suitable for discussion or reflection. As you read this book, consider journaling as a way to learn and understand. As you reflect and write, be honest with your thoughts and hopes, without ignoring your fears. As questions arise, or if you need more information, don't hesitate to search the Internet, where information is only a click away, much of it reliable. In some cases, one search leads to another, and you are well on your way toward self-education, a lasting and valuable form of learning.

---

1. "Proto-orthodoxy" refers to those Christians eventually recognized by the dominant group of Christians as adhering to "right" or orthodox belief, that is, as conforming to the creeds developed at Nicaea (325 CE) and at subsequent ecumenical church councils.

PART I

The Pagan Experience

Chapter 1

The Role of Religion in Antiquity

THE FIRST HUMANS WERE animists; they were conscious that nature was spirit-infused. Their life was holistic; individuals and groups alike viewed the natural, social, and spiritual dimensions as profoundly integrated. Primal cultures—that is, tribes or communities having no scriptures, literate sources of guidance, or linear sense of history—represent primitive attempts to establish harmony with the powers such groups sensed directing human life. Spirituality, for primal peoples, means direct relationship between human beings and the deeper realm around and within them, which they view as more powerful and real than the realm they experience through the senses. While we cannot speak of primal religious systems in the singular, whether in Asia, Australia, Africa, or America, nonetheless, there are sufficient common or similar elements in these to speak of each region in a collective singular.

To understand primal cultures, a good place to begin is with their sense of embeddedness. This starts with the tribe, apart from which there is little independent identity. Through the tribe, individuals participate with nature in a unified order. Despite the cultural variety represented by these traditions, three common patterns are evident in their spirituality: (1) the solidarity of human beings with the natural world, (2) the centering of individual human existence in the social community, and (3) the reciprocity of the human spirit with the world of spirits transcending the human. Significantly, each of these holds together elements of reality that have undergone systematic alienation in Western culture.

In the Greco-Roman world, there were many religions, including Judaism and Christianity. In the Roman empire, religion was prominent in society, and virtually everyone was religious. It was rare for anyone to be atheistic. Pagans were clearly religious, as everyone accepted the existence of the gods. Not everyone worshiped the gods, but all accepted their existence. Religion was needed, people agreed, because they knew they were powerless over the forces of life that could harm them. As mortals, they knew they were limited in their ability, unable to control such things as drought, war, or disease. They knew there were matters even in their own personal lives that were beyond their control, such as whether their children would be healthy, their spouses remain loyal, or their crops grow. Religion was a way of getting what they couldn't provide for themselves. In other words, people needed someone more powerful than themselves, a role fulfilled by the gods.

Ancient religions were almost entirely polytheistic. Prior to the emergence of Christianity and Islam, the only exception was Judaism. Everyone else in the Roman world worshiped many gods, for their gods were not sovereign, omnipotent, or exclusive. Each god had a role, controlling some aspect of human life. There were national gods; gods of localities (each city had its own god); gods of places (such as of rivers, meadows, and forests); gods over every function (such as of one's home, of the pantry, and of the hearth; gods of crops, of healing and rain, of childbirth, and so forth).

Religion in the ancient world was a way of worshiping these forces, a way of currying favor with benevolent deities while avoiding offending their capricious nature. Worship involved the performance of cultic acts such as performing sacrifices on their behalf and offering prayers as a sign of humility and submission. The root of the word "cultic" in the sense of devotion comes from the Latin phrase *cultus deorum*, meaning "care of the gods." The gods, like humans, had needs, and devotees took care of the gods in order that the gods might take care of their needs. Worship, in this sense, was mutually beneficial. Humans felt the gods' needs could be met through sacrifices, preferably by offering animals or things that were grown, items valuable to humans as well. Sacrifices could be offered in one's home, preferably before one's meals, in the form of a libation poured out or as a burnt offering on a family altar. Larger or more elaborate sacrifices, such as that of animals, were conducted in public temples, many of these places of gathering and worship led by priests and other officials appointed by local authorities to serve as intermediaries with the gods.

Each locale and region had its religious festivals, which citizens and residents of communities sponsored for public well-being. Festivals often celebrated the birthdate of a god or commemorated beneficent deeds on the part of the local or national deity. Many of these festivals were sponsored by the state. In addition to state religions, each region and town had its own god, and it was common for each family to have a preferred god or goddess.

What is common to pagan religions is the absence of beliefs. Believing specific things about the gods was not significant to personal religion. What mattered was that the needs of the gods be met through cultic sacrifice and prayer. It was necessary that one believe in the existence of the gods, of course, and in the obligation of sacrifice, but beliefs about specific aspects of the gods, such as their nature, their demands, or what they wanted devotees to believe about them, these were private matters, unessential to worship and practice. Such things might be relevant to mythology—the stories about the gods—or matters for philosophers to discuss or debate, but they were irrelevant to personal religion.

As odd as it might seem to us, ancient Greek and Roman religions had no beliefs to affirm, theologies to embrace, or creeds to recite. When people went to the temples, they performed sacrifices. They did not recite creeds or confess theological beliefs. As a result, in all religions of the Greco-Roman age, there was no such thing as heresy or orthodoxy, because there was no insistence on right belief or criticism of wrong belief, only an emphasis on the cultic acts necessary to appease the gods. Interestingly, there were no ethical standards associated with these religions. Religions did not establish particular rules of morality. Although the gods were offended by such acts as patricide, they seemed unconcerned with misbehavior such as adultery or cheating on taxes. Such deeds did not disqualify one from worship. Even the gods were known to behave immorally or hypocritically. Such things mattered philosophically, but they were not issues that concerned the gods.

The one exception to matters of behavior and belief in the ancient world was Judaism. Judaism emphasized specific beliefs, such as belief in the one true God who called Israel to be his people and instructed them how to live in community and to worship him alone. However, Judaism was a minority religion, comprising about 7 percent of the population during the period of the Roman empire. Furthermore, the Jews did not condemn Gentiles for worshiping many gods. Their God had chosen them, and they in response had chosen to worship their God alone. Through much of their history to this point, the Jews were henotheists, worshiping one God among many. Others could choose to worship different gods, but God was the god they had chosen, and their loyalty and worship was to their God alone. This God had given them a scripture—the Torah—a set of sacred books with laws only they were obligated to keep. Greco-Roman religions did not have sacred books—they were not scripturally based, as were Judaism and Christianity.

Christianity began as a sect within Judaism. Unlike other religions, including Judaism, Christianity was, from the outset, a religion that emphasized belief. It stressed that Jews, along with all other unbelievers, needed to believe that Jesus was the Messiah, God's long-awaited redeemer who would save believers from their sins. We see this belief in Jesus as Redeemer already in the earliest Christian sources, the letters of Paul, written between twenty to thirty years after Jesus' death, well before the appearance of the first Gospels. In his letters, Paul indicates that Jesus is the fulfillment of the written scriptures of the Jews. For Paul, belief in Jesus is essential, the only way to be right with God.

From the beginning, then, Christianity was structured as a religion that de-emphasized cultic acts such as sacrifice and emphasized proper belief. Christians did not perform sacrifices to their God because they believed Jesus was the perfect and complete sacrifice. Their religion was based on accepting the sacrifice of Jesus on their behalf, rather than on performing sacrifices on his behalf. In this respect, Christianity was a religion of belief rather than of cultic act.

Moreover, unlike other religions of the Greek and Roman period, Christianity was exclusivistic. No other religion—perhaps excepting Judaism, although, as we shall see, ancient Judaism was not as exclusivistic as we might think—insisted that to worship their god, you could not worship other gods. Ancient religions were inclusivistic, accepting one another. If someone decided to worship a new god, such as when one moved to a new town and wished to adopt its deity, that didn't require giving up one's former god or gods. Many gods were believed to exist, all desiring worship. Christianity, however, claimed that the only way to be right with God was through belief in Jesus. This teaching made other religions wrong, and Christianity right. Faith or belief in Jesus made Christianity unique in the ancient world, its missionary consciousness contributing to its expansion and widespread growth.

This emphasis on belief also brought Christianity into contact with pagan philosophical schools prevalent in Greco-Roman culture. Many educated Christians, together with certain Hellenized Jews, engaged philosophically with their pagan counterparts, intellectualizing and mythologizing their belief system to make it more accessible, attractive, and compatible with philosophical tradition. The emphasis on exclusivism, however, exaggerated the need for proto-orthodox Christians to be correct in what they believed, adhering more literally to the developing apostolic tradition, refining what it meant to believe in Jesus. As a result, they felt they had to be precise about Jesus, who he was and what he taught, and what Christians needed to believe if they were to be right with God. If salvation depended upon belief, Christianity needed to clarify what had to be believed. As it turned out, different opinions emerged as to who Jesus was and what it meant to believe in him. Different theologies, christologies, and soteriologies developed and came to be embraced. Controversies ensued and soon creeds came into being, different Christian groups affirming different beliefs.

Each group needed its own authority for what it believed, and each claimed that its beliefs were rooted in the teachings of Jesus' apostles and, through them, to Jesus himself. In particular, each group stressed that its authority was based on its own sacred writings, allegedly produced by one or more apostles of Jesus. Distinct groups emerged, favoring certain writings over others.

THE PRIMACY OF SCRIPTURE IN JUDAISM AND CHRISTIANITY

The Christian idea of having written authority for beliefs about God is said to go back to Jesus, who, as a Jew, based his views on the sacred authority of the Hebrew scriptures. While there was not yet, in Jesus' day, a final canon of Jewish scriptures, there existed a widely accepted group of sacred writings based on the Torah, the five books of law attributed to Moses (Genesis, Exodus, Leviticus, Numbers, and Deuteronomy). Eventually there would be a set canon consisting of twenty-four books (or, as numbered in the Christian Old Testament, thirty-nine books), divided into three sections: *Torah* (Law, which includes the five books attributed to Moses), *Nebi'im* (Prophets, which includes the historical and prophetic books), and *Kethubim* (Writings, which includes the wisdom and poetic books of the Hebrew Bible).

By the start of the first century CE, when Christianity emerged, most Jews subscribed to the special authority of the Torah. Not all accepted the authority of the Prophets (for example the Sadducees did not), but most mainline Jews, including the Pharisees, certainly did. Jesus quoted from some of these books, as did Paul and other New Testament authors, so we can assume that all accepted them as authoritative. The third part, the Writings, was not yet completed in the first century, but one of its major components, the book of Psalms, was already in use in synagogue worship. Indeed, this book was so important that the third part of the Jewish canon could be referred to simply as "the Psalms." This usage is found in Luke's Gospel, from the late first century, which refers to "the Law of Moses, the Prophets, and the Psalms" (Luke 24:44).

It is no surprise that a faith firmly anchored in the sacred texts of its parent religion would develop scriptures of its own. Christians did develop their own scriptures, but not immediately. The first generation proclaimed its message almost exclusively by word of mouth and saw no pressing need to assemble its own sacred tradition, since it expected Christ to return shortly. As the expected return of Christ was delayed, and as the number of believers continued to expand, the need for written documents became manifest. With the passing of the first generation of Christians, the need arose to preserve those crucial stories and lessons that had given shape to their community; continuity and order were at stake.

Jesus, as a Jewish rabbi, accepted the authority of these sacred scriptures, and he interpreted them for his followers. In other words, Jesus based his teachings on the authority of a sacred text. In the Gospels, we find Jesus quoting from these scriptures as divinely revealed authority. For example, when a rich man asks him what he must do to inherit eternal life, Jesus replies, "Keep the commandments." When the young man asks him to be specific, Jesus begins naming them (see Matt. 19:16–19). By so doing, Jesus is stating that these commandments, based on scripture, are authoritative for determining how one can be in right standing with God. On another occasion, an expert in the Law comes to Jesus to ask him which commandment is most important, and Jesus responds by quoting scripture. He is not speaking from his own authority, but quoting passages from Leviticus 19 and Deuteronomy 6, accepting scripture as authoritative for how people should live.

It is important to note, however, that Jesus follows up his quotations with interpretation. For example, in Matthew's version of the Sermon on the Mount, Jesus cites scripture repeatedly, saying, "You have heard that it was said," but "I say to you," and then proceeds to give a unique interpretation of that scripture (see Matt. 5:21–48). This section, consisting of so-called antithetical sayings, contains not contradictions but rather interpretations of Hebrew Torah. While a literalist might say, "I have not broken the law against murder, adultery, or retaliation," Jesus would reply, "Let's look at the larger context of specific scriptures, and when we do, we realize that anger, insults, and lustful thoughts are on a continuum with laws against murder, adultery, and retaliation, and, in God's sight, their violation. Furthermore, let's look more closely at these laws and their intended meaning. God's laws don't represent lines in the sand. There is always failure and always room for growth and improvement. Therefore, if someone strikes you on the cheek, turn the other also. If someone asks for a favor, be generous by giving her twice as much as she requests. And if the law states, hate your enemy, I say love your enemies, and pray for those who persecute you. In all cases, prefer mercy to justice." Jesus, then, had scriptures that he believed make clear how one relates to God and others.

After his death, Jesus' followers continued to accept the Hebrew scriptures as authoritative, mostly in their Greek translation (known as the

Septuagint), which were read widely by Jews both in Palestine[1] and in the Diaspora,[2] since Hebrew was largely unknown at the time, replaced by Aramaic in Palestine and by Greek in the Hellenic world.

However, for their understanding of Jesus and the new relationship with God that he had taught, his followers began turning to new authorities. Belief was important to them, and since they were exclusivistic, they began by interpreting the Hebrew scriptures messianically and christologically, viewing Jesus as their fulfillment (see 2 Cor. 1:20). At the same time, they began taking the words of Jesus authoritatively, as authoritative as the Hebrew scriptures, a phenomenon already present in the New Testament. For example, in 1 Corinthians 7:10, Paul quotes a saying of Jesus as if it were scripture. "To the unmarried," Paul says, "I give this command—not I but the Lord—that the wife should not separate from her husband . . . and that the husband should not divorce his wife." Here Paul gives a commandment—on the par with scripture—given by Jesus, prohibiting divorce (Mark 10:11–12). Likewise, near the end of the first century, a follower of Paul cites two sayings about the importance of paying preachers and teachers, calling both "scriptures." The first, about not muzzling an ox while it is treading out the grain, comes from Deuteronomy 25:4. The second, "The laborer deserves to be paid," is a quotation from Jesus (Luke 10:7).

Soon thereafter, the writings of Jesus' apostles came to be seen as authoritative, on a part with scripture. The apostle Paul, for example, understood himself to be an authoritative spokesperson for the truth (Gal. 1:8–12). Paul's letters, written occasionally to specific congregations and individuals, were reverently saved and shared with Christians in other places. Shortly thereafter they began to assume the authority of scripture, at least among some Christians (2 Pet. 3:16). In fact, Paul's authority was becoming so significant that documents written by others were being ascribed to him (see 2 Thess. 2:2; also, the Pastoral Epistles and disputed letters like Hebrews, which some biblical versions attribute to Paul). Eventually other writings, such as the four canonical Gospels; the book of Acts; 1 and 2 Peter; 1, 2, and 3 John; Jude; and the book of Revelation, became viewed as authentic writings of the apostles or their associates, all said to derive from the initial community of Jesus and his immediate followers. In the next century a host of additional gospels, epistles, and apocalypses appeared, vying for authenticity. The author of Luke's Gospel openly admits that "many writers"

---

1. Scholars use this term in reference to the "Holy Land," the territories of Galilee, Judea, Samaria, and the Transjordan (the Jewish area east of the Jordan River) in Jesus' day.

2. This term refers to Jewish exiles living outside of Palestine, from biblical times to the present.

had preceded him in the attempt to "draw up an account of the things that have happened among us" (Luke 1:1).

This movement to consider apostolic writings as sacred authorities makes considerable sense, for Christianity is rooted in the life and teachings of Jesus. However, Jesus left no writing. If he had, they would have become Christian scripture. But since he did not do so, his apostles became the only link to Jesus. If later Christians wanted access to Jesus, they needed to go back through the apostles. This became necessary for each group within early Christianity, whether orthodox or heterodox.[3] Each group claimed its own Gospel or set of Gospels, and each group established its own claim to apostolic succession, tracing the teachings of its leaders back to the first followers of Jesus. This lead to a proliferation of writings in the second century alone, allegedly produced by the apostles themselves, but all pseudonymous, that is, forged in the name of an apostle or a group of apostles, some even attributed to female followers of Jesus such as Mary Magdalene.

By the third century, more than twenty gospels were in circulation, all claiming, like the Gospel of Peter or the Gospel of Philip, apostolic derivation. Notable among them was the Gospel of Thomas, consisting exclusively of isolated saying attributed to Jesus. The abundance of gospels was due mostly to the growth of gnostic sects within Christianity, especially in the second century. The vast majority of Gnostics were "dualists," believing that human beings were spiritual entities trapped in an evil material world, and that they could be freed, or saved, only through secret knowledge. They shared in common a tendency to produce texts that claimed to distill new revelation. It is no coincidence that the first canonical lists began to appear among orthodox scholars and theologians shortly after the emergence of gnostic sects.

The process that led to the formation of the Christian canon is complex but fascinating. The four Gospels now found in the New Testament, together with the other canonical writings, may have been produced by diverse, even antithetical communities, but all were viewed to be sufficiently orthodox to make the final cut. However, during the second, third, and fourth centuries, Christians continued to debate the acceptability of certain writings. The arguments centered on three criteria:

- *Apostolicity*: the book in question had to have derived from the initial community of Jesus and his disciples.

---

3. Instead of the pejorative term "heretical," it is better to call individuals or groups holding alternative views "heterodox," meaning "other belief."

- *Orthodoxy*; the book in question had to be valued as inspired and revelatory, that is, as derived directly from God and hence harmonious with the rest of the New Testament.
- *Catholicity*; the book in question had to be accepted and used by a wide range of communities, especially those considered authoritative or apostolic.

At first, a local church had only a few apostolic letters and perhaps one or two Gospels. During the course of the second century most churches came to possess and acknowledge a canon that included the present four Gospels, Acts, thirteen letters attributed to Paul, 1 Peter, and 1 John. Seven books still lacked general recognition: Hebrews, James, 2 Peter, 2 and 3 John, Jude, and Revelation. On the other hand, certain Christian writings, such as the first letter of Clement, the letter of Barnabas, the Shepherd of Hermas, and the Didache, were accepted as authoritative by several ecclesiastical writers, though rejected by the majority.

Paradoxically, Marcion, the second-century heretical Christian preacher, was responsible for the first canon of the New Testament. Unable to reconcile the Old Testament's portrayal of God as violent and vengeful with the New Testament's portrayal of God as good and loving, he created a restrictive canon that excluded all of the Old Testament and any Christian literature that had Jewish overtones. Marcion's teaching prompted a hearing before other clergy in Rome that resulted in his condemnation. Soon afterward, other church leaders began to form their own canon or list of approved books. The most famous of these is the Muratorian Canon, dated to the church at Rome circa 190. It included the four Gospels; the Acts of the Apostles; thirteen letters attributed to Paul; Jude; and 1 and 2 John, as well some books later excluded, including the Apocalypse of Peter and the Wisdom of Solomon. What is unusual about the latter is that despite being a Jewish work, written prior to the birth of Christianity (in the first century BCE), it is listed here as a Christian text.

Strangely, the development of a definitive canon of scripture took orthodox Christians nearly four centuries to complete. The earliest surviving list to include all twenty-seven books now known as the New Testament is from the year 367, appearing in an Easter letter written by Athanasius, bishop of Alexandria, to congregations in the eastern section of the church. In the west, the twenty-seven books of the New Testament were accepted at the subsequent councils of Hippo (393) and Carthage (397).

The process toward theological consensus fragmented Christianity, the mainstream declaring adherents of different beliefs heretics and apostates. In some cases, opponents of orthodox beliefs were exiled and banned, their careers destroyed; some were tortured, others merely ignored. Many conformed, but only through coercion. In the end, consensus was achieved, but only temporarily, too narrowly defined, and at too high a cost.

QUESTIONS FOR DISCUSSION AND REFLECTION

Select one or more of the following questions and write your answer(s) in a journal. If you are in a group study, be prepared to share your answers with those in the group.

1. In this chapter, what positive qualities describe ancient pagan beliefs and practices? Do you find these qualities attractive and applicable to your current life? If so, how, and why?

2. In antiquity, practically everyone was religious, something that doesn't seem to apply today. How did loss of faith (belief?) come about? Might it be more accurate to say that most people today continue to be inwardly religious, only in different ways? Explain your answer.

3. Except for primal or very traditional societies, modern humans have abandoned the ancient practice of sacrificing to the gods. Explain why this change occurred.

4. In pagan antiquity, what made Judaism distinct as a religion?

5. In pagan antiquity, what made Christianity distinct from Judaism?

6. In your estimation, should current Christians de-emphasize belief? If so, what should the new emphasis be?

7. What role did scripture play in early Christianity? Why? What role does it play in your religious life and practice today? Explain your answer.

8. Of those criteria used by Christians in finalizing their canonical process, which do you find most compelling? Explain your answer.

9. Assess the author's statement that canonical consensus came at too high a cost.

Chapter 2

The Role of Philosophy in Pagan Antiquity

IN ANTIQUITY, PHILOSOPHY WAS the deeper religion of most intelligent people. Its concepts provided thinkers—pagan, Jewish, and Christian—with an intellectual framework for expressing their ideas. At the beginning of the Hellenistic period we find six main schools—Platonism, Aristotelianism, Pythagoreanism, Cynicism, Epicureanism, and Stoicism, of which those of Plato and Aristotle soon lost ground, although the former in the Neoplatonism of Plotinus later became once again prominent. On the border between philosophy and religion was Pythagoreanism. Pythagoras of Samos (c. 570–c. 490 BCE) paid great attention to numbers. He gathered about himself a group of followers to whom he communicated secret symbols and metaphysical lore, including belief in the transmigration of souls. Members of the Pythagorean brotherhood were vegetarians and viewed the body as the seat of all impure passions. Ultimately, certain aspects of Pythagoreanism were adopted by various Gnostic systems of the early Christian period. Though Gnosticism took many different forms, a characteristic teaching of all Gnostics was the fundamental antithesis between the material and the spiritual universe. Only the spiritual element in humans could receive redemption, gained through a secret knowledge or *gnosis* concerning knowledge of God and of the origin and destiny of all living beings.

Pythagoreanism and Platonism (known as Middle Platonism) enjoyed a revival from the first century BCE, but the three schools that held the stage were the Cynic, Epicurean, and Stoic. The aim of all three may be summed up as the self-sufficiency of the individual and his or her indifference to external circumstances, although they differed in the forms by which they gave expression to this ideal.

The Cynics opposed conventional standards, defining virtue as the capacity to reduce one's desires to a minimum. The typical Cynic was the famous Diogenes of Sinope (c. 412–323 BCE), of whom many stories were told, including his reply to Alexander the Great who, when he asked what he could do for Diogenes, the latter replied, "Get out of my light!" By practicing extreme frugality, humans could learn to be independent of externals and thus attain true happiness. For Cynics, salvation lies in a return to nature. Later Cynics appeared as itinerant evangelists, bringing their teachings to common people. In their preaching and exhorting they developed the literary form known as diatribe. Though in modern usage the term became confined to denunciation, originally a diatribe was like a homily or sermon, and was characterized by a lively and vivid semi-conversational style.

Epicureanism has suffered from a misunderstanding of its ethical ideal. Epicurus (347–270 BCE) was a far greater person than the word "epicure" suggests. Epicurus distrusted the dialectic and metaphysics of idealists such as Plato. Suspicious of abstract terms, he appealed to people's common sense. Human wisdom lies in the pursuit of pleasure (by which he meant genuine happiness, not sensual enjoyment), and this entails avoiding excess of all kinds. Subject to later misinterpretations, Epicurus's concern was not on sensual pleasure, but on achieving serenity or impassiveness, even in the midst of adversity. The gods, if they exist, live in serene detachment and have nothing to do with human existence. Epicurus had been deeply impressed by the atomism of Democritus, and made it the foundation of his system. Since everything results by chance from a fortuitous combination of atoms, the body and soul are dissolved at death. There is no future for people to fear. Religion, and ideas of immortality, are false. Death brings a final dispersion of the atoms that constitute one's body and soul. Due to limited appeal, chiefly in scientific circles, Epicureanism had little influence on Judaism or Christianity.

The most successful and influential school was the Stoic (see the extended discussion below), which offered acceptable solutions both to the metaphysical and the practical problems of the age. Unlike Epicureanism, which tended to foster atheism and self-indulgence, Stoicism encouraged the development of religious and moral fiber. The universe, according to Stoics, was not meaningless, nor was humanity's place determined by blind fate. Pervading the whole of the material order is divine Reason, and the duty of humans is to live in accord with this Reason or "natural law." The soul is a divine spark or seed of the universal Reason; thanks to one's soul, a person can rise above adverse circumstances, and in the face of difficulties can maintain serenity (hence the modern usage of the word "stoical").

Stoicism was developed most fully by Posidonius of Apameia (c. 135–c. 51 BCE), the last truly original Greek thinker, who constructed a system combining Stoic and Platonic thought that would become the dominant philosophy of the later Hellenistic age. In later Stoicism, the original doctrine of God was modified in two directions: on the one hand, a greater measure of transcendence was allowed to God, while on the other hand, Posidonius admitted some hope of immortality, and least for the great and good. Admission of partial immortality opened the way for a more general hope, such as was offered by the mystery religions. Stoicism would also provide the vocabulary of the thought of Philo of Alexandria, the Jewish thinker who read the philosophy of Posidonius into the Old Testament. The ethical teachings of later Stoics, such as Seneca (a contemporary of Paul), Epictetus, and the Roman Emperor Marcus Aurelius, contain superb examples of moral wisdom. Since, however, there is no personal God, the Stoic creed, though noble and elevated, remained a philosophy and never made a religious appeal to the masses.

From the earliest days of Christianity, the attraction and interaction of Christian theologians with pagan philosophy was pervasive. On the one hand, Gentile Christian theologians recognized their deep indebtedness to their Jewish heritage, with its historical and this-worldly emphasis. On the other hand, they were profoundly attracted to what we might call a higher spirituality—the soul's desire for higher things—one found in the Hellenistic philosophical tradition, with its allegorical and vertical concerns.

However, if one had nothing but pure allegory and a vertical spirituality, one is a Gnostic, concerned with rejecting material things and becoming entirely spiritual. Such a stance implies rejection of the Jewish roots of Christianity. Thus, early intellectual Christians attempted to hold together both dimensions—the horizontal and the vertical—but to do so required a non-literal or allegorical reading of scripture.

When we examine the interaction between early Christians and pagans, we turn to philosophy, for ancient philosophy was a form of spirituality, by nature religious rather than anti-religious. While ancient philosophers were skeptical of religious mythology, they were very much interested in the deeper truths believed to underlie mythology. Hence, pagan philosophers criticized Christianity, not for its religious nature, but because they believed they offered a better or higher spirituality. They blamed Christians for being too Jewish, meaning overly materialistic, too invested in natural and earthly pursuits.

In antiquity, educated Christians viewed philosophy as essential to a good education, much as we view the study of science today. Hence, Christian scholars and theologians were attracted to philosophy, and could not avoid interacting with it. The central themes of ancient philosophy were wisdom and happiness, stemming from the overarching philosophical question, "what is happiness?" To be clear, the Greek word we translate as "happiness" did not mean joy or pleasure, as we think today. Rather, happiness meant something like "true success or true fulfillment in life," closer to what today we call "the meaning of life." So the question, "what is happiness?" couldn't be answered by assuming that happiness is what makes us feel good, or even what makes us feel healthy, because such qualities were seen as means to an end, rather than ends in themselves.

While there were certainly hedonists in antiquity, such philosophies were not attractive to ancient Christians. Rather, learned Christians pursued the most widely accepted view of happiness among ancient philosophers, shared by Stoics, Platonist, and Aristotelians, namely, that happiness consists in a life of wisdom. In their estimation, wisdom was valuable for its own sake. Wisdom was the goal of all other values in life, whether money, power, or health; for ancient philosophers, pagan and Christian alike, all cultural values were secondary to wisdom.

To become a person of wisdom required both knowledge and understanding. The majority of ancient Christians, particularly those rooted in early Christian orthodoxy, gave biblical answers to philosophical questions. To the question, "What is happiness?" such Christians answered, "everlasting life," which in the Bible is not confined to life after death, but rather something realized in the present as well as in the afterlife. According to the Gospel of John, "everlasting life" is to know God and Jesus Christ (17:3).

Thus, for early Christian philosophers, happiness was the goal of life, and happiness consisted of a certain kind of wisdom, viewed as "the wisdom of God in Jesus Christ." To possess this wisdom was to possess everlasting life, and in order to possess happiness, Jesus Christ was the wisdom Christians seek. In 1 Corinthians, Paul calls Jesus "the power of God and the wisdom of God" (1:24). Early Christians noted that the Old Testament book of Proverbs speaks of wisdom as being in the beginning with God (8:22–31), and they found the same teaching in the Gospel of John, where Jesus is called the Word with God in the beginning (1:1–5). Based on such correlation, early Christians naturally associated Jesus with God's eternal wisdom. For them, to know Christ was to know the wisdom of God, and to have happiness was to know Jesus Christ, the wisdom and power of God.

In this chapter we focus on four philosophical movements in the Greek world, all influenced by traditions stemming from Plato and Aristotle, who lived in the fifth and fourth centuries BCE. All four movements—Platonism, Stoicism, Hermeticism, and Neoplatonism—were pagan or secular. All influenced Christian thinkers, contributing to the development of early Christian orthodoxy.

PLATONISM

Human beings have always been fascinated with the universe, including their place in the order of things. Over time, they devised models of reality to help explain their experience and to guide their conduct. The ancient Greek philosophers were deeply interested in this endeavor, developing cosmological models to explain their understanding of reality. In the fifth century BCE, two pre-Socratics, Parmenides and Heraclitus, set the stage for later thinkers, arriving at diametrical conclusions about the universe. Parmenides, a monist, argued for the unity, permanence, and eternity of reality, declaring that all things in the universe are made of one thing, which he called Being. A rationalist, he arrived at his model of the universe through reason, rather than through the senses, which he distrusted. Heraclitus, an empiricist, focused on change and diversity in the universe. His observations led him to conclude that there is no permanence, for everything changes. As he put it, "no one steps into the same river twice." Unlike Parmenides, whose focus was on Being, Heraclitus was concerned with Becoming.

Two successors, Plato (427–347 BCE) and Aristotle (384–322), championed their concerns, developing comprehensive views of reality. Plato's model, the first grand synthesis, explained permanence and change dualistically. Plato posited two realms to reality, the Physical World, consisting of "particulars" (temporary things such as trees, horses, chairs, and triangles), which are always in flux, and the Ideal World, consisting of "universals" (ideals, essences, or "forms" such as treeness, horseness, chairness, and triangularity), which are eternal and unchanging. Concerned with permanence (Being), Plato viewed objects in the Physical World as copies of forms in the Ideal World.

In Plato's Ideal World, forms are related hierarchically, meaning there are lesser forms (such as treeness and triangularity), intermediate forms (such as beauty and justice), and a supreme form or highest ideal, which Plato called The Good. Using a mathematical model for reality, Plato ingeniously combined the views of Parmenides (Being) and Heraclitus (Becoming), creating a model that demonstrated the superiority of permanence over change.

For Plato, there are two kinds of being, nonmaterial and material. Nonmaterial reality, consisting of forms or essences in the Ideal World, he called "intelligible being," and he contrasted these with "sensible being." Both are perceptible, although not in the same manner. Some things are perceived by the senses, and some perceived only by the intellect. Intelligible things are absolute or unchanging, ranging from such things as mathematical truths to principles of virtue and ethics. They are perceptible only by the intellect. Sensible things, however, being material, are perceptible only through the senses.

To visualize a thing perceived by the intellect, imagine yourself in math class, learning about the Pythagorean theorem. Initially you don't understand it, until finally you say, "Aha, now I get it, now I see it!" What you see Plato called "intellectual vision," seeing not with the bodily eye but with the intellect. What you see, we might say, is an eternal nonmaterial truth, something called spiritual or divine truth. Such truths are not physical, yet physical things can be understood as made in the image of the intelligible form, such as a horse made in the image of "horseness," or a chair in the image of "chairness." If all horses or chairs were to disappear from earth, their ideal prototypes would still exist, for all such "forms" or "ideas" remain eternally in the Ideal World.

As Plato understood them, intelligible forms are not simply abstraction. Rather, they are more real than the sensible images we see with our physical eyes. Sensible things come and go—mere imitations, shadows, or reflections of their forms, which are unchanging and eternal and therefore truly real. For Plato, the eternal world is the real world, and it is nonmaterial. In this respect, Platonists give Christians a nonmaterial way of thinking of the soul and of God. For Plato, the soul (the intellect), originating in the eternal world, has intellectual vision, which is the highest form of reason. The soul is not like the body, material or sensible. Though the soul takes up no space and cannot be seen, nevertheless it is more real than the body, which is changing,

Plato, at one with his teacher Socrates, rejected the intellectual skepticism and moral relativism of his day, which was based on the teachings of Sophists, then the reigning school of Greek epistemology (way of knowing). Led by Protagoras, Gorgias, and Thrasymachus, Sophists traveled across Greece, questioning everything. Believing that humans could not know anything with certainty, they nevertheless viewed humans as the standard-bearers for truth, alone determining the standards for knowledge. Plato painted a rather unflattering picture of Sophists as having no genuine interest in discovering truth, trained only to win debates and make a point. Our word "sophistry," which describes the skill of using plausible but deceptive arguments, stems from Plato's critique. Protagoras appears to have limited knowledge to sense experience, which is relative and subjective because everyone's perceptions are different. Plato's harsh judgment reflects his disdain for Protagoras's famous dictum, "Man is the measure of all things." Gorgias rejected Protagoras's view that truth is relative and declared that truth does not exist. Thrasymachus took this radical skepticism to its conclusion, teaching that truth is opinion, and that individuals should seek their own self-interests by continually asserting their own wishes. It remained for Socrates, Plato, and Aristotle to probe the deeper questions of knowledge.

For these thinkers, humans can know certain things with certainty. Socrates and Plato argued that there are absolutes (norms, ideas, and ideals), and that they are knowable—not by experience or by opinion—but through reason. Truth refers to things that are knowable, discovered through reasoning, using what we call "the Socratic method," a process of dialogue and discussion that asks careful questions and proposes reasoned answers to discover truth. In Plato's estimation, the resultant truth is said to be certain because it is based on his theory of "recollection," that is, on the principle that eternal knowledge is originally within each soul, but is lost when it goes through the "River of Forgetfulness" prior to birth. Reason, these philosophers posited, is the function of the soul, itself a divine spark trapped in a material body.

A human being, in Plato's view, is a dualism of mind and body. The mind or soul is eternal, while the body exists merely as a temporary vehicle for the soul. When a person is born, according to this view, the soul, fallen from the eternal realm, is united for a lifetime to a body. However, at death the soul flees from its physical prison as a bird from its cage. The soul's true desire is to return to its heavenly abode, but before it can return, it is judged according to its moral conduct on earth and then experiences rebirth until it arrives at ultimate release, whence it makes its final ascent to the eternal realm from which it originated.

In his *Republic*, Plato used a famous image to describe the upward journey of the soul to the light of the sun by means of a gradual emancipation from the land of shadows in which we habitually dwell. He considered human beings to languish as prisoners in a cave, where they ignorantly suppose that reality consists of the shadows cast by the light of the fire on to the back wall of the cave. The soul has to be gradually turned around and led up into the light of the sun, to whose brilliant rays it is gradually accustomed. The sun in the allegory stands for the supreme idea, the idea of the Good, the source of reality and value to the rest of the universe.

In some of Plato's writings, such as the *Phaedrus* and the *Symposium*, the supreme form is that of beauty and not of goodness. The ascent to beauty is less a matter of being led upwards from shadows to reality, than of following the natural attraction each of us has for beauty and sublimating it, so that we pass from the love of beautiful physical objects, to love of beautiful actions, and thence to love of absolute beauty. For Plato, the contemplation of absolute beauty is the highest human ideal. It is impossible to exaggerate the influence of such language on the development of Christian thought and on the ensuing Christian mystical tradition.

Plato's approach to epistemology led him to conclude that the possibility of knowledge, and therefore of morality, is the preexistence of the soul, from which he inferred its immortality. These twin beliefs in the existence of "ideas" (universals, forms, or ideals) and the immortality of the soul were foundational to Plato's religious perspective.

Aristotle, Plato's pupil, seeking unity *in* the universe, disagreed with Plato's dualistic approach, using a biological model to explain how things can change, yet remain the same. Aristotle claimed there is only one reality—the physical—arguing that the form (essence) of a particular thing is within the object. Using analogies from nature such as how acorns become oak trees, he explained that what changes is the matter, but not the form of an object. Building on Heraclitus's principle of Becoming, Aristotle postulated that all things change, going from potentiality to actuality, and that all motion or change originates with a Prime Mover or a First Cause, which he called the Unmoved Mover. For Aristotle, this first cause of motion is itself unmoved, unchanged, and unalterable. Aristotle's "God," though eternal and perfectly fulfilled, is impersonal and therefore indifferent to the world, a "do-nothing God" occupied solely in self-contemplation.

Aristotle's interest spanned many disciplines (logic, biology, psychology, ethics, metaphysics, politics, and art), and while he contributed to each of these, perhaps his single most important achievement was his contribution to epistemology. By dividing human knowledge into several broad fields, he laid the foundation for much of Western philosophical and scientific study. Unlike the Sophists, Aristotle declared that knowledge consists of facts and the meaning of facts. Knowledge includes observation and theory, fact and interpretation. Everything in the universe is a combination of matter and form, potentiality and actuality. The closer things are to pure actuality, the more form they contain.

For Aristotle, at birth the mind begins as an empty tablet, but it contains the abilities of sensation and of thought. Reason, therefore, has the potential to obtain knowledge of reality, but it must do so thoroughly, probing and analyzing until it reaches its conclusions. Thus, by using reason, unaided by any higher power, humans can attain conclusions that are reliable and true.

STOICISM

The word "stoic" derives from the Greek word "*stoa*" or porch, the location in the Athenian *agora* (marketplace) where Zeno (c. 336–264) conducted his school. Unlike Plato, who in his distinction of sense and intellect was a dualist, Zeno and his followers were all materialist monists. For ancient philosophers, "materialism" meant that everything is composed of one or more of the four elements of life: earth, water, air, and fire—all physical things. Light, for example, is said to be made from fire—a material thing. If God is light, which many Stoics believed, then God is a material being. At death, the human soul, conceived as a "fiery breath," returns to God, its source.

The most perfect substance, permeating all things, is perfect reason, which is, in effect, God. The Stoics tolerated worship of popular Greek gods, although later Stoics allegorized the mythological, anthropomorphic Homeric deities. Stoics viewed the world as God's body, and they believed that God inhabits the universe as its soul, conceived as the Logos or divine principle of rationality. Viewing God as the soul of nature, they encouraged people to live in harmony with nature and one another. Unlike Platonists, Stoics believed the human soul to be corporeal, the noblest and purest form of matter. Because all humans possess reason—a spark of the divine—they are equal. After death, all souls, as all reality, return to God, as waves return to the sea.

However, it was by their ethical teaching rather than their metaphysics that the Stoics exerted influence. They were the most influential moral philosophers of the ancient world. For them the end of life is happiness, and this is achieved by "life according to nature." This entails acceptance of whatever happens and a severe restriction of desire to what lies within one's power, namely, one's moral choice. They were non-hedonists, believing that the road to wisdom is a life of virtue free from passion. Mastery of all disordered feelings and passions—*apatheia*—became for Stoics the necessary means for gaining true happiness. They emphasized the natural virtues, such as kindness, patience, courage, and honesty, recognizing that the virtue lay not in knowing how to act, but rather in living according to these ideas. A life of virtue is a life of excellence. One who lives in this manner is wise. A person of wisdom is not driven by passion (by emotion), but rather by reason, by the responsible will. To live this way is to be free. For later Alexandrian philosophers like the Jewish Philo and the Christian Clement, *apatheia* became a necessary stage in the acquisition of contemplation, the ultimate end of life.

To modern people, passion is generally viewed as a good thing, for it is what makes us human and not machines. Ancient people did not have machines, so their greatest fear was to lose control of their behavior, and therefore to act inhumanely, like a beast. In the ancient world, a good person lived according to reason, not passion—freely, not compulsively or obsessively.

HERMETICISM

In antiquity, a surprising number of pagans were attracted to a body of literature associated with the divine revealer named Hermes—the Greek messenger god who transmitted communications among the gods and between the gods and human beings—and the Egyptian god Thoth, the scribe of the gods. The basic features of Hermeticism are remarkably similar to the views of the Gnostics. According to Hermetists, our true self is our soul or intellect, which is a fragment of the divine. Our true existence is immaterial and unchanging. Nonetheless, we are imprisoned in this world of material change, dwelling in bodies that impede our knowledge of God and matters of eternal truth. Because we are divine in our true selves, God wants us to know him, much as God wants to know us. However, this communion between God and human beings cannot take place as long as we live in ignorance—thinking that the material world is our true home and that our bodies are our true selves.

The first step in overcoming ignorance is philosophical study. At some point, a Hermetic initiate must have an experience of enlightenment (a rebirth)—a vision of or contact with God. Through this rebirth, the Hermetist becomes divine and gains immortality. Obviously, he or she is still a composite of body and soul, still tied to this changing world of matter, but the initiate becomes a god by achieving *gnosis* of God and of the true divine self within.

NEOPLATONISM

The doctrine of the incomprehensibility of God, shared by Christians and pagans, is not a uniquely religious notion. Rather, it has a philosophical component, one developed by the great third century Neoplatonist philosopher Plotinus (205–270), an important thinker for Christian theologians of the fourth and fifth century who were defining the Christian doctrine of God.

Neoplatonism, an adaptation of the ideas of the Greek philosopher Plato, was formulated by Plotinus and his biographer Porphyry (c. 234–c. 305), and further developed by philosophers such as Iamblichus (c. 250–320) and Proclus (412–485). Like the Gnostics, Plotinus sought to achieve *gnosis* of the ultimate God, but unlike the Gnostics, this new approach emphasized humanity's essential connection to God rather than its state of alienation from God. Like the Gnostics, Plotinus believed in a remote and indefinable source of all that is, which he called The One. The One thinks, and his thinking produced the first emanation from him—Mind or Spirit. In turn, Mind generated Soul, the principle that gives life to all, so that all human souls participate in this divine Soul.

Thus, when Plotinus thought of God, he thought in terms of threes. While not speaking of God as personal, he conceived of God as three "hypostases" (a hypostasis is a complete individual being, entity, or divine principle),[1] using a term that profoundly influenced later Trinitarian Christians. The three hypostases represent a hierarchical or descending arrangement, remaining eternally distinct from each other. Yet despite this distinctness, reality is also a continuum, and for Plotinus there are no sharp lines drawn across the map of the universe. The clearest illustration of this conundrum is the doctrine that the soul is never totally fallen, but always remains in the realm of Mind above it.

In his *Timaeus*, Plato had asserted the existence of three primal principles, but he had established no relation among them. Plotinus organized them in a descending triad; from this divine triad, all of reality emanates. For Neoplatonism, it is not quite right to say that The One exists, for the One is Being itself. From The One, all being emanates through Mind and Soul, creating new levels of reality that are both lower than and contained in The One. Everything that exists is thus an emanation from or a level of reality within The One. Everything derives from The One, and everything is intended to return to The One. Plotinus agreed with the Gnostics that the material world is not true being, but he did not believe that there was a clear separation between spiritual reality and the material world. Rather, everything exists on a continuum.

Plotinus's idea of the divine Mind—his middle hypostasis—influenced Christianity directly. It is a Platonic element, related to intelligibility. As we noted earlier, intelligibility is what gives us "aha" moments, moments of awareness, recognition, or deep insight. These occurrences are said to be evidence of the divine Mind, which, according to Platonist philosophy, is full of "ideas." Prior to the use of "methodical doubt" by René Descartes in the seventeenth century, Western thinkers did not imagine themselves having autonomous ideas. All such thinkers thought Platonically, assuming

---

1. The later Latin tradition would substitute the word "*persona*," meaning person or mask, for the Greek hypostasis. A hypostasis can be a person, but also a cat, a tree, or anything that is complete in itself. A hand, however, is not a hypostasis, because it is a part of something greater, and not a complete individual entity.

that "ideas" are of divine origination. Prior to Descartes, the only being said to have "ideas" was the divine Mind or God. Ideas, for Plato, are eternally intelligible forms, essences, or truths such as beauty, justice, or goodness. For Plato and his intellectual descendants, to know these ideas was not to figure them out or arrive at them autonomously, but rather an intuitive way of seeing. When you "get it," you are experiencing intelligible truth, when time touches eternity. To think this way, to see intuitively, is to experience the divine Mind, which is all-seeing and all-knowing—pure intelligence perceiving intelligible truth.

This way of seeing, however, is not the highest level, for the highest way of seeing belongs only to The One. Our minds have many ideas, but The One, being singular, has no parts and thus, no manyness. One way to conceptualize this way of seeing is to imagine a geometric point—an abstract point without space or time, having no dimensions of depth, height, or width—and to consider all of geometry as driven by this simple, divisionless point. This is a metaphor, but it is how the concept of The One works in Neoplatonism. The One has no parts or division and yet is the source of all the manyness of life, including all of science, mathematics, and ethics—all things are said to be generated by The One.

According to Neoplatonism, the divine Mind is "eternally generated" by The One—and this is precisely the same vocabulary used by the bishops at the Council of Nicaea to speak of the Son, who is said to be eternally generated by the Father, begotten not once but eternally so. Hence, the begetting of the Son occurs outside of time, meaning that though he came into being, there was "never a time when he was not." For church theologians, the concept of eternal generation was incomprehensible—necessarily so. For Nicene theologians, because the Father is incomprehensible, so is the Son, the Father's equal in every respect.

Christianity differs from Neoplatonism at this crucial point, because for Plotinus, when The One generated or begot divine Mind, it begot a lesser entity, less than itself. Platonists thought hierarchically—what is generated is lower than its source. This is precisely what the Nicene doctrine of the Trinity denies. Though the Son's source is the Father, the Son is equal with the Father. Thus, while there was a hierarchy in the Neoplatonic triad, there would be no hierarchy in the Christian Trinitarian doctrine of God. However, like the Neoplatonist One, the Christian God is incomprehensible because God is not intelligible, having no structure or parts to understand. In Christianity, God would be understood as the geometric point that gives all things definition, yet is itself singular and therefore incomprehensible.

Though Plotinus viewed the body as distinct from the true self, he did not set the soul and the body in opposition. Instead, the unity and beauty of the body manifest the presence of the soul, which animates the body. Like the body, the material world is not a flawed imitation of the spiritual world but the visible manifestation of that world. The cosmos gets its unity and beauty from the divine Soul, which gives it life. As the body is not the true self but a manifestation of the true self, so, too, the true self is not independent of its source. Rather, the self consists of layers of being, and the deepest or most central layer remains in The One. Presently, humans exist both in heaven and on earth, both in The One and apart from it. Describing the One as Being, Plotinus also depicted the One as The Beautiful and The Good. Because everything that exists has its being from The One, all things are necessarily good because they participate in The One's Goodness and receive goodness from The One. Things vary in goodness based on their proximity to The One and on how deeply they participate in The One. Thus, evil does not exist as a separate reality, but is simply a deficit or privation of goodness.[2]

Because everything derives from the One, everything is intended to return to The One. Of course, humans are seldom conscious of their connection to The One. Rather than attending to their higher selves, they become distracted by lower, less real concerns. Instead, they should cultivate awareness of the true being at the center of their selves. Aware of this ignorance and distraction at the center of human existence, Plotinus focused on a program of return or ascent in five stages, not sharply distinct from each other. In practical terms, seekers should (1) study philosophy and (2) live disciplined lives that are not focused on material needs and concerns. Furthermore, they should (3) practice contemplation and try to heighten their awareness of the connection to The One. This practice of consciousness and (4) purification, which for Plotinus was the same as acquiring moral and spiritual virtues, leads (5) to fleeting experiences of true *gnosis*, times in which individuals see Beauty itself and stand fully within the divine. As in Hermeticism, humans need not wait for some future moment to return to The One—they can do so now. According to his biographer Porphyry, Plotinus achieved this unitive state four times in his life.

Neoplatonism influenced the thought and behavior of educated Christians for centuries, influencing not only its theology but helping mold the ensuing Christian mystic tradition.

---

2. The doctrine of evil as a privation of goodness became central to Augustine's doctrine of creation.

QUESTIONS FOR DISCUSSION AND REFLECTION

Select one or more of the following questions and write your answer(s) in a journal. If you are in a group study, be prepared to share your answers with those in the group.

1. Assess the influence of pagan philosophy on early Gentile Christianity.
2. Assess the merits of allegorical approaches to biblical interpretation.
3. Assess the author's statement that "ancient philosophy was a form of spirituality."
4. Briefly define the Greek concept of happiness and its relation to living wisely.
5. In your estimation, why were early Christians more attracted to Platonism than to Aristotelianism?
6. Why did ancient Jews and Christians find Stoicism attractive?
7. In your estimation, how did Plotinus influence the development of the Christian doctrine of the Trinity?
8. Assess Porphyry's program of the soul's return or ascent to the divine.

PART II

The Jewish Experience

Chapter 3

The Emergence of Monotheism

WHEN WE EXAMINE THE structuring theological elements in Jewish scripture, we discover that the basic symbolic vocabulary reflects on two axes of thought, one vertical and the other horizontal. The Bible links the people of God, whether Israel or the church, to the divine through the *vertical axis* of revelation, divine providence, and the created order. This stable relationship is supplemented with a *horizontal or historical axis*, characterized by loyalty to God, obedience to God's will, care for God's earth, and love for one another. This chapter investigates the vertical dimension by examining the development of the doctrine of God in the Old Testament.

The Bible addresses reality by speaking of God: "In the beginning . . . God created the heavens and the earth" (Gen. 1:1). Likewise, when the Bible speaks of humans, it describes them by speaking of God: "And God said, 'Let us make humans in our image'" (Gen. 1:26–27). When the secular world speaks of the divine-human relationship, it reverses the dynamic from divine to human initiative, inferring that because humans are meaning-seeking creatures, they are spiritual.

It is not my intention to offer a solution or even clarification on the distinctions between these perspectives, only to affirm that as soon as men and women became recognizably human, they responded to the human experience creatively, through religion and art. While there may have been some desire to propitiate powerful forces, these early faiths were more interested in expressing the wonder and mystery that seemed always to have been an essential component of the human experience. "Like art, religion has been an attempt to find meaning and value in life."[1]

WHICH GOD DO JEWS WORSHIP?

The principle figure in the Bible—as in life—is God, and the central theme of the Bible—as of all mystical experience—is the relationship between humans and God. But when Jews worship, which God do they worship? The radical God of Abraham, the capricious God of Sarah, the legalistic God of Moses, the nationalistic God of David, the exclusive God of Isaiah? How about Christians? Do they worship the surprising God of Mary, the empowering God of Peter, the sentimental God of Mary Magdalene, the loving God of Jesus; the mystical God of Paul, the orthodox God of Augustine, the impassive God of Aquinas, the gracious God of Luther, the sovereign God of Calvin, the puritanical God of Jonathan Edwards, the just God of Martin Luther King, the redeeming God of Billy Graham, or the progressive God of Pope Francis? While the explanations for the varied views of God held by these individuals are historical, linguistic, social, cultural, and theological, they are also biblical.

When Karen Armstrong, former Catholic nun and now leading religious scholar, began to research the history of the idea and experience of God in the three Abrahamic faiths (Judaism, Christianity, and Islam), she was surprised to discover that eminent monotheists in all three traditions, instead of advising devotees to wait for God to take the initiative in the relationship, encouraged them to create a sense of God for themselves. Some spiritual masters discouraged believers from expecting to experience God objectively, as a reality "out there," suggesting that in an important sense God was a product of the creative imagination. A few highly respected monotheists, thinking philosophically, denied God's existence while emphasizing that God was the most important reality in the cosmos.[2] While ideas like these boggle Western rationality, such paradox is central to authentic spirituality.

Historically speaking, there is no one unchanging idea in the word "God"; instead, the word contains an entire spectrum of meanings, some of them contradictory and even mutually exclusive. Indeed, the statement "I believe in God' has no objective meaning, but like any other statement only means something in context. The same is true of atheism. Since one cannot logically say for certain that there is no God, people dubbed atheists usually

---

1. Armstrong, *History of God*, xix.
2. Ibid, xx.

deny particular conceptions of the divine. Had the notion of God not had sufficient flexibility, it would not have survived to become one of the great human ideas.

THE EMERGENCE OF MONOTHEISM IN THE BIBLE

Building on the contributions of dialectical philosopher Georg Wilhelm Friedrich (1770–1831), evolutionary scientist Charles Darwin (1809–1882), and cultural anthropologists Sir Edward Tylor (1832–1917), critical religious scholars of the nineteenth century considered it axiomatic that all religions go through evolutionary stages of development, moving from the simple to the complex. When the distinguished German biblical scholar Julius Wellhausen (1844–1908) examined the stories and laws that appear in the Hebrew scriptures, he concluded that Israelite religion evolved in stages from primitive animism to ethical monotheism. Critical scholars have detected as many as five such stages:

- Animism—belief that all natural objects are inhabited by souls. While enhancing awareness, in this phase religious attention is directed toward appeasing these souls. Hints of this mindset have been found in the talking serpent of Genesis 3, in Abraham's conversing with angels by the oaks of Mamre in Genesis 18 (some scholars suggest that Abraham may have been communicating with spirits that inhabited the trees), in Jacob's visions of a heavenly ladder while sleeping on a stone pillow at Bethel (Genesis 28:18 suggests that the stone became a cult object), and in the commandment to make altars only from uncut stone (Exod. 20:25), supposedly to avoid offending the spirit within the stone.

- Totemism—a clan or group is represented by a particular animal; images (totems) of the animal are worshiped. Religious attention is focused on a few objects only. Critical scholars find an example of totemism in the making of a golden calf at Sinai (Exod. 32:4; cf. 1 Kgs. 12:28; Acts 7:41). Archaeological digs in Israel have unearthed a bronze bull in an ancient Israelite cultic site, dated from the period of the judges (c. 1200 BCE). This figurine, symbolizing power and fertility, apparently was associated with the worship of Yahweh (Israel's deity) as well as Baal (a deity of the neighboring Phoenicians).

- Polytheism—recognition of many higher powers, friendly and unfriendly. All are ranked higher than humans and have designated functions such as deities of war, love, agriculture, rain, and so forth.

Polytheism is alleged to exist in the Pentateuch, where the chief title for God is Elohim, a term with a plural ending.

- Henotheism (also called "monolatry")—one god in a certain territory. This transition stage between polytheism and monotheism, based on the idea that each tribe, clan, or nation is ruled by a single god, suggests there are as many gods as there are nations or ethnic groups. This is alleged to be evident in the Israelite religion, which pitted the national god, Yahweh, against the gods of surrounding nations such as Baal and Astarte, deities of the Phoenicians (Judg. 2:11–13), or Dagon, god of the Philistines (Judg. 16:23).

- Monotheism—belief in the existence of only one God. According to Wellhausen, this stage was not consistently reached until the period of Israel's classical prophets.

What are we to make of the presence of religious evolution in the Bible? Was there a time when the Israelites were animists, totemists, or polytheists? Of course, given what we know about biological, social, and cultural evolution, and if we go back far enough, say to the Paleolithic (Old Stone) Age, everyone's ancestors were animists to some extent. That, however, is not the question we are asking. Rather, what we want to know is, does the Bible provide evidence that at some point in biblical history, say during the patriarchal period, the Israelites were animistic, totemistic, or polytheistic?

Admittedly there are references to such beliefs and practices in patriarchal times, (otherwise how can one explain mention of "household gods" in Genesis 31:19–35?), but such references, including the examples given above about altars made out of unhewn stones, Jacob's stone pillow, and Abraham's residence by the oaks of Mamre, can be explained otherwise and need not be animistic. Nineteenth-century biblical scholars cautioned against applying an evolutionary straightjacket on cultural and religious history in general, including Israelite history. Some considered animistic references in the Bible to be holdovers from ancient times. However, before we fault Wellhausen for arguing that Israelite religion had developed in five stages, we must note that he also espoused Wilhelm Vatke's notion that Israelite religion had developed in three stages: the nature/fertility stage, the spiritual/ethical stage, and the priestly/legal stage.

We need to remember several things about Wellhausen's theory of evolutionary development, namely, that (1) according to the romantic ethos of the nineteenth century, which Wellhausen inherited, to label something as "primitive" is to hold it in esteem; and that (2) progress is not always one way or in a straight line. There is regress and decay. Wellhausen admired the passion of the eighth-century prophets but disparaged the legalism of the Deuteronomic Reform and the ritualism of the priestly writers. For Wellhausen, the religion of Israel ended in decay, preparing the way for the new religion of Christianity.

A helpful place to start our discussion of the theology of ancient Israel is 1 Kings 19, a passage that records a memorable experience of the prophet Elijah on Mount Sinai. Elijah (his name means "Yahweh is my God"), persecuted by Jezebel (King Ahab's Phoenician wife) for his faithfulness to Yahweh, has fled to Mount Sinai, where he prepares for an encounter with the divine: "Now there was a great wind, so strong that it was splitting mountains and breaking rocks in pieces before Yahweh, but Yahweh was not in the wind; and after the wind an earthquake, but Yahweh was not in the earthquake; and after the earthquake a fire, but Yahweh was not in the fire; and after the fire a sound of sheer silence" (1 Kgs. 19:11-12; these last few words are traditionally translated "a still small voice").

This passage is often cited as a landmark in the history of Israelite religion, for it reveals an emerging distinction between polytheism and monotheism. In polytheism, the forces of nature may be inhabited by the gods, or loosely equated with them. But in the monotheism that was developing in Israel, there would be greater distance between nature and divinity.

Most Jews and Christians, whether observant or not, know that at the heart of the Torah lies the famous faith statement known as the Shema: "Hear O Israel: The Lord is our God, the Lord alone" (Deut. 6:4). While that translation, taken from the NRSV, neither affirms nor denies monotheism (the Hebrew words can also be translated: "The Lord our God is one Lord," or "The Lord our God, the Lord is one," or "The Lord is our God, the Lord is one"), when Jews recite these words, they are clearly affirming monotheism. We cannot assume, however, that such was the original meaning.

In its biblical context, the statement "Hear O Israel" (Deut. 5:1; 6:4) is proclaimed with great urgency. While Moses is said to be speaking at a time when the memory of the Exodus is still fresh and the people are faced with the hazards of entering Canaan, it is quite clear that the author has in mind another audience. Deuteronomy is primarily being addressed to a later generation, to "those who are not here with us today" (29:14-15). Biblical scholars tell us that the Shema—and its view of God—does not come from the eleventh century BCE (the Mosaic period) but rather from the seventh century BCE (the reign of Josiah and the time of the classical prophet Jeremiah), suggesting that monotheism, as we know it today, emerged relatively late in Israelite history.

The idea that other gods exist, but are not to be worshiped, is evident in the Ten Commandments. Understood as having been given by God, they represent the very heart of the law of the Jews. They begin with an interesting statement: "I am the Lord your God, who brought you out of the land of Egypt, out of the house of slavery; you shall have no other gods before me" (Exod. 20:2). This text clearly presupposes the existence of other gods, but they are not to take precedence over the God of Israel. The text declares the God of Israel to be the only God for the Israelites, but it doesn't state that there are no other gods. Quite the contrary!

Eventually a strain of monotheism developed within ancient Israel, as is evident in Isaiah 45:5: "I am the Lord, and there is no other; besides me there is no god." However, this passage is dated to the sixth century BCE, long after Moses. Even as late as the time of Jesus, Jews who were monotheists also believed in divine beings such as angels and archangels, far more powerful than mortals. The basis for such beliefs is found in the Hebrew Bible, which mentions divine beings coming to earth as humans. Sometimes God also is said to appear on earth in human or some other form. Already in the book of Genesis Abraham is said to have an encounter with three "men"; later in the story, two are revealed to be angels and the third is God.

Another occurrence of an angel being identified as God occurs in Exodus 3, at the burning bush. Here Moses is addressed by the "angel of the Lord" (Exod. 3:2), who is later identified as "the Lord" (Yahweh) and as God ("Elohim"). Other passages of the Bible tell us that angels can be called sons of God (see Job 1:6) or God himself, and that they become human. Perhaps the most famous instance of a "man" identified as God is the story of Jacob's wrestling match at Bethel in Genesis 32:24-30. Jacob's divine adversary had to vanish before sunrise, but not before giving Jacob a new name.

Viewing the doctrine of God as having changed through Israelite history contradicts what we were taught in church. Most of us never envisioned God as having evolved at all. We learned that God was there in the beginning, fully formed, that God gave form to everything else, and that the earliest humans, including Adam and Eve, the patriarchs, Moses, and Israel's religious leaders, were monotheists from the start. But that's not really the story in the Bible, at least not the whole story. "If you read the Hebrew Bible carefully, it tells the story of a god in evolution, a god whose character changes radically from beginning to end."[3]

The view that Israelite religion reached monotheism only after a period of henotheism (exclusive devotion to one god without denying the existence of others) is now widely accepted by biblical scholars, including by many practicing Jews and Christians, but things get more controversial when you

---

3. Wright, *Evolution of God*, 101.

suggest that there was a long time when Yahweh was ensconced in an Israelite pantheon, working alongside other gods. Let's examine the archaeological, biblical, and historical evidence, starting with the biblical account of the conquest of Canaan, to see if we can determine why a gap exists between scholars and rank-and-file Christians, most of whom believe monotheism was revealed to Moses, who then created a theocracy based on monotheistic faith.

THE ARCHAEOLOGICAL EVIDENCE[4]

According to the book of Joshua, the Canaanites, wicked polytheists, were conquered by monotheistic Israelites, led by Joshua: "Joshua defeated the whole land, the hill country and the Negeb and the lowland and the slopes, and all their kings; he left none remaining, but utterly destroyed all that breathed, as the Lord God of Israel commanded" (Josh. 10:40). Religious conservatives rely on the findings of William Albright, sometimes called the founder of biblical archaeology, for support of this scenario. In his book *From the Stone Age to Christianity*, published in 1940, Albright affirmed that artifacts unearthed in Palestine (today's nation of Israel) paint a clear picture: Israelites had marched into Canaan from Egypt and swiftly destroyed and occupied Canaanite towns, rapidly replacing indigenous paganism with a radically different Yahwism. In his estimation, archaeological excavations showed an abrupt break between the Canaanite culture first encountered by the Israelites and the culture they built to replace it. Albright was a devout Christian, something that clearly impacted his findings. His views now lack foundation.

Recent decades of painstaking excavation and scientific archaeological research in the region supposedly conquered by the Israelites fail to provide evidence of a violent conquest by the Israelites. There isn't even much evidence to support a competing theory, that of a gradual, more peaceful influx of desert nomads gradually displacing Canaanites. While biblical archaeologists disagree about many things, there is now consensus that the Israelites who first settled in the highlands of Canaan were not foreign invaders but rather that they were Canaanites all along.

In the twelfth century BCE, as the Bronze Age was giving way to the Iron Age, there was political and economic disruption across the Middle East. Amid this chaos, new settlements, clearly Israelite, arose in Canaan. In all likelihood, the Israelites emerged from a particular line of Canaanites, a group which may have absorbed exiles from Egypt. One of these early Israelite settlements yielded an artifact that illustrates the cultural continuity

---

4. This segment is adapted from Wright, ibid., 106–9.

between Israel and Canaan. The artifact is a small figurine of a bronze bull, exactly the kind of "Canaanite" idol that the Bible condemns.

In addition to figurines of Baal, recent archaeological digs in Israel have unearthed in ancient Israelite settings testimony of extensive devotion to Asherah, the Canaanite goddess of fertility and the wife of El. In the late twentieth century archaeologists discovered inscriptions, dating to around 800 BCE, at two different Israelite sites, one in the northern Sinai and another near Hebron in Judah. Both inscriptions invoke blessings "by Yahweh and his Asherah." In both cases the implication is that Asherah is a consort of Yahweh. The word "his" puts a suggestive spin, corroborated by a passages in 2 Kings 23:6, reporting that near the end of the seventh century (around 620 BCE), Asherah was worshiped in Yahweh's temple in Jerusalem.

As one would expect, there are numerous references to Asherah in the Bible, all disparaging. Her symbol was a sacred pole in a grove of trees near an altar (1 Kgs. 16:33; 2 Kgs. 21:3). The biblical writings regularly command destruction of these symbols (Deut. 7:5; 12:3; 16:21). A crucial development in the evolution of monotheism occurred when a priest who didn't favor polytheism "brought out the image of Asherah from the house of the Lord, outside Jerusalem, to the Wadi Kidron, burned it at the Wadi Kidron, beat it to dust and threw the dust of it upon the graves of the common people" (2 Kgs. 23:6). These passages attest to the pervasive polytheistic practices of the Israelites, late in the prophetic period; the fate of monotheism lay in the balance.

Such finds would not have surprised William Albright, for the Bible indicates that the Israelites occasionally worshiped idols. But the biblical story views such episodes as lapses in monotheism, a belief system brought to Canaan by Moses. However, few biblical scholars today agree with this assessment. They do not view biblical accounts of Moses to be historically reliable. Rather these stories are believed to have been recorded centuries after the events they describe, and then further redacted later by monotheists who wished to give their theology greater authority.

Increasingly it is suspected that an early pure Yahwism may never have existed except among a small minority of Yahweh devotees, or perhaps only in the minds of later revisionists such as the Deuteronomistic historians. The evidence seems to point to later Yahwism having emerged out of a greater Canaanite religion or out of a Yahwism indistinguishable from the Canaanite religion.

HOW YAHWEH BECAME YAHWEH[5]

From an objective standpoint, there is no reason to assume that the advent of Israelite monotheism took place anywhere other than Canaan, after centuries of immersion in Canaanite culture. It is also possible that Yahweh, who in the Bible expends so much effort denouncing Canaanite gods, actually started as a Canaanite deity.

Such a hypothesis is helpful because it addresses numerous problems in the biblical text, including (a) references to God speaking in the plural (see Gen. 1:26-27; 3:22; 11:7. This use of the first-person plural by God, in both the P and J sources, seems to indicate that this language was originally part of the Israelites' tradition); (b) references to the "divine council" (Ps. 82:1. Traditional explanations suggest that this reference is to angels, the heavenly host, or other supernatural beings, but Psalm 82:1 and 6 refer to "gods," and none of the above qualify as gods); and (c) the many titles for Yahweh in the Bible that include the word El:

- Elohim ("God"; "gods")
- El Elyon ("God Most High"; "Exalted One")
- El Shaddai ("God Almighty"; "God of the Mountain")
- El Olam ("God of Eternity"; "The Everlasting God)
- El Roi ("God of Vision or Divining"; "God Who Sees")
- El Berith ("God of the Covenant")

Of these, the phrase El Shaddai is especially intriguing, for its meaning remains unclear; it seems to refer to mountains, not omnipotence. This name probably refers to El's localization in a mountainous region or to his theophany in mountain storms (cf. the "thunder and lightning" associated with the Sinai theophany, Exodus 19:16, and the "wind, earthquake, and fire in 1 Kings 19:11-12). In the time of the patriarchs the deity was identified with the storm god Hadad, often known as Baal among the Canaanites. After the patriarchal period, the original meaning of "Shaddai" was eclipsed, and the name occasionally was used as a synonym for "Yahweh." The author of Job favors this name, for it expressed the majesty and omnipotence of deity. The Septuagint renders "Shaddai" in the book of Job as Kurios ("Lord") or Pantocrator ("Almighty"), expressing aspects of God attractive to later Jews and Christians.

While El is the generic Semitic name for "God" or "deity," it was also the name for the Canaanite high god. "Given that the Canaanite El appears

5. Ibid., 110-15.

on the historical record before the Israelite god Yahweh, it is tempting to conclude that Yahweh in some way emerged from El, and may even have started life as a renamed version of El."[6] For instance, there are a few times in the Bible when the term El applied to Yahweh seems to be a proper noun. According to Genesis 33:20, Jacob "erected an altar and called it El-Elohe-Israel." This concept could be translated as "god, the god of Israel," but uncapitalized it wouldn't make much sense. Some English translations of Genesis render the expression as "El, God of Israel." Perhaps an even closer link between Israelite religion and El can be found in the word "Israel," which ends in "el" and means "El does battle," "El contends," or "El perseveres." In ancient times names were often inspired by gods, and names ending in "el" typically referred to the god El.

For present purposes, of interest is the way "El Shaddai" is used in Exodus 6:3, in a conversation between Moses and God. God says: "I am Yahweh. I appeared to Abraham, to Isaac, and to Jacob as El Shaddai, but by my name Yahweh I did not make myself known to them." Here even Yahweh claims to have started life in Canaan with the name El.

If you were crafting a history of your god, would you add such an odd twist, saying that he used to go by another name? Wouldn't such an oddity fit better if one were trying to convince two religious groups—one worshiping a god called Yahweh and another a god called El—that they actually worship the same god? This is precisely the suggestion of the Documentary Hypothesis, that at some point in Israelite history there were two geographically distinct traditions to reconcile, one worshiping a god named El (the E author lived in the north, closer to the heartland of El worship) and one worshiping a god named Yahweh (the J author lived in the south, in part of Israel known as Judah).

Certainly the Bible holds hints of once separate groups having united. It describes Israel at the end of the second millennium BCE, before it evolved into a monarchical state, as a confederation of twelve tribes. The merging of Israel's tribes is also reflected in the patriarchal story: Abraham begat Isaac, who begat Jacob. Few scholars consider this lineage accurate, but most think it significant.

The idea that Israel coalesced near or in the region of El worship and only adopted Yahweh later, while absorbing tribes from the south, gains support from the famous Merneptah Stele, an ancient Egyptian stone inscription from 1219 BCE, on which the name "Israel" first appears historically. The word clearly refers to a people, not a place, but the people seem to have been Canaanites. The stele does not mention Yahweh; its only possible allusion to

6. Ibid., 111.

any god is the "el" in Israel. And centuries would pass before a text would mention both Israel and "Yhwh" (the ancient spelling of Yahweh, before Semitic languages were written with vowels). Intriguingly, there are separate Egyptian references to "Yhw" even earlier than that first reference to Israel, but here "Yhw" seems to be a place, not a god. And that place "seems to have been somewhere around Edom, in southern Canaan, which makes sense if a Yahweh-worshiping people from the south eventually merged with an El-worshiping people to the north."[7] As the name Israel indicates, over time a group of Israelites transformed the concept "El the warrior" to Yahweh the warrior, styling itself nationally after this deity. At first Yahweh came to be regarded as Israel's God and only long afterwards as the God of the universe.

Most of us grew up hearing stories about Elijah, a classic Israelite prophet who defended monotheism without compromise in his conflict with Jezebel and the prophets of Baal, but even this great hero cannot be considered a monotheist, since he advocated monolatry rather than true monotheism. He didn't necessarily deny Baal's existence (the monotheistic position), just that Baal was not worthy of Israelite worship. The first "effective monotheist" seems to have been the prophet Amos, although later classical prophets developed his ideas further. It took an event and a person to develop monotheistic belief most thoroughly, an event known as the Babylonian Exile and an unknown prophet called Second Isaiah. It was this event, called "the furnace of adversity" (Isa. 48:10), that led to the monotheistic standard the masses would accept.

Two themes catapulted Second Isaiah to popularity, first within Judaism and later in Christianity. The first theme is that God alone is the God of the whole earth: "I am the Lord, and there is no other; beside me there is no god" (Isa. 45:5); "I am the Lord, who made all things, who alone stretched out the heavens, who by myself spread out the earth" (Isa. 44:24). Biblical scholars cite Second Isaiah as a landmark, and deservedly so. Finally, after centuries of monolatry, monotheistic declarations come with clarity and force. The second theme, that God will "bring forth justice to the nations," gets as much attention as monotheism. What kind of God is this God? What is God's stance toward the world? The answer is inspiring: God is universal not only in power but also in concern, and this gives God's people a momentous mission: "I will give you as a light to the nations, that my salvation may reach to the end of the earth" (Isa. 49:6). What this mission means for the world is discussed in chapters 4–7.

---

7. Ibid, 114.

CONCLUSION

While the cult of Yahweh is the principle concern of the Old Testament, it may not have been the principle religious concern of the Israelites. The common masses participated in syncretistic beliefs and practices throughout the pre-exilic period, while a small minority were monolatrists, belonging to what scholars call the "Yahweh alone" movement. This minority wrote the biblical texts and projected their beliefs into the distant past to give the impression their monotheism was the norm from which Israelites deviated.

In the early 1970s Morton Smith became the first biblical scholar to propose seriously that the Yahwism-alone movement was a minority religio-political movement in the pre-exilic period, in opposition to the royal cult and all popular or familial forms of religion. Smith traced the movement's development through five stages:

1. During the pre-monarchic and monarchic periods, Israel shared the common religious perspective of the ancient Near East. Each region had a national deity and Yahweh was the national god of Israel. Properly speaking, Yahweh was the deity of the dynastic rulers in Judah and Israel (his status was like that of Chemosh in Moab or Milcom in Ammon. Perhaps a few elements within Israel had a proclivity to worship one universal god, but their impact was minimal).

2. From the time of David (1000 BCE), the court of Judah may have been responsible for popularizing the worship of Yahweh among the masses.

3. In the northern nation of Israel, a move toward monotheism began with the Omride conflict (850–840), when Jezebel persecuted and killed Yahwistic prophets. However, the overthrow of the Omrides (kings Omri and Ahab) resulted from their foreign connections rather than from a desire to elevate Yahweh monotheistically.

4. Classical prophets and the Deuteronomic Reform movement brought the message of practical monotheism to the masses. Amos and Hosea were forerunners among the prophets in 750 BCE. Despite attempts at reform (probably more political than religious) by kings Hezekiah (c. 700 BCE) and Josiah (621 BCE), by 580 BCE monotheism appears to have been in the minority once again.

5. In the exilic and post-exilic eras the people became monotheists, for by then people living under foreign rule and influence had to make a clear decision about participating in those cults. Restraint in the fact of such pressure makes people true monotheists.

The constant biblical rhetoric against syncretism and idolatry should not be seen as evidence of monotheism, but rather as admission that pure Yahwism was in the minority. During the pre-exilic period most Israelites were polytheists, worshiping Yahweh along other gods, and they saw this as perfectly acceptable. Initially, the elevation of Yahweh for exclusive veneration was an act of nationalistic expression, as one might find in a time of crisis. Ultimately, in the post-exilic era, priestly laws separated the Jews from others and encouraged pure monotheism.

QUESTIONS FOR DISCUSSION AND REFLECTION

Select one or more of the following questions and write your answer(s) in a journal. If you are in a group study, be prepared to share your answers with those in the group.

1. Is your understanding of spirituality dependent upon human or divine initiative? Explain the difference.

2. When you worship, which God do you worship? The God of Moses or of Jesus? The God of Aquinas or of Luther? The God of Martha or of Mary? The God of Jonathan Edwards or of Martin Luther King? Explain your answer.

3. Assess the merits of the notion that Israelite religion evolved through distinct stages in its understanding of God. Can we square this concept with the popular notion among conservative Jews and Christians that ancestors of their faith such as Abraham and Moses were monotheists, having ideas of God received through divine revelation rather than through a human process of understanding and discovery? Explain your answer.

4. Assess the merits of the statement, "If you read the Hebrew Bible carefully, it tells the story of a god in evolution, a god whose character changes radically form beginning to end."

5. In your estimation, do the Ten Commandments reflect the perspective known as henotheism or that of monotheism? Explain your answer.

6. If you were to accept the conclusions of most biblical scholars that the Israelites were Canaanites in origin rather than foreign invaders, would this change your views of biblical authority? Explain your answer.

7. Assess the merits of the notion that the various biblical names and titles for God reflect polytheistic rather than monotheistic understandings of God. Were the first Israelites pagan? Explain your answer.

Chapter 4

Judaism in the Exilic Period

JUDAISM IS SAID TO have emerged during the Babylonian Exile. Prior to that time, going back to the United Monarchy under kings David and Solomon, Israel had been a monarchical state. The biblical books of Samuel and 1 Kings narrate how Israel was transformed from a loose confederation of tribes into a nation with a dynastic monarchy and a permanent temple in Jerusalem. David's rule marked the beginning of "royal theology" in Israel, the view that God had established a special covenant with David, promising to establish David's throne securely through all generations (2 Sam. 7:1–17). Royal theology sets forth the ideology of theocratic kingship, merging politics with religion, the building of a palace with the erection of a temple, a fusion achieved in Jerusalem by Solomon prior to 900 BCE.

After Solomon's death in 922, his empire split into two kingdoms, southern Judah and northern Israel. While Judah kept the capital of Jerusalem with its temple, the kings of Israel retreated to the northern city of Samaria. With their control of the strategic pass of Megiddo, they were more cosmopolitan and more inclined to take an interest in other cultures and religions than were the more introverted rulers of Judah. The ten northern tribes did not favor a hereditary principle, for though Judah was ruled throughout her history by one dynasty, no royal line managed to maintain itself for more than a couple of generations in the north.

The Northern Kingdom fell to the Assyrians in 722 BCE, following a lengthy siege. In accordance with Assyrian policy, inhabitants of Israel were deported and captives from elsewhere were relocated there. During this time many refugees migrated south and settled in Judah, which survived the onslaught through diplomacy, the payment of tribute, urban fortification, and, according to the biblical record, through divine assistance (see Isa. 37:33–35). It was only a matter of time before its demise would come as well.

During the last two decades of its history, the kingdom of Judah was caught in a power struggle between imperial Egypt and Babylon, each striving to fill the power vacuum left by Assyria, whose capital at Nineveh had fallen to the Babylonians in 612 BCE. Josiah, the last great king of Judah, had died in 609, killed while attempting to prevent Egypt from bolstering the declining Assyrian empire in its struggle with Babylon. Jeremiah the prophet, viewing Babylon as a tool of God's power, was accused of being a traitor and condemned to a dungeon. In 587 the Babylonian king Nebuchadrezzar (Nebuchadnezzar) attacked and destroyed Jerusalem and its temple, deporting many of its inhabitants to Babylon.

After more than a century as vassal to Assyria, the Southern Kingdom fell to the Babylonians, marking the start of the Babylonian Exile. Actually, the first deportation of exiles had taken place earlier, in 597, when Nebuchadrezzar launched his first attack on Judah, laying siege to Jerusalem and taking captive Jehoiachin—a grandson of Josiah and the newly crowned eighteen-year-old king of Judah—the queen mother, and a large number of the royal establishment, some ten thousand people in all (2 Kgs. 24:12, 14). In place of Jehoiachin, Nebuchadrezzar installed his uncle, Zedekiah, as king.

Zedekiah's reign lasted eleven years. At first Zedekiah was a loyal vassal of the Babylonians, but around 590, with the support of neighboring states, he stopped paying tribute and took the side of pro-Egyptian sympathizers in his court. The Babylonians retaliated with a full attack against the cities of Judah, ending with a lengthy siege of Jerusalem. The city was eventually captured and burned, the temple plundered and destroyed, and Zedekiah was taken prisoner. At Nebuchadrezzar's command, Zedekiah's sons were executed. Then Zedekiah was blinded, put in chains, and sent to Babylon. Thus ended the dynasty established by David, founded upon an unconditional covenant of royal theology instituted by God and believed to last forever (2 Sam. 7:16; Ps. 89:4, 29, 36–37). Gone, too, was the Solomonic temple, and with it the sense of unconditional divine protection. Much of Jerusalem's population was also taken to Babylon, joining Ezekiel, Daniel, and others who had been deported in 597. Some Jews were allowed to remain in Judah, however, and tension increased between them, the Babylonian exiles, and neighboring peoples such as the Samaritans to the north, the Ammonites of the Transjordan to the east, and the Edomites to the south.

Among the remaining Jews in Judah was the prophet Jeremiah who, while believing that the future of Judaism lay with the exiles in Babylon, did not join them when given the chance. The final phase of Jeremiah's career, as recorded by his scribe Baruch in Jeremiah 40-44, was interwoven with the troubles that accompanied the remnant left in the ruins of Judah. Following the assassination of Gedaliah, the first Persian governor of Judah, by a Jewish patriot, the Judean military chiefs fled to Egypt for refuge, taking with them the unwilling Jeremiah and Baruch. The subsequent deportation of additional Judeans by the Babylonians in 582, mentioned in Jeremiah 52:30, may been a reprisal for this short-term revolt.

We last hear of Jeremiah in Egypt, denouncing the colony of exiles for reverting to the worship of the Queen of Heaven, Ishtar. The exiles justified themselves by recollecting that in the days before Jerusalem's fall, when they worshiped the mother goddess in Judah, they had plenty of food and experienced prosperity (Jer. 44:17-18). Jeremiah, however, insisted on monotheism, confident in God's promises to Israel, despite the ambiguities of historical experience.

VERUS ISRAEL (TRUE ISRAEL)

According to the Jewish scholar Yehezkel Kaufmann, "The Fall of Jerusalem is the great watershed of the history of Israelite religion. The life of the people of Israel came to an end; the history of Judaism began." How would the survivors react? The book of Jeremiah reveals the tension between the exiles in Babylon and those who remained in Judah. This tension would grow in the days ahead, each group claiming to be the "true Israel."

The prophets Jeremiah and Ezekiel were contemporaries, both deeply affected by the deportations of Judeans to Babylon. With his emigration to Egypt in the late 580s, Jeremiah was in Judah during the destruction of Jerusalem, witnessing the catastrophe personally, while Ezekiel had been taken to Babylon in the first deportation and learned of Jerusalem's destruction secondhand.

The book attributed to Ezekiel is the most unusual of the prophetic books, as rabbinic tradition recognized when it debated whether the book should be admitted to the Jewish canon of scripture. Ezekiel contains elaborate and somewhat fantastic visions, surrealist in nature. Yet the author is an optimist, who believes that the relationship between God and Israel will be restored. Alongside the optimism seen in this book's ending—a vision of Jerusalem restored, its temple repaired, a fertile, healing river flowing from its base—the description in Ezekiel 40-48 is highly idealized, even utopian. Access to the restored temple, however, is restricted to Israelites, with foreigners barred from admission.

As Ezekiel sees it, the restoration of the people is to be preceded by punishment of Israel's oppressors, among them Edom (Ez. 35) and "the Gog of the land of Magog" (Ez. 38–39; see also Rev. 20:7—21:2); whereas in Ezekiel Gog and Magog serve as a veiled reference to Nebuchadrezzar and Babylon, in the book of Revelation they symbolize all forces opposing God's will (in both cases, their defeat is described in highly mythological language). After divine victory over these enemies, Israel will be fully restored, "like the garden of Eden" (Ez. 36:35).

In Ezekiel's vision, exile is not a permanent condition, for God will lead the people from Babylon back to the Promised Land. This theme of a new Exodus is also elaborated by Second Isaiah (Isa. 40:3–5; 55:12–13). However, alongside the optimism of Ezekiel is evidence of developing tensions over the identity of the true Israel. In this respect, Ezekiel and Jeremiah are in agreement. Those who had not been exiled are "bad figs," so bad that they must be destroyed. The exiles are "good figs," whom God will restore to the land (Jer. 24). Those who remained in Judah disagreed. When some of the exiles returned, beginning in the late sixth century BCE, these conflicting views would be addressed. From their resolution came what we call Late or Second Temple Judaism.

From the first exile of Judeans to Babylon in 597 and ever since, Judaism has been a religion with two distinct geographies. One continued as Palestinian Judaism, associated with the Promised Land and the city of Jerusalem. However, a significant number and eventually a majority of what we call Jews (a word derived from the name "Judah") were no longer living in Judah, but had been forcibly exiled to Babylon or had fled elsewhere. This group emerged as Hellenistic Judaism. Those who were dispersed—the Diaspora (meaning "dispersion")—frequently found themselves in tension with those who remained in Judah. In actually, the beginning of that tension occurred during the Assyrian conquest of the Northern Kingdom of Israel in 722, at which time the Assyrians captured and burned Samaria, the capital of the kingdom of Israel, deporting many of its inhabitants (known in legendary lore as "the ten lost tribes of Israel") and resettling the conquered territories with outsiders. Many of these intermarried with the remaining Israelites, worshiping foreign gods alongside Yahweh.

These tensions continued in the postexilic period. One of the major differences between the historical books written during this period (Ezra–Nehemiah and 1 and 2 Chronicles) is that while Ezra–Nehemiah is hostile toward Judah's northern neighbors as well as to others in the region not considered the "true Israel," Chronicles is more inclusive. For the Chronicler,[1] the ideal is one Israel, all twelve tribes united. Nevertheless, the Chronicler was aware of the tensions between the northern and southern regions, siding ultimately with Judah while virtually ignoring the Northern Kingdom of Israel, which in the sixth century became the Persian province of Samaria. Over time, the division between these regions became acute, and the Samaritans came to be equated with Israel's ancient enemies, the Edomites and the Philistines. Eventually a complete break developed between the Samaritans and the Jews, each with its own temple and each claiming to be the authentic Judaism and to possess the legitimate temple and the only authoritative version of the Torah. While this schism had its roots in the pre-exilic and exilic periods, it is less prominent in the Hebrew scriptures than in the New Testament and in later rabbinic writings.

Although Ezekiel had envisioned a reunion of the two houses of Israel—the tribes of the north and the south—this dream did not materialize. The remnant of the Northern Kingdom (later known as Samaritans) and the descendants of the Southern Kingdom (Judeans, Jews) became divided by such deep rivalry that in New Testament times it could be said that "Jews do not share things in common with Samaritans" (John 4:9). Jesus, of course, worked to overcome this division, as we learn in John 4, in Luke's parable of the Good Samaritan (Luke 10:29–37), and elsewhere in the canonical Gospels.

Egypt became one of the main centers of the Jewish Diaspora. The Egyptian Diaspora was pre-exilic. Writing in the eighth century BCE, Isaiah of Jerusalem indicates that prior to the Exile there were five cities in the land of Egypt that spoke the language of Canaan (probably Aramaic rather than Hebrew) and observed a particular form of Yahwism that flourished in the Egyptian Diaspora. Second Isaiah, writing around 550, that is, a century and a half after First Isaiah, mentions Jews living in Sinim, that is, Syene, at the first cataract of the Nile, on the southern border of Egypt (Upper Egypt). To this place, settling on an island in the Nile named Elephantine, Jewish mercenaries came in the time of the Egyptian king Psamtik II (Psammetichus II), who ruled from 594 to 589 BCE, to help the Pharaoh protect the frontier against Ethiopian invaders. In time, this Jewish colony erected a temple where Yahweh (or Yahu) was worshiped, together with the goddess Anat (known from Canaanite religion as the warrior goddess as well as the sister and consort of Baal, the storm god also worshiped as the creator of humanity). Despite their departure from mainstream Mosaic tradition, these Jews recognized their allegiance to the temple in Jerusalem.

---

1. Scholars use the term "Chronicler" to refer to the author, or as is more likely, the authors or team of authors that produced the books of 1 and 2 Chronicles.

The Babylonian Exile prompted various waves of migration to Egypt. Jeremiah speaks of one such wave in 41:16—"soldiers, women, children, and eunuchs"—actions he opposed on principle. The emigrants settled in the Delta region of Lower Egypt (Migdal and Tahpanhes) and at Patros in Upper Egypt. Thus, Jews spread across Egypt, from the southern frontier to the Mediterranean coast. Their number was probably small, and there is evidence that most of them became assimilated with the Egyptians, primarily through intermarriage. In those days Egypt was not yet the center of the Diaspora, which was in Babylonia.

Yet another wave of immigrants came to Egypt about 525, when the Persian ruler Cambyses conquered Egypt and annexed it to Persia. At this time the Jewish mercenaries at Elephantine wisely switched allegiance to the Persians. By 410, conditions had changed for the Jewish exiles in Egypt. The previous year, Egyptian priests of the god Khnum bribed the Persian governor to order the destruction of the Jewish temple at Elephantine. It is doubtful to call this act "the first anti-Semitic outbreak," as some historians have done, for this event was local and not part of an extensive or ongoing campaign and hence, not a sign of anti-Semitism. In fact, the settlers at the military colony contrived to receive pay and rations from the royal treasury.

In their efforts to have their temple rebuilt, the Elephantine Jews wrote to Johanan, the high priest in Jerusalem, and to Bagoas, governor of Judah, enlisting their support. Understandably, neither responded to their request. A Jewish temple outside of Jerusalem was in violation of the Deuteronomic Code (see Deut. 12:10–14). Two years later, further letters were sent, this time to the authorities in Samaria, including two brothers who were acting on behalf of their aged father Sanballat, governor of Samaria. Evidently, the Jews at Elephantine regarded authorization from Samaria as valid as from Jerusalem, for they regarded the religions of both regions as the same. This time there was a reply, approving the rebuilding of the temple but authorizing only meal offering and incense. No mention was made of animal sacrifices, something only possible at the temple altar in Jerusalem.

Independent of the military organization, the Jewish colony was civilian in its way of life. While including non-Jews, the Jewish population at Elephantine formed a religious community of the kind later, in the Hellenistic period, called *politeuma*. Under this arrangement, an elected president and other officials represented the community, which gathered in assembly whenever necessary. They wrote, and likely spoke, Aramaic. All signs indicate that Jews in Egypt lived on equal terms with the natives, transacting business with various peoples and races and even intermarrying with them. In 404, the Pharaoh regained independence, and, conveniently, the Jewish forces followed suit, loyal once again to their adopted homeland. Eventually, important Jewish settlements arose in Alexandria and in other Egyptian cities and towns, growing numerically to around one million by the first century CE, a figure no doubt augmented by conversions. Nevertheless, Jeremiah, Ezekiel, and Second Isaiah were proven right. The future belonged not to the exiles in Egypt, or to the remnant left in Judah, but to the exiles in Babylon, particularly to those who preserved the traditions of their past and who eventually returned to Palestine to begin reconstruction.

LIFE FOR THE JEWISH EXILES IN BABYLONIA

The fall of Judah, with its utter destruction of Jerusalem and the temple, brought to an end political, social, and religious life in Judah. The culture shock caused by deportation, the problem of adaptation, and their resentment against God for letting it happen made this the strongest test the Jews had undergone. Their survival required nothing less than the reinvention of their identity.

In every respect, Babylonian culture seemed superior to the modest way of life the Jews had known in Judah. In contrast to the hilly farming and grazing land of Judah, the rich alluvial land of Babylonia was a scene of thriving agriculture and teeming industry. The capital city of Babylon, built on both sides of the Euphrates River, must have made Jerusalem seem like a ghetto. The city encompassed an area of two hundred square miles, in comparison to the city of David, extending precariously beyond its walled base of some fifteen acres, its architecture, size, and population dwarfed by comparison, its population no more than a few thousand. In fact, the entire territory of Judah was only about a thousand square miles in size, of which a large part was desert. Nine-tenths of the city of Babylon consisted of parks, fields, and gardens, in addition to the city's canals and waterways. The city's entryway was the beautiful Ishtar Gate, leading to the palace, which supported on its roof the famous "Hanging Gardens," one of the seven wonders of the ancient world. The proud temple of Jerusalem, gutted by Babylonian soldiers, paled into insignificance before the marvelous temples of Babylon. Many Jews must have wondered whether the high level of Babylonian culture might not be due to the superiority of Marduk, the God of Babylon, over Yahweh, the God of Israel, and of Babylonian paganism over their traditional faith.

In addition to the culture shock of deportation, the most serious adjustment for the Jews of Babylonia was religious. Their faith had been oriented to Zion (Jerusalem) and to the land of Palestine, the Promised Land God had given them as an inheritance, and to the temple in Jerusalem, the place where God "tabernacled" in Israel's worship. The greatest danger was that in time the Jewish faith, torn from its geographical and historical base, would drown in the sea of Babylonian culture.

The problem faced by the Jews in Babylonia was fundamentally the same as that faced by early Israelites in their transition to the land of Canaan. The Jews believed that God's sovereignty had been manifested in Palestine, particularly in the Jerusalem temple. But could their God be worshiped in a strange land, where other gods seemed to be in control? Even the most devout Jews, who remembered the joy they had one shared with worshipers in Jerusalem, raised the bewildering question. This mood is reflected in Psalm 137, which concludes with a terrible imprecation against the Babylonians who devastated Jerusalem and against the Edomites who gloated over its destruction.

Things did not go badly for the exiles in Babylon, however, for they were granted a significant amount of social freedom and economic opportunity. Many Jews came to thrive in this setting, for anti-Semitism was unknown at that time. The Jewish community eventually flourished in Babylonia, many of its members participating fully in its commercial life. In time, Babylonia became one of the major global centers of Jewish life and learning, rivaling and exceeding the Palestinian homeland for centuries to come.

Before the fall of Jerusalem, Jeremiah and Ezekiel uttered menacing oracles to lead the people of Judah to repentance; after the fall, these prophets proclaimed oracles of hope. Jeremiah promised a new covenant (Jer. 31:31–34), and Ezekiel, a new beginning (Ez. 37:1–14; also chapters 40–48). During the Exile, an unknown prophetic interpreter whom scholars call Second Isaiah used the typology of the Exodus to reignite the confidence of the people, assuring them of imminent delivery from captivity. Cyrus II of Persia would be God's "messiah" to deliver them (Isa. 45:1–3).

In 539 BCE the Persians under Cyrus defeated the Babylonian army. Cyrus, a tolerant and enlightened leader, issued an edict liberating the Jews from captivity and permitting repatriation. It is a tribute to Jewish tenacity and vitality that the Mosaic faith not only survived the Exile but was immeasurably deepened and enriched. Though some Jews must have capitulated to the pressures of Babylonian culture, others were bound more closely to their tradition and community. Surprisingly, the sense of belonging to the covenant community was intensified, rather than weakened, by life under captivity. In the Exile the people devoted themselves to preserving the Torah, studying and searching the tradition intensely for its meaning while preserving their scripture in writing for future generations. The Exile was thus a time of religious activity and of concentrated and consecrated attention to Israel's religious heritage. Considerable editing of the prophetic and historical literature was done in this period by anonymous priests and redactors. The role of the priests, no longer sacramental, became one of teaching and preserving Torah. To them the tradition was not just a museum piece from the past, but a living tradition through which God spoke to their contemporary situation. Whatever the origin and early stages of the Pentateuch (the Torah), it may be regarded as certain that its final compilation took place during the Babylonian Exile. The Deuteronomistic History, compiled in the years before Jerusalem fell, was also brought into final shape at this time.

Another benefit of the Exile was the realization that God could be worshiped anywhere, even in a foreign land and apart from the temple. Undoubtedly, a number of prayers in the book of Psalms were composed during the Exile by unknown individuals who cried to God "out of the depths" (Ps. 130:1). It is likely that the institution of the synagogue originated during the Exile as well. The presence of these organized local assemblies would become essential to later survival, when the Jews came to be scattered throughout the countries of the Dispersion (the Jewish Diaspora).

During the Exile, the people of Judah sought a new understanding of the community that still bound them together despite national disaster. The severe dislocation of the Exile, as with all world-shaking events, produced a double—and seemingly contradictory—effect on the lives of the exiles. Such crises can produce a conserving reaction, a renewal of national and traditional loyalties, but also a wider, liberating vision of a progressive and unified humanity. This twofold perspective came to expression during the Exile.

The collapse of the nation brought about an intense awareness of the uniqueness of Israel's calling, a point of view championed by the prophet Ezekiel and the Jerusalem priests who produced the Priestly version of the Pentateuch, known as "P," revising the older narratives and adding the books of Numbers and Leviticus, drawing upon older sources such as the Holiness Code (a collection of seventh-century laws now found in Leviticus 17–26) and other laws, genealogies, and ritual texts. About 398 BCE, long after the Jews received permission to return to their homeland, Ezra, a Jewish priest and scribe and the Persian minister of Jewish affairs, was commissioned by the Persian king Artaxerxes II to institute judicial reform in the land of Judah. Ezra brought with him from Babylon the Jewish Torah that Jewish priests compiled there, making it the basis of the postexilic community. Ezra's reform marks the beginning of classical Judaism, earning him the title "the Father of Judaism." From this point on, Judaism would be centered on three institutions: temple, priesthood, and Torah. The text that Ezra brought was clearly unknown to the people, who wept when they heard it. Ezra's text was not the original Torah, but something new and unexpected. Earlier biblical writers had worked in the same way, radically revising the texts they had inherited. Revelation had not happened once and for all time, but it was an ongoing process. Classical Judaism would be concerned not merely with the reception and preservation of revelation but with its constant reinterpretation.

By the time of Ezra there were two established categories of scripture: Torah and the Prophets. After the Exile, another set of writings was produced that became known as the Writings, consisting of liturgical writings called Psalms, additional historical writings such as Ezra–Nehemiah and 1 and 2 Chronicles (the works of the Chronicler are essentially commentaries on the historical books of Samuel and Kings), and a number of books constituting the Wisdom tradition, written by Jewish sages but associated with King Solomon (three Wisdom books were attributed to Solomon: Proverbs, Ecclesiastes, and Song of Songs). By the second century BCE, Wisdom became associated with Torah, and the historical book of Daniel with prophecy.

While the exilic and postexilic community came to regard the surrounding cultures as a threat to its faith and identity, the Exile also awakened a new world-consciousness, enlarging the Jewish faith by the vision of new horizons that had never been seen so clearly before, not even in the cosmopolitan age of Solomon. The exiles came to realize that they must look beyond their own limited community to the entire civilized world if they would behold fully God's purpose in history. The time was ripe for a deeper understanding of Israel's calling to be God's agent in bringing blessing to "all the families of the earth" (Gen. 12:3).

A new understanding of Israel's special place in world history is magnificently expressed by Second Isaiah, whose writings are found in Isaiah 40–55. In contrast to Jeremiah, Ezekiel, or even Isaiah of Jerusalem, whose scroll includes the writings of this author, we know nothing about his life or personal career, and so scholars call this poet Second Isaiah (or Deutero-Isaiah). Despite his anonymity, he is considered one of the greatest prophets of the Hebrew scriptures.

Known for his scorn of the pagan gods and for his unbridled monotheism ("I am the Lord, and there is no other; besides me there is no other god; Isa. 45:5),[2] Second Isaiah's triumphalism, reflecting the needs of a beleaguered community, is checked by his portrayal of a mysterious figure, a Suffering Servant entrusted with the task of establishing justice throughout the

---

2. This passage contains the first unequivocally monotheistic statement in what became the Hebrew Bible.

world, but in a nonviolent way. This figure is despised, bruised, and rejected, yet his suffering redeems his people, including righteous Gentiles. It is God's intention that the Servant—perhaps a reference to Second Isaiah himself, a faithful remnant within Israel, or a future figure yet to come—should be "a light to the nations," enabling God's salvation to reach to the ends of the earth, thereby demonstrating that the Gentiles—that is, the non-Jewish peoples of the world—are also included within the divine promise (see Isa. 42:5–9; also 45:23: "To me every knee shall bow"; see also Phil. 2:10).

There is a broad universalism in Second Isaiah's message, yet also the conviction that Israel occupies a special place in God's historical plan. Second Isaiah's universalism is reminiscent of a poem found in both Isaiah 2:2–4 and Micah 4:1–5, which announces that in the end-time all nations will flow to God's temple in Jerusalem in order to hear God's teaching and follow God's ways. Second Isaiah's universalism runs deeper still, proclaiming that God actively achieves world salvation through his chosen agent, Israel. Through the witness of Israel's life and faith, all the families of the earth will experience divine blessing. This perspective represents the broadest implication of Israel's election, a realization that emerged during the Babylonian Exile.

Periodically throughout Judah's history, particularly in times of national crises, there was a deep nostalgia for the brief Golden Age of David and Solomon and a longing for its return. The thousand-year-period between David and Jesus Christ (viewed as the "Son of David") served effectively as a preparatory millennium of Christian history, for that span of time established two key notions that would shape Christian thought and imagery, namely (1) *Kingdom hope*: hope for rule by God, so important in both the Old and New Testaments, and (2) *Messianic hope*: hope for a Davidic ruler that would guarantee the promissory terms of the Davidic covenant. After the end of the Davidic dynasty, elements of royal ideology continued to play an important role in later Jewish and Christian traditions.

QUESTIONS FOR DISCUSSION AND REFLECTION

Select one or more of the following questions and write your answer(s) in a journal. If you are in a group study, be prepared to share your answers with those in the group.

1. Explain and assess the view that Judaism emerged during the Babylonian Exile. In light of this view, how would you reply to someone

arguing that Judaism had its origins in the time of the patriarchs, certainly by the time of Moses?

2. In his denunciation of the Jewish colonists living in Egypt, Jeremiah condemned the exiles for worshiping gods other than Yahweh. In your estimation, provide a rationale for both perspectives, those of Jeremiah and of the exiles. If you were living at that time and place, would you have been a monotheist or a polytheist? Explain your answer.

3. In your estimation, did God cause the Babylonian Exile, or was it simply one more episode in the trials of ancient Jews, living precariously in a land surrounded by powerful empires?

4. In your estimation, who constituted the "true Israel" at the time of the Babylonian Exile, the exiles in Babylon, or those who remained in Judah? If you were to adapt that question to modern times, who are the "true Israel" today, progressive or traditionalist Jews? Or progressive or traditionalist Christians? Explain your answer.

5. Assess the merits of the author's statement, "The future belonged not to the exiles in Egypt, or to the remnant left in Judah, but to the exiles in Babylon."

6. Explain and assess the message and role of Jeremiah.

7. Explain and assess the message and role of Ezekiel.

8. Explain and assess the message and role of Second Isaiah.

Chapter 5

Judaism in the Postexilic Period

As we ponder the postexilic period in Palestine, an era known as the Restoration[1] but also as the Second Temple period,[2] we must consider the sweeping historical changes transpiring in the Near Eastern world around the middle of the sixth century BCE, keeping in mind that for centuries the center of world civilization had been the Fertile Crescent. This term refers to the vast arc of fertile land extending northwestward from the Persian Gulf, across Mesopotamia, and south along the coast of Canaan toward Egypt. This region, also known in as the "cradle of European civilization," was linked in antiquity by shared culture, related languages, and, for most of that period, especially during the second and first millennium BCE, by the domination of Semitic empires, beginning with Hammurabi in the eighteenth century BCE and ending with a succession of empires, the old Babylonian empire followed by the Assyrian empire and then the Neo-Babylonian (or Chaldean) empire. Immediately south of the western arm of the Fertile Crescent was Egypt, which in many periods exerted considerable influence beyond its borders.

---

1. Technically speaking, the Restoration concluded shortly after 400 BCE, ending after the missions of Nehemiah and Ezra.
2. The term "Second Temple" refers to the period from the construction of the second Jerusalem temple in 515 to the destruction of Jerusalem and the Herodian Temple Mount by the Romans in 70 CE.

THE HISTORICAL CONTEXT

The Neo-Babylonian empire was short-lived, lasting not much longer than its first and greatest emperor, Nebuchadrezzar (605–562), whose death triggered a period of instability, causing the throne to change hands three times in the space of seven years. Like its predecessor the Assyrians, the Neo-Babylonian empire was overextended and thus vulnerable. The principle threat came from the east, in the Iranian plateau. There two related groups, the Medes and Persians, had coalesced in 550 under the leadership of Cyrus, who had become king of Persia in 559. The last Chaldean king, Nabonidus, who ruled from 556–539, spent much of his time in Arabia, perhaps securing trade routes to the west and southwest, leaving his son Belshazzar as coregent in Babylon. In 559 Cyrus defeated and captured Nabonidus, shortly thereafter entering Babylon unopposed. The year 539 marks the beginning of what is called the "Persian period" in ancient Near Eastern history. The Persian period lasted until the conquests of Alexander the Great, ending with the looting and destruction of the Persian capital city of Persepolis in 330 BCE.

The sudden and surprising collapse of the Babylonian empire and the rise of the Persian empire gave the Jewish exiles a new lease on life. Cyrus, the enlightened Persian ruler (550–530), permitted those Jews who so desired to return to their homeland and reconstitute their community life under cultural and religious autonomy. There could be no native monarchy now, for the Persians allowed no such independence. Therefore, the temple and its priesthood became the center of Jewish identity for the next five hundred years, forming an institution that would remain until the destruction of Jerusalem in 70 CE.

The first task of the returning exiles was to rebuild their temple, then the walls of Jerusalem. About the year 398, nearly a century and a half later, Ezra inspired the struggling Jewish settlement in Jerusalem to accept the Torah as its constitution. The Torah proved an indispensable instrument for uniting and governing the Jewish community. Though a priest, Ezra instituted a major reform that stripped the priests of their religious and intellectual leadership, leaving them in charge only of the conduct of the temple ritual. Instead of a hereditary priesthood, which all too often exhibited the marks of decadence and moral corruption, the spiritual leadership of the people became vested in scholars. Recruited from all classes, they represented a non-hereditary, democratic element. The creative impulse in Judaism was henceforth centered in the synagogue, in which all Jews were equal and which became at once a house of prayer, study, and communal assembly.

The importance of this revolution, unparalleled in ancient religion, can scarcely be exaggerated. Ezra's successors, the scribes and rabbis, not only preserved the Torah but also gave it new life. By their painstaking study and interpretation of the biblical text they endowed the Jewish tradition with some of its most noteworthy characteristics—its capacity for growth and its fusion of realistic understanding and idealistic aspiration. Their activity made the Bible relevant to the needs of later generations confronted by new problems and perils. They contributed not only to the survival of the Jewish people but also to the background from which Christianity arose, for they formulated many of the basic teachings shared by Christianity and Rabbinic Judaism.

During the Second Temple period, both the Law and the Prophets became scripture, a sacred core of authoritative books to which the entire people looked for guidance. As we know, the Law, which was the province of the priest and later of the scribe, and Prophecy, which was the experience of the prophet and later of the apocalyptist, did not exhaust the range of spiritual activity in early Judaism. A third strand was supplied by Wisdom, which was cultivated by the sage or the elder. Wisdom was essentially an intellectual discipline, concerned with the education of upper-class youth. The sage was a professional teacher whose function was to inculcate in his pupils all the elements of morality aimed at achieving worldly success. Wisdom had a timeless quality, transcending time and culture. Though ancient sages reflected on problems of society as they knew them, these were human problems found in varying forms in every society.

To head the first contingent of Jews returning from exile, Cyrus appointed "a prince of Judah" as governor, one who bore the Babylonian name Sheshbazzar. The return described at the beginning of the book of Ezra seems to have been of a small group. According to Ezra 3, as soon as this group arrived in Jerusalem, they built an altar to reestablish the regular sacrifices to Yahweh. In the second year the returnees began the reconstruction of the temple that had been built by Solomon. After laying the foundation, the work came to a halt, disrupted by local opposition and by a sense of frustration; the foundations were not nearly as magnificent as those of the original. About 520, work on the temple resumed under dual leadership. Political leadership lay with Zerubbabel, who succeeded Sheshbazzar as governor. Like Sheshbazzar, Zerubbabel was a descendant of Johoiachin, the young king of Judah who had been exiled to Babylon in 597. Religious leadership lay with the high priest Joshua. This shared leadership and their efforts to reconstruct the temple had the support of the postexilic prophets Haggai and Zechariah, who speak of Zerubbabel and Joshua in exalted language, addressing them in messianic and apocalyptic terms (see Hag. 2:2–9, 20–23; Zech. 3:1—4:14; 6:9–14).

The book of Zechariah, like Isaiah, is a composite work. Chapters 1–8 deal with the late sixth century, especially the issues of leadership in the restored community in Judah and the reconstruction of the temple, completed in 515 BCE. Chapters 9–14 are different in style and content and come from a later period, probably the fifth century BCE. For this reason, scholars distinguish between "First Zechariah" and "Second Zechariah" (or "Deutero-Zechariah"). First Zechariah reflects a time of vindication, hope, and optimism for the future, reflected in his closing statement, "In those days ten men from nations of every language shall take hold of a Jew, grasping his garment and saying, 'Let us go with you, for we have heard that God is with you'" (Zech. 8:23). Second Zechariah, by contrast, uses oracles cast in a bizarre apocalyptic form popular in Judaism in the late postexilic period. The oracles in Second Zechariah are linked by a common theme, the "Day of the Lord," but unlike earlier prophets, Second Zechariah's language is cryptic, abounding with marvelous visions of the future and of a coming dramatic finale when God's foes are shattered and God's dominion is established cosmically over all the forces of evil.

The two centuries of Jewish history during the period of Persian rule are of great significance, for in this period we see a people becoming great through weakness. At a time when Judaism lacked everything that is usually connected with greatness, it underwent a transformation that contributed to the development of religion far exceeding the contributions even of India or Greece. If, when Jerusalem was sacked and the best of its people deported, the nation of Judah had followed the example of other nations in similar plight, it would either have ceased to exist, or else after a time it would have grasped at some semblance of its former state. As the latter was not immediately possible, it found a kind of greatness that was new to the world.

Fortunately, Judaism had as guide in this task the writings of Second Isaiah, one of the great religious geniuses of all time. Second Isaiah set out to interpret history as displaying the intention of God. But unlike other interpreters of history, Second Isaiah did not wait until the events had passed before explaining them. Rather, he explained contemporary history and that yet to come in terms of an ideal of conduct (righteous, vicarious suffering) that no one had preciously imagined possible.

Second Isaiah was the inheritor of a perspective of earlier prophets, particularly Isaiah and Jeremiah, a viewpoint espoused only by a select few and yet unknown anywhere else in the world, namely, that a God of perfect moral character ruled supreme over the universe. The number of Jews who adopted this view initially was small in number, but they were strong enough in their conviction to influence history. The great majority of Jews continued to hold the traditional belief that Yahweh was the God of Israel alone. Perhaps those who accepted the new universalistic truth did not realize that the two views were incompatible, and for a time, both views must have continued together. However, it took the destruction of the nation and its temple to free the wider truth from its nationalistic bonds.

Monotheism became the defining characteristic of Judaism, followed by Christianity and Islam. The ancient words of the Shema became reinterpreted as a monotheistic declaration, from "The Lord is our God, the Lord alone" (Deut. 6:4) to "The Lord our God, the Lord is one," reiterated in the pronouncement of the apostle Paul, "for us there is one God, the Father, from whom are all things and for whom we exist" (1 Cor. 8:6), and in the Muslim profession of faith, "There is no god but God."

The majority of exiles, however, bemoaned the loss of homeland and of sacrificial worship, hopeful of their restoration. However, the sense that they alone knew the truth about God unified them in a way they had never been before. Three outward signs distinguished Jews from non-Jews. The first is their opposition to idols: God was not material, and could not be depicted in any copy, form, or image, as Second Isaiah emphasized (see Isa. 40:18-20; 42:17; 44:9-20), not, of course, to persuade Babylonians to abandon idolatry, but to give the Jews a clearer sense of identity. The second distinguishing mark of the Jews is circumcision, not so much a religious rite as a legal requirement, a sign of allegiance and membership in the covenant people. The prophets, more concerned with inward piety, had little interest in external rites: Jeremiah twice refers metaphorically to the circumcision of the heart (4:4; 9:26; see Ezek. 44:9; Rom. 2:25-29; Gal. 5:6). The third mark is Sabbath observance. As a distinctive duty of the Jews, it is prominent in Nehemiah, and before him in Third Isaiah (see Isa. 56:58), and is also emphasized by Ezekiel and in Jeremiah 17.

Our knowledge of Jews in both Judah and Babylon in the Persian period is fragmentary, for which we have some literary evidence in the Hebrew Bible. Following the destruction of Jerusalem, some Judeans stayed in the land, as we have noted, continuing to harvest their crops. While many of the cities, especially those that served as fortresses, like Jerusalem and Lachish, had been destroyed, others continued to be occupied. This largely rural population would form the nucleus of the restored Judean community, whose claims to the land were contested by the returnees from Babylonia.

THE LITERARY CONTEXT

To the Judean survivors we can attribute some of the literature of this period, including the book of Lamentations, a collection of detailed reaction to the fall of Jerusalem in 586. A different perspective on the fall of the city, that of the exiles in Babylon, is found in Psalm 137 and also in Ezekiel. The book of Obadiah, the shortest book in the Hebrew Bible, may also have been written shortly after the fall of Jerusalem. Devoted to the divine judgment of Edom, the nation that had seized a part of Judah's territory after its fall to Babylon, Obadiah denounces the pride and treachery of Edom and announces its future destruction, something that happened in the fifth century BCE, when Arab tribes began pressing into Edomite territory from the Arabian Desert.

By the fourth century these invaders, known as Nabateans, had conquered the Edomite mountain acropolis of Sela (Obad. 3), carving into its red limestone cliffs the fabled capital of Petra—today one of the supreme archaeological attraction in the world. From Petra, the Nabateans eventually controlled the surrounding trade routes. For four hundred years they thrived in the region, eventually extending their kingdom as far north as Damascus.[3] At their peak, around the time of Christ, the Nabateans were trading not only with Palestine, Egypt, and Syria, but also with Greece, Rome, and even China. The Romans conquered Petra in 106 CE, adding to its splendor, until an earthquake destroyed buildings and damaged the vital water system that piped water into the city. The ruins of Petra were an object of curiosity in the Middle Ages and were largely abandoned after that.

Other biblical projects attributed to the Judean survivors include the final edition of the Deuteronomistic History (the historical narrative found in the books of Joshua, Judges, Samuel, and Kings, which together comprise the "Former Prophets" in the Hebrew Bible), as well as the editing of several prophetic books, including Jeremiah. The material assigned to the prophecy of Jeremiah shows evidence of a complicated literary history. Rather than being a finished composition, it was subsequently expanded and edited by other writers. This editorial activity applied particularly to chapters 30–33, often called "The Little Book of Comfort," a segment that includes the famous vision of the restored community expressed in the prophecy of the new covenant (Jer. 31:31–34), which influenced later prophetic tradition

---

3. In Galatians 1:17–18, Paul notes that after his conversion he made a trip to Arabia (probably Syrian Arabia, namely, the Nabatean kingdom east and south of Damascus). We may conclude from 2 Corinthians 11:32 that Paul had incurred the anger of King Aretas IV (currently ruling the Nabatean kingdom with at least some jurisdiction or influence in Damascus), possibly due to evangelizing activity in the region, perhaps even in its major city, Petra.

and eventually provided the name to the canon of the Christian writings ("New Testament" means "New Covenant"). Material added to the Jeremiah text during the early post-exilic period possibly includes oracles against the nations in Jeremiah 46–51. The oracle against Edom contains material similar to verses in Obadiah (compare Jer. 49:9 and Obad. 5; Jer. 49:14–16 and Obad. 1–4); chapter 52, an appendix to Jeremiah, is also late. This segment, taken from the Deuteronomistic History (see 2 Kgs. 24:18—25:30), narrates the fall of Jerusalem and its aftermath.

The major source for our knowledge of Jewish life in Palestine during the Persian period is two books of the Old Testament, Ezra and Nehemiah, which in the Hebrew Bible is a single work, though compiled from different sources (this conclusion is supported by the use of Aramaic rather than Hebrew in Ezra 4:8—6:18 and 7:12–26). Aramaic, a Semitic language originally spoken in Aram (modern-day Syria), came to be used as an international language of diplomacy and commerce by the Assyrians. It resulted in part from the Assyrian practice of deporting the elite of conquered regions. The use of Aramaic took hold during the Persian period, as is attested in inscriptions and official Persian documents as far east as India and throughout the Levant, including Syria, Palestine, and Egypt. Thus, Aramaic was the ordinary spoken language of Galilee in the first century CE. The New Testament Gospels, though written in Greek, quote Jesus speaking Aramaic on several occasions. Some of the Dead Sea Scrolls were also written in Aramaic, as were the earliest Targums (Aramaic translations of the Hebrew scriptures).

The books of Ezra and Nehemiah probably were completed in the early fourth century. The contents can be outlined as follows:

Ezra 1–2: The return from exile

Ezra 3–6: The early restoration

Ezra 7–10: The mission and memoirs of Ezra

Nehemiah 1:1—7:5: The mission and memoirs of Nehemiah

Nehemiah 7:6–73: List of returnees (nearly identical to that in Ezra 2)

Nehemiah 8:1—12:26: Ceremonies of renewal, including a census of Jerusalem residents and other lists

Nehemiah 12:27—13:31: Continuation of the memoirs of Nehemiah

These books cover a considerable period, beginning in the second half of the sixth century and continuing into the fourth. A close study of these books reveals numerous peculiarities, including chronological problems and overlap issues, with frequent shifts from third-person narrative to fictional autobiography. Because the opening verses of the book of Ezra duplicate the concluding verses of 2 Chronicles, earlier scholars assumed literary relationship, perhaps even the same author, for the books of Chronicles, Ezra, and Nehemiah, something modern scholars dispute, due to significant differences in language, style, and content. Based on internal evidence and on a comparison with other Jewish literature of the period, the Chronicler is said to have written in the late fifth or the early fourth century (since the historian copies almost verbatim the autobiographical "Memoirs of Nehemiah," while using the "Memoirs of Ezra" as an additional source), certainly before Hellenization made a significant impact on Judaism. While I Chronicles 29:7 mentions the "daric," a Persian coin named for Darius I (522–486), there is no sign that the author was influenced by Greek thought.

The Chronicler's work represents a fundamental revision or reinterpretation of Israel's history, using the story of Ezra–Nehemiah as the final phase of the unfolding story that begins with David. The Chronicler's focus is singular, namely, that Israel is called to be a community centered in the temple. For the Chronicler, Israel's history is essentially the account of a worshiping community, a "kingdom of priests and a holy nation," its life viewed as a liturgy to the God dwelling in Zion, the Holy City.

Problems arise when we read the Chronicler's account in its final form. For example, the Chronicler believed that Ezra came first, and dates his appearance in Jerusalem in the seventh year of Artaxerxes I (458 BCE). However, as we now know, there were at least four kings named Artaxerxes, and the chronology works better if we assume that the Persian ruler referred to in Ezra 7:7 is Artaxerxes II (398 BCE), rather than Artaxerxes I. There is no doubt about the date of Nehemiah's arrival, which took place in 445 BCE, but it seems that Ezra came some fifty years later. Nehemiah's mission was legal, having been sent to Judah on two official missions, representing Persia as governor of Judah for twelve years, and then a brief return sometime later. Nehemiah had held the important position of king's cupbearer in Babylon, and as a Jew, he sought royal approval to go to Jerusalem and rebuild it. Upon his arrival, an inspection revealed a dire situation: the city's defenses were in ruins. Nehemiah began to reconstruct the walls, but immediately faced opposition, both from the local Judeans and from the leaders of neighboring provinces. Nehemiah skillfully foiled their plots, completing the rebuilding of the walls.

Throughout his first term as governor, as well as during the second term that began in 432, Nehemiah introduced various reforms to bind the Jews into a closely-knit community, reforms inspired by powerful threats from external forces in Samaria, as well as from the Ammonites and Edomites. At first, these adversaries accused the Jews of plotting a revolution against

Persia; then they ridiculed the feeble strength of the walls around Jerusalem; and finally they threatened to attack. The Persians, however, encouraged the refortification of Jerusalem. From 460 to 454, a revolt against Persian rule took place in Egypt, a revolt supported by Persia's rival, Athens. For the Persians, it made strategic sense to strengthen Jerusalem, viewing the Jews as an ally near Egypt.

Furthermore, Judah's neighbors viewed a strong Jerusalem as a threat, suspicious that the leaders of a revived Judah might attempt to exert control over the surrounding region. To allay such fears, some of the Jews, especially members of the wealthier class, took a relaxed attitude toward their neighbors, even to the point of mingling and intermarrying with them. To meet these circumstances, Nehemiah enforced a policy of exclusivism, thereby intensifying the division between Jews and Gentiles, particularly between Jews and Samaritans.

According to Nehemiah, membership in the Jewish community was determined by two standards. The first was birth. When the walls were built, Nehemiah enrolled all the citizens according to genealogy (Neh. 7:5-69; Ezra 2). During his second term, Nehemiah strictly prohibited intermarriage. He banished a priest from office when it was discovered that he was married to a daughter of Sanballat, the Samaritan governor. Ezra carried these measures further, not only denouncing mixed marriages but also forcibly breaking up those already in existence (Ezra 10:2-5). The second qualification for membership was adherence to the Torah, including strict observance of the Sabbath and faithful support of the temple. Thus a strong wall was built around the Jewish community—not just the wall of Jerusalem, but the wall of exclusivity based on birth and religious loyalty. The desire to maintain purity had political implications, but it was more fundamentally a struggle to preserve Jewish identity and distinctive faith in the face of tremendous cultural pressures.

Unlike Nehemiah's mission, Ezra's was primarily religious. A member of the exilic community in Babylon, as well as a member of a priestly family and "a scribe skilled in the law of Moses" (Ezra 7:6), Ezra sought permission from the king to return to Jerusalem to impose the requirements of the Torah, especially those forbidding marriage with non-Jews. Apparently, such intermarriage was frequent, for it took several months to identify the men who had married "foreign" women. The book of Ezra ends abruptly, its last words obscure, but the gist of the statement is that the "foreign" women and their children had been sent away or at least ostracized from the community.

Ezra is mentioned again in Nehemiah 10 as the officiant of a lengthy ceremony of renewal, at which he read the "book of the law of Moses," with which they were unfamiliar,[4] and during which the fall festival of Booths was celebrated. The ceremony concluded with a commitment to observe all God's commandments, focusing on three features: prohibition of intermarriage, insistence on Sabbath observance, and the requirement to support temple personnel with tithes of agricultural produce and an annual tax.

After Ezra's reading from the Law, the returnees celebrated Passover, together with "all who had joined with them and separated themselves from the pollution of the nations of the land" (Ezra 6:21). The latter group of participants presumably referred to the Judeans who had remained in the land, but who accepted the religious authority of the new leaders, especially as it related to qualifications for membership in the community. For the author of Ezra, the Restoration required the reconstruction of the temple, the reestablishment of proper worship, and the installation of the proper priesthood.

The problem of syncretism had haunted Israel from its original occupation of Canaan. The threat of cultural assimilation persisted and intensified in the postexilic period, especially after the rise of Alexander the Great, who made a conscious effort to absorb all religions and cultural differences in a synthesis known as Hellenism. The surprise was that Judaism harnessed assimilation, creatively transforming what was borrowed from others into a vehicle for expressing its own faith. While some Jews would compromise or even relinquish their distinctives, as we note in ensuing chapters, Israel's calling was to be holy—meaning distinct and separate—a "peculiar" people set apart from the nations. It is easy to criticize the narrow theological focus of Judaism under Nehemiah and Ezra, with the line strictly drawn between "us" and "them," but this distinctive community would preserve the spiritual heritage that deeply affected the course of Western civilization.

After Nehemiah, Ezra, and the Chronicler, our sources are silent until the mid-fifth century BCE. Furthermore, there is no mention in Persian sources of the tiny province of Judah (also called Jehud). From the Persian perspective, Judah was a relatively unimportant part of their empire; scholars estimate that the entire population of Judah at this time was no more than ten thousand, and that of Jerusalem fewer than a thousand.[5]

The period from the completion of the Second Temple in 515 to the coming of Ezra to Jerusalem in 398 BCE spans about four generations. In this period, Persian culture reached its greatest height, as evidenced by the impressive ruins standing at Persepolis, the main capital of the Persian

---

4. The text that served as the basis of the covenant renewal could have been the Holiness Code, the book of Deuteronomy, the Pentateuch in its entirety, or some form of the Priestly edition of the Pentateuch (the Priestly Code).

5. Coogan, *Brief Introduction to the Old Testament*, 344.

empire. Both Darius I and Xerxes, builders of the magnificent capital, waged campaigns against Greece, only to be defeated at the famous battles of Marathon in 490 and Thermopylae and Salamis in 480. Since the Jewish historians leap over this period in order to speak of the missions of Nehemiah and Ezra, we rely on postexilic prophets for some light on the conditions in Judah during this period.

In addition to Obadiah, we have the writings of Third Isaiah (Isa. 56–66), written after the completion of the temple in 515, possibly as late as the fifth century BCE. No specific historical references make this writing impossible to date precisely. One group of foreigners, the Edomites, is singled out for divine vengeance, their participation in the destruction of Jerusalem having been condemned earlier in Psalm 137 and by Obadiah. In the postexilic period, disciples of Second Isaiah continued their master's message, reinterpreting it to new situations. Whereas Second Isaiah pulses with the excitement of a new Exodus and the return to the Promised Land, Third Isaiah reflects the disillusionment and dissensions within the Palestinian postexilic community, and it does so by moving from the plane of history into a suprahistorical realm of religious imagination, marking a turn from prophecy to apocalyptic, a highly symbolic and idealized form of literature that flourished in the postexilic period.

The focus of apocalyptic is the nearness of the Day of the Lord, a time when God will assert sovereignty over history and the nations. It is characteristic of apocalyptic that specific historical events recede into the background, and the context between God and evil forces assumes a cosmic scale. The purpose of apocalyptic writers was to encourage the faithful to remain steadfast in perilous times. Such themes also appear in "the little apocalypse" of Isaiah (chapters 24–27 and 34–35), added to the earlier Isaiah tradition during the postexilic period, much as Second Zechariah was appended to the Zechariah scroll. Second Zechariah ends with the mysterious comment, "There shall no longer be Canaanites in the house of the Lord on that day" (Zech. 14:21), a possible reference to the exclusion of non-Israelites from the recently restored community, also a concern of the book of Ezra. For Second Zechariah, the temple, as all of Jerusalem, is sacred to Yahweh, and foreigners will be barred from it.

While the "Isaiah Apocalypse" lacks precise historical references, it vividly describes the end-time, when all creation comes under divine judgment. In this new age, Death will be swallowed up (Isa. 25:8), and the dead among God's people will be restored to life (26:19), perhaps the earliest biblical example of belief in the resurrection of the dead.[6]

---

6. The earliest unequivocal reference to bodily resurrection and to the rewards and

Two other prophetic books from the Minor Prophets are dated to the postexilic period, the short books of Joel and Malachi. The book of Joel can be divided naturally into two parts: a vivid lament occasioned by an infestation of locusts, interpreted as a form of divine judgment that can be halted only by communal repentance (1:1—2:27), and an apocalyptic description of the end-time in which Judah's enemies are punished and the land is restored to glorious abundance (2:28—3:21). Later apocalyptic literature makes use of themes from Joel, including the image of locusts elaborated vividly in Revelation 9:3-11. Christian tradition also sees the promise of the outpouring of the divine "spirit" (Joel 2:28-29) fulfilled in the Christian "new age" (Acts 2:16-21).

The book of Malachi, the last book of the Old Testament in the Christian canon, is one of the latest of the prophetic books, usually dated to the end of the fifth century, about 400 BCE. The temple has been rebuilt and a sacrificial system is in place. We find no reference to a king, but rather to a governor (Mal. 1:8), the usual title of the administrator of the Persian province of Judah. The book also includes topics such as marriages between Judeans and foreigners, divorce, and tithing, concerns of Nehemiah and Ezra. The author, who may have been a priest or a Levite, refers to himself as a divine messenger (the term "Malachi" in the opening verse is probably not a person's name but rather a title; see "my messenger" in 3:1). The book concludes with a reference to the return of Elijah before the "day of the Lord" (4:5), understood by Christians as a reference to John the Baptist, the precursor of Jesus Christ, that is, of Jesus "the Messiah" (Malachi 3:1 is quoted in Matthew 11:10 and Mark 1:2, although Mark's Gospel erroneously attributes the quote to Isaiah). During the early postexilic period, hope persisted in the restoration of the Davidic dynasty, perhaps in the person of Zerubbabel, as witnessed by the prophets Haggai and Zechariah. But that hope was disappointed, and the idea of a future Davidic ruler, a messiah, was postponed to a more remote future.

Although prophecy remained alive in the early postexilic period, over time prophecy became a written activity, preserved in scrolls. After Ezra's time, the belief emerged that the age of charismatic prophecy had ended and would not resume until the coming of the Messianic Age. In the later postexilic period, prophecy found a new form of expression in apocalyptic literature, as noted above. Although this type of literature was anticipated by Ezekiel, Third Isaiah, and Zechariah, it flourished later in Judaism,

---

punishments in the afterlife is Daniel 12:2-3, the last book of the Hebrew Bible to be written. This passage was recorded in the context of one of the darkest moments in early Jewish history, during the forced Hellenization and persecution by the infamous Antiochus IV Epiphanes, who ruled from 175 to 164 BCE.

beginning with the Maccabean period and continuing into the second century CE, its chief example in the Hebrew Bible being the book of Daniel.

Despite the troubles facing the struggling Jewish community during the postexilic period, the Jews of Palestine presumably enjoyed security under Persian sovereignty. The story of the Jewish community breaks off with the account of the Restoration under Nehemiah and Ezra and does not resume until 1 Maccabees, a book outside the Hebrew Bible that covers events of the second century (175–132 BCE). Much of the interim, especially the fourth century BCE, is obscure or blank, perhaps indicating that Judah was relatively secure for a century or more after Ezra. However, the times were destined to change, Israel's history soon plunging and swirling along a turbulent course.

During the time of reconstruction, the majority of Jewish exiles remained outside the homeland. Two biblical books speak of their experience, both written no earlier than the fifth century, possibly toward the end of the Persian period in the fourth century BCE. The first is the book of Jonah, an account presented in the story of a prophet who lived in the classical period of Israelite prophecy, the middle of the eighth century (the time of Jeroboam II and of the prophets Amos and Hosea; see 2 Kgs. 14:25).

The book of Jonah expresses a prophetic universalism reminiscent of Second Isaiah. The story tells how God commissioned Jonah to go to the Assyrian capital of Nineveh and proclaim its imminent destruction because of its wickedness. Jonah rebels and gets sidetracked, is thrown overboard during a storm, swallowed by a great fish, and after three days and nights in the fish's belly, is disgorged onto dry land. Jonah eventually proclaims God's word of judgment, and to his shock and displeasure, the city repents and is converted. Jonah's message was based on judgment, but he learned that there is a wideness to God's mercy (see Jonah 4:2).

Jonah, representing restored Judaism, was troubled by a Mosaic teaching, echoed across the Hebrew Bible, that God is "merciful and gracious, slow to anger and abounding in steadfast love and faithfulness" (Exod. 34:6). At the very time when the policies of Nehemiah and Ezra foster narrow nationalism and doctrinaire exclusivism, an unknown prophetic author writes the book of Jonah as a counterbalance, focusing on the mystery of God's mercy. Scholars debate the book's essential message. Is the book rejecting intense nationalism and suggesting that God controls history for good and not for woe, or is the central message one of divine forgiveness as a response to repentance? The book of Jonah ends with a question, a rhetorical question perhaps, but one that suggests that various levels of interpretation are possible.

The second book, the story of Esther, reflects a different spirit. Despite its apparently nonreligious character (the book contains not a single explicit reference to God), later writers wrote additions to the Hebrew scroll to give the story a more religious tone. Some additions are found in the Greek Septuagint, and the translator of the Vulgate, Jerome, placed these extra passages at the end of the biblical narrative, after Esther 10:3. While some rabbis later questioned Esther's inclusion in the canon, the popularity of the Feast of Purim, with which the book is associated, eventually caused such doubts to fade.

Esther's story is placed during the reign of Ahasuerus (Xerxes I, who ruled from 486 to 465). The writer constructs the story around the ancient hostility between Israel and the Amalekites, a conflict that began in Moses's time and reached its peak during the reign of Saul, Israel's first king. Two of the story's main characters, Mordecai the Jew and the Persian vizier Haman, represent Saul and the Amalekites respectively. When Haman tells Xerxes that the Jews refuse to assimilate, the king grants him permission to issue an edict for the wholesale massacre of Jews. However, due to Mordecai and Esther's intervention, Haman is executed, along with his ten sons, bringing the last of the "Amalekites" to an end and sparing the Jews. The story concludes with a celebration of the survival of Judaism, instituting the festival of Purim in remembrance of the lot (Hebrew *pur*) that Haman had cast to determine the day of vengeance. The story of Esther clearly recalls the threat to Jewish survival in the Diaspora. The story became popular during the Maccabean period, when the separation of Jews from Gentiles occasioned violent persecution. Throughout subsequent history, Haman symbolizes Gentile leaders who carry out vicious anti-Semitic policies.

According to the historian Charles A. Beard, one of the lessons of history can be summarized by the proverb, "The bee fertilizes the flower it robs." This is particularly true of the Jews during the Exile and the Restoration period. Although the experience of change and dislocation seemed bitter to many at the time, the people came to realize that God was working for good. The view that world-shaking events may have a double and seemingly contradictory effect on people's lives also characterized a small but highly literate and influential group of Palestinian Jews living in Judah under Persian rule during the fourth and fifth centuries BCE. These sages flourished during this "Golden Age of Wisdom," a peaceful era of two hundred years aided by a common lingua franca (Aramaic) across the Persian empire, a new sense of Jewish identity, and a new internationalism. During this period the books of Job and Ecclesiastes were written and the wisdom material found in the book of Proverbs was collected and finalized.

In the centuries after the return from Babylon, the Jews in Palestine were repeatedly faced with the prospect of more powerful cultures overwhelming their own and overpowering them. The period of the Restoration, which followed the return from exile, was challenging and difficult for the tiny, modest, and insecure Jewish community, surrounded as it was by a welter of foreign peoples—Samaritans, Edomites, Moabites, Ammonites, Philistines, and later, Greeks and Romans. The small Jewish settlement was a tributary of the great Persian, Ptolemaic, Seleucid, and Roman empires, which arose in succession and for five centuries held sway over the Jewish community in this part of the world.

The way of wisdom would play a central role in shaping future Jewish thought. Rabbis who searched the Torah for answers to life's existential questions eventually inherited the role of sages as leaders of Jewish life, thought, and worship.

THE CULTURAL CONTEXT

While the reconstruction in Palestine united the Jews and gave them a sense of oneness, the Diaspora saved Judaism from spiritual inbreeding and extinction. There were numerous migrations and forcible resettlement of peoples in antiquity, but the Jewish experience is without analogy.

The device of deportation, invented perhaps by the Hittites and applied subsequently by all their successors (Assyrians, Babylonians, Persians, Greeks, Romans, and others), was not an attempt to exterminate enemies, but rather to break their natural cohesion. Over time, the colonists deported and resettled detached psychologically from their respective cities. But the Jewish Diaspora continued to consider Jerusalem its hearth and home: "If I forget you, O Jerusalem, let my right hand wither!" (Ps. 137:5). On the other hand, since the structure of Near Eastern monarchies was essentially feudal, there was neither the need nor the wish to assimilate.

Had the restoration of Jerusalem occurred a century earlier, the result might have been far different. When the Assyrians conquered Samaria in 722, they established a military colony there. As a result, the Ten Tribes, deported to Assyria, could never return. Since there were already military colonies of Assyria in Palestine (Samaria, Gezer, etc.), Nebuchadrezzar did not wish or need to send new settlers to Judah. Further, though the Babylonians were savage in battle, they took no delight in useless destruction or wholesale slaughter. The remnant of Judah was not exterminated or tortured to death. Unlike the case of Samaria, there was a cultural and legal vacuum that the Restoration could fill.

The exceptional feature of Jewish history is the reluctance of so many exiles to return. They remained in Mesopotamia but, paradoxically, continued to care for the Holy Land generation after generation, to this day. This Diaspora clung to its unique God and to Jerusalem, the center of lawful worship. Nevertheless, the God of Zion was not only the God of the Jews. He was, for an ever-growing number of Jews, the sole God in heaven and earth, and the deities of the pagans but vain idols. Hence, the polarity of Jerusalem and the Diaspora "had its ideological counterpart in the paradoxical combination of universal monotheism and particularism, in the conception that the sole Lord of the Universe dwells on the hillock of Zion. This theological paradox held the Jews of the Dispersion together, and from all points of the compass they directed their eyes to the Lord's Temple in Jerusalem."[7]

Despite the continuation of the reforming work of Jewish leaders during the fifth and fourth centuries BCE, it would be a mistake to believe that Judaism after Ezra was a community governed by extreme strictness, or that faithful Jews remained immune to foreign influence until the coming of Alexander, the bringer of Hellenism, late in the fourth century. Archaeological evidence shows that in this period, Palestine formed part of an eclectic, Greco-Egyptian-Persian culture, which extended from the Nile Delta to Asia Minor. Greek painted pottery, Phoenician amulets, and Egyptian figurines were the same across the Levant, and kitchen pots, bronze amulets worn by girls, weapons used by warriors, and other cross-cultural paraphernalia were all shared in common.

The commercial influence of Greece, for example, was so great in Palestine that Athenian coins became the principal currency for trade transactions in the fifth century. While the Jews were convinced that God had set them apart from the nations (Lev. 20:24), yet they called him the God of Heaven, the same title of Ahuramazda, the deity of their Persian rulers. The Jews imagined they were living according to the Law of Moses, while the synagogue, unknown to the Torah, became a fundamental part of devotional life. Some Jews in Egypt erected temples, contrary to the biblical command for centralization of worship.[8]

Another mistaken conception is that of postexilic exclusiveness. In the Persian period, Jews were the first peoples to open entrance to proselytes. Ancient cults were exclusive; in most cases, foreigners were prohibited even

---

7. Bickerman, *Ezra to the Last of the Maccabees*, 8.

8. Centralization of worship is implied across the Hebrew Bible, such as in the command in Deuteronomy 12:3, a command stressed repeatedly in that chapter by the Deuteronomist; see also the references to Shiloh in Jeremiah 7:12–15 and 26:4–6, and the many commands prohibiting worship in the Canaanite "high places," a reference to regional sanctuaries, generally for local deities.

from sacrificing to the deities of a city not their own. Yet the Jewish law allowed a stranger sojourning among the Jews to keep the Passover with the congregation of Israel (Ezra 6:21; see also Exod. 12:49; Lev. 19:34). Equally startling for the ancient world was the idea of proselytism, the appeal to the nations to join themselves to Israel, which begins with Second Isaiah (Isa. 49:6), continues in Third Isaiah (Isa. 56:6–8), and is repeated by later prophets (see Zech. 8:23). Thus, the postexilic community establishes a new and revolutionary principle: Thus says the Lord, "my house shall be called a house of prayer for all peoples" (Isa. 56:7).

Conversely, in antiquity, pagans make little or no efforts to convert strangers. All peoples were true believers, in their opinion, if they worshiped their ancestral gods. Jews, to the contrary, naturally proselytized Gentiles and admitted converts to the worship of their God. While only Jews were true believers, everyone was welcomed to enter the congregation of the Chosen People.

While conformity to Torah stipulations was a major characteristic of postexilic Judaism, there were different opinions among Jewish groups about interpreting the laws of the Torah, as we see during the Greco-Roman period, when groups such as the Essenes went so far as to segregate themselves in the Judean desert, considering other Jews apostate. Other Jews, such as the Sadducean elite who controlled the Jerusalem priesthood and the banking industry, adopted a policy of tolerance and compromise—an understandable attitude, since they came from families of priestly prestige and political influence. The Pharisees, in one sense stricter than the Sadducees, in another sense were more liberal, for they accepted the teachings found in books outside the Torah, such as the Prophets. Moreover, the Pharisees believed that in addition to promulgating the written Torah, Moses had also endorsed a body of oral law to interpret the meaning of what was written. This oral Torah, which they called "the Tradition of the Elders," was eventually codified in the Mishnah (about 200 CE) and finally resulted in an expanded edition known as the Talmud (completed about 500 CE).

The early Christian movement can be seen as stemming from controversies over how to apply the laws of the Torah to everyday life, and the degree to which non-Jews were bound to abide by them. In time, shaped by the theologies of Augustine and Luther, a sharp antithesis developed between "grace" and "law" in Christian circles—an antithesis postexilic Jews and early Christians would not have recognized.

QUESTIONS FOR DISCUSSION AND REFLECTION

Select one or more of the following questions and write your answer(s) in a journal. If you are in a group study, be prepared to share your answers with those in the group.

1. Explain why Second Isaiah considered Cyrus, a Persian ruler, to be a messiah (see Isa. 44:28—45:1).
2. Explain the role and message of Nehemiah.
3. Explain the role and message of Ezra.
4. Explain the role and message of Zechariah.
5. Explain the role and message of Third Isaiah.
6. Describe the turn from prophecy to apocalyptic during the Restoration period. What are the central tenets of the apocalyptic perspective, and where in the biblical literature does this perspective appear? In your estimation, was Jesus an apocalyptist? Explain your answer.
7. Explain the role and message of Jonah.
8. Explain the role and message of Esther.
9. In your estimation, why did Jewish sages flourish under Persian rule? Which books of the Bible comprise "wisdom literature"?

Chapter 6

Judaism in the Hellenistic Period

A MAJOR TURNING POINT in the history of the eastern Mediterranean world occurred in the 330s BCE, when the Persian empire was conquered by an army of Greeks and Macedonians. Greece, torn by the Peloponnesian wars from 431 to 404,[1] was ripe for control from without. Beginning in the 350s, Philip, king of Macedonia to the north, was able to dominate Greece militarily and politically. Philip had reigned for twenty-three years, all the time preparing the military machine that would crush Persia.

Philip's son, Alexander the Great (356–323), succeeded to the throne of Macedonia as a twenty-year-old, upon his father's assassination. As a young man, Alexander studied under Aristotle, one of Greece's greatest philosophers, and Alexander dreamed of conquering the world for Greek culture. Historians refer to this process as Hellenization, a term derived from *Hellas*, the Greek name for Greece.

In 334, Alexander crossed the Hellespont, the body of water dividing Europe from Asia. In a series of brilliant military successes, he quickly conquered Asia Minor, with its many cities of Greek tradition. The decisive battle was at Issus, a narrow strip of land between the mountains of Cilicia and the Mediterranean Sea, north of Syria. As we reconstruct the scene, our eyes should be set, not on the battlefield but on Syria, Egypt, Tyre, Sidon, Samaria, and Judah. None of these loved Persia, despite its benevolent strategy of conquest, which, unlike the Assyrians and Babylonians, allowed

---

1. The Peloponnesian wars, won by the Spartans, were fought by the Delian League led by Athens against the Peloponnesian League led by Sparta.

conquered peoples to return to their native regions and to live and worship there in relative freedom. Was this an auspicious time to revolt and seek political autonomy, while Darius III, the current Persian monarch, was fully occupied with the new invader?

It seemed impossible that Alexander could win the battle; his forces were greatly outnumbered, only one-tenth the size of Darius's army. Perhaps there were rumors from Greece about the new kind of army that Philip had created. In any case, the semi-independent nations waited, hoping for a stalemate that might weaken both sides. The news, when it came, was staggering. The defeat of the Persians was so complete that Darius had to flee on horseback. There was no question now that Issus spelt the defeat, not of Persia alone, but of the entire Mediterranean world.

At first, the Jews took a vacillating approach, proudly boasting they could not break their oath of allegiance to Darius. However, shortly thereafter, the Jewish high priest and all his company went out in procession from Jerusalem in their priestly robes and surrendered to Alexander, who entered Jerusalem as conqueror. This surrender came just in time, for the fate of Tyre and Egypt, who resisted, was catastrophic.

The city of Samaria revolted in 332, and Alexander, after putting down the revolt, settled Macedonians there. From Josephus we learn that when a group of Samaritans offered their help to Alexander, they received in return permission to build a temple of their own on Mt. Gerizim. It was this act that finalized the schism between the Jews and the Samaritans, a division aided by postexilic policies such as the refusal of the Jews to allow the Samaritans to help build the temple in Jerusalem in 520, and by the policy of forbidding mixed marriages pursued by Nehemiah and Ezra. Favoring their own ancestral traditions, the Macedonian colonists had no interest in the God of Israel. Over time, this group appropriated the geographical term "Samaritans," relinquishing the religious term "Israel" exclusively to Judah.

After defeating Syria and laying siege to the coastal cities of Tyre and Sidon, Alexander subdued Samaria and Jerusalem before conquering Egypt, where he founded the city of Alexandria in 331. Alexander eventually marched into the heart of Persia, overthrowing Darius and extending his territories as far east as India. Arguably the greatest conqueror in Western history, Alexander returned to Babylon, which he intended to make the capital of his vast empire. In the summer of 328, he was struck by a fever and died at the age of thirty-two years. Having failed to appoint his successor, his seven ruling generals began to quarrel among themselves. Several successors proved ineffectual, resulting eventually in a fourfold division of the empire. The region of Palestine (as the land of Israel came to be known in Roman times) came to be controlled by two rival kingdoms: the Egyptian kingdom founded by Ptolemy, and the Syrian kingdom ruled by Seleucus.

After some wrangling concerning the allocation of Palestine, which lay halfway between Syria and Egypt, the region was finally annexed by Ptolemy about 320. During the following 122 years, the Jews came under the jurisdiction of the Ptolemaic dynasty, experiencing a time of relative peace and security. Several events of this period are indicated in the summary in Daniel 11:5–45. At this time the Jews were governed by a succession of their own high priests, subject ultimately to the rule of Egypt. Overall, Ptolemaic rulers were tolerant, not interfering with the religious beliefs and practice of their subject peoples.

However, under Ptolemaic rule, as political boundaries shifted and rulers and kingdoms came and went, Hellenism flourished, certainly in major urban centers, though probably far less in rural areas. By this point a blend of Greek and Middle Eastern elements, Hellenism became a vehicle to promote unity through social change. To aid this strategy, the Greek city (*polis*) featured institutions such as gymnasiums, theaters, and public baths, as well as shrines to the Greek gods. The coinage in use under Greek rule pictured Greek gods and addressed the rulers with divine titles. The entire eastern Mediterranean came to be connected by a new lingua franca, *koine* (common) Greek (a simplification of classical Greek dialects), supplemented by Greek customs, institutions, traditions, and religions. Thus, more than at any time in previous history, Hellenism produced a form of cultural unity based on cosmopolitanism, that is, on global rather than local values.

THE JEWISH DIASPORA

Although Jews have a special connection to the land of Israel (known by such varied names and titles as Canaan, Palestine, Judea, or the Holy Land), from an early period they became widely scattered, beginning with the deportation of the Northern Kingdom to Media by the Assyrians in 722. However, since the northern tribes were apparently lost by assimilation or absorption, the Jewish Diaspora became connected more specifically with the migrations and deportations of Jews from the Southern Kingdom by the Babylonians in 586.

For a thousand years after liberation by Cyrus, well-organized Jewish communities lived in Babylon. Remaining in contact with Jews in Palestine, they eventually gave the world the Babylonian Talmud. Nevertheless, Jews spread to the north, south, and west of Palestine as well. Shortly before the conquest of Alexander the Great, the unscrupulous Persian ruler Artaxerxes

III traveled across the Middle East on a conquering rampage, subjecting the Philistine port city of Sidon to such a terrible siege in 345 that its 40,000 inhabitants committed mass suicide by setting their city on fire. From there Artaxerxes conquered Egypt in 342, subjecting its people to barbaric cruelty. Between these events, about 343, Artaxerxes took a large contingent of Palestinian Jews into captivity at Hyrcania, near the Caspian Sea, an event labeled by the scholar T. K. Cheyne as "the third of Israel's great captivities." Though Artaxerxes III only lived four years after his brutal triumphs over Sidon and Egypt, his deportation of Jews to the remote Caspian Sea, on the boundary between southeastern Europe and northwestern Asia, is often overlooked because the greater disturbance of Alexander's invasion followed only a decade later, affecting the whole of western Asia and obliterating both memories and written records.

Scholars are uncertain about the first stages of Jewish migration from Palestine to Egypt in the Hellenistic period, due to a lack of clear evidence. According to the first-century CE Jewish historian Josephus, the process was started by Alexander, who is said to have given the Jews permission to settle in Alexandria on the basis of equality of rights with the Greeks, a favor they received in return for their loyalty to him. Historians question this report, as it is not supported by more reliable sources of the Hellenistic period.

More accurate information tells us that when Ptolemy I (ruled 323–283) annexed Palestine in 320, he precipitated a sizeable Jewish immigration to Egypt. The sources preserve contradictory statements regarding Ptolemy's attitude to the Jews. According to a tradition preserved by Hecateus of Abdera, a Greek writer contemporary with Ptolemy I, the Jews, headed by their high priest Hezekiah, went to Egypt voluntarily, having heard of Ptolemy's "kindness and love of mankind." The second tradition, supported by Agatharchides and Aristeas, historians of the second and third century BCE, depicts Ptolemy I as a "hard master" to the Jews, who brought to Egypt multitudes of captives from Jerusalem. Aristeas, an official under Ptolemy II Philadelphus, tells of 100,000 Jewish captives brought to Egypt in the time of Ptolemy I; 30,000 of these, men of military age, Ptolemy placed in fortresses, and the rest (old men and children), he gave to his soldiers as slaves.

Ptolemy II (ruled 283–246), upon ascending the throne, freed these Jews from slavery. While the figure of 100,000 captives seems exaggerated, for such a large number would have depleted Palestinian Jewry, it may be accepted as factual that the Jewish diaspora in Hellenistic Egypt began under Ptolemy I, and that the vast majority of the Jews left their native country under compulsion.

While the number of Egyptian Jews in Hellenistic times was sizeable, we have no means of determining it precisely. According to Philo, they numbered one million by the first century CE, a report generally accepted by scholars as accurate. That figure, however, is probably also exaggerated, as a separate numbering of the Jews was not practical either under the Ptolemies or in Philo's day. According to Josephus, the total number of inhabitants of Egypt in the first century CE was 7.5 million, excluding Alexandrians, whose population numbered 300,000. It is hard to imagine that every eighth person in Egypt was Jewish.

In addition to significant numbers of Jews in Babylonia and Mesopotamia, where they had lived since the Babylonian Exile, Jewish influence was also significant in Adiabene, a small kingdom on the banks of the Tigris River, its kings converting to Judaism in the first century CE. Jewish presence in Asia Minor can be traced back to the reign of the Seleucid Antiochus III, who transferred 2,000 Jewish families from Babylon to Asia Minor in the period 210 to 204. Having heard of rebellion in the region of Lydia and Phrygia, Antiochus believed the Jews would serve loyally as soldiers and keepers of the Persian fortresses there. Those families, then, laid the foundation of the Jewish diaspora in Asia Minor. Their presence across Asia Minor is also attested by the New Testament book of Acts, from inscriptions, and by Philo, who indicates that by the first century CE Jews had spread to even the most remote places in Asia Minor.

The same holds true for Syria, whose figures rival those of Asia Minor. Josephus tells us that Jews were more numerous in Syria than in any other country, due to Syria's proximity to Palestine. In Roman times, Jews, like Christians, settled in cities such as Antioch, Alexandria, Ephesus, Corinth, and even Rome, places that attracted foreigners by their size, population, security, and amenities. Records show that by the second century BCE, the Jewish dispersion had reached Cyprus, Crete, Greece, and Macedonia. Jews also migrated from Egypt to Cyrene (a North-African country in modern-day Libya). According to Josephus, Jews were sent to Cyrene by Ptolemy I when he conquered the region. The fact that the Hellenistic author Jason, whose five-volume narrative is the basis of 2 Maccabees, was a native of Cyrene, indicates the high cultural level of the Jewish community in that country. In the Roman period, the Jewish population in Cyrene developed considerable strength, and at the end of the reign of Emperor Tiberius, made a desperate attempt to rebel against Rome, resulting in the destruction not only of the Jewish population of that country but also in a violent pogrom against the Jews in Alexandria in 38 CE.

As the evidence makes clear, the Jewish population was considerable in the Greco-Roman world, especially in the eastern half of the Mediterranean world. Jews and pagans would have met frequently in large cities. However, their common life confronted both groups with difficult questions. According to the influential Hellenistic scholar Victor Tcherikover, "the 'Jewish question' faced the Greeks, and later the Romans, with the same urgency that it faces the cultural world of our own day."[2]

PALESTINIAN JUDAISM UNDER THE SELEUCIDS

The comparative tranquility of the Ptolemaic era came to an abrupt end at the start of the second century BCE. In 198, Antiochus III, the enterprising ruler of the Seleucid dynasty, managed to wrest Palestine from Egyptian control and annex it to Syria. Life for the Jews became very different and much more difficult. Thirty years later, in 168, religious and cultural survival became a crisis for Palestinian Jews.

Initially, the fundamental nature of the Jewish community remained unchanged; it was primarily a religious association headed by the high priest, whose position combined civil and religious authority, aided by the council of elders, known as the *gerousia*. Judea remained a relatively small, self-contained area having only loose contact with the rest of Palestine; yet everywhere a process of Hellenization was taking place. The most concrete evidence of the cultural change was the existence in this period of the *polis* or Hellenistic city—in the Philistine plain, Gaza, Ashdod, and Ashkelon; on the coast, Joppa and Ptolemais; inland, Samaria and Beth-shan (Scythopolis); and in the Transjordan, Gadara and Philadelphia (Rabbah). Greek fashions and ways, which eventually entered Jerusalem, began posing a threat to the Jewish way of life. The impact of Greek culture and ideas on Palestinian Judaism varied. Some Jews adopted Hellenistic modes of life and thought with enthusiasm, others only opened slightly to pagan influences, while still others, called Hasidim ("pious one"), fanatically resisted acculturation.

We can see contrasting examples in two Jewish wisdom books written in the Hellenistic period, the book of Ecclesiasticus (Sirach) and the Wisdom of Solomon. These are not part of the Hebrew Bible but belong to the collection referred to by Protestants as the Apocrypha and by Roman Catholics as the deuterocanonical literature. Both books, however, were included in the Septuagint (the Greek translation of the Hebrew scripture), and therefore were read as scripture in antiquity by Jews and Christians.

Written originally in Hebrew by Jesus Ben Sira and then translated into Greek by Sira's grandson in 132 BCE, the Hebrew version of Sirach was composed in the period between 195 and 180. Ben Sira was a conservative

---

2. Tcherikover, *Hellenistic Civilization*, 295.

Jew who did not welcome Hellenism. In his book, which resembles Proverbs, he asserts that true wisdom comes from Yahweh, the God of Israel, and not from pagan philosophy. True wisdom, which existed before the creation, is embodied in the Law of Moses, known as Torah. According to Ben Sira, the evidence of God's rule in human life is to be seen in the leaders God has raised to establish and guide Israel. In a homage to Israel's leaders (found in chapters 44–50), Ben Sira singles out his contemporary Simon the high priest, who served in that office from 220 to 195 BCE. For the author, Jewish identity is found in three resources: reading and appropriating the Bible, celebrating God's historical guidance of Israel, and participating in the proper worship of God in the temple.

The Wisdom of Solomon, also called the book of Wisdom, advocates a warmer embrace of Greek culture. Written by an unknown but well-educated Jew living in Alexandria, Egypt, the book is dated by scholars to the late first century (around 20 BCE). The association with Solomon derives from the middle section of the book, where the unnamed speaker is recognized as King Solomon. Composed in elegant Greek, this book is a highly Hellenized work. It evidences interaction with Greek culture, especially Greek philosophy. Its literary style is that of the diatribe, in which the author publicly debates issues, raising questions and offering solutions. Featuring imaginary dialogues, this literary device, common to the Greek philosophical tradition, is also used by Paul in his letter to the Romans, particularly in chapters 2 and 3, where rhetorical questions set up dialogues with imagined objectors. The diatribe style also helps us to interpret Romans 7, where Paul conducts a complex argument regarding the role of religious law for Christians.

For the author of Wisdom, the virtues that wisdom instills are those of Stoic philosophy: temperance, prudence, justice, and fortitude. As in Sirach, the history of Israel is retold in Wisdom, but here it is recounted not so much as a celebration of the past but as a kind of parable or metaphor of the journey of the soul that leads to knowledge of God and of God's purpose and will for humanity. In this respect, Wisdom's approach is similar to that of Philo of Alexandria, the first-century CE Jewish scholar known for interpreting the details of the Mosaic Torah in allegorical fashion, or of Plotinus, the third-century CE Neoplatonist pagan philosopher who speaks of the ascent of the soul from ignorance to union with God.

According to Josephus, when Antiochus III defeated Egypt and annexed Palestine, Antiochus was gracious to Jerusalem, ordering the repair of damages suffered in the past and providing an allowance for temple expenses. He also allowed the framework of local government to continue, aided by tax exemptions. However, when Antiochus intervened in international affairs, he had to answer to Rome, paying a bitter price in the treaty of Apamea (188), when he was forced to evacuate Asia Minor and pay a severe indemnity. The need for money required further military campaigns, leading to his premature death in battle in 187.

He was succeeded by his son Seleucus IV (187–175), while a younger son, Antiochus (later named Epiphanes), was held hostage in Rome in lieu of full payment of the indemnity. During Seleucus's reign, his chief minister Heliodorus went to the Jerusalem temple to obtain additional funds. Heliodorus then killed Seleucus, making way for Antiochus IV, recently released from Rome, to assume royal power. Antiochus adopted as throne name the title of Epiphanes (manifestation of the divine Zeus); however, his subjects nicknamed him Epimanes (madman). His policy was one of unity (and therefore the Hellenization of all his subjects) and expansion, and this required large sums of money.

Our best literary sources for this period of history are the books of 1 and 2 Maccabees. Written from the perspective of those who strongly resisted the imposition of Hellenistic culture, these books condemn the Hellenizers, while at the same time providing a narrative of current political and social events. 1 Maccabee, written by an ardent Jewish patriot living in Jerusalem, is a stirring narrative. As the Hasmonean court historian under John Hyrcanus, the author wrote his book about 100 BCE. The unknown author, dependent upon archives of historically valuable material, wrote a sober and straightforward account of the Maccabean uprising against the policies of Antiochus IV, covering about forty years (175–134). 2 Maccabees, written around 125 BCE, deals with a period of about fifteen years, covering the period of Antiochus IV's rule (175–164) and ending about 160. The author, likely an Alexandrian Jew, indicates that he has epitomized a larger work, consisting of five books composed by Jason of Cyrene. 2 Maccabees begins with the pre-Maccabean history, relating the causes that provoked the Jewish rebellion, starting with the unsuccessful attempt by Heliodorus, envoy of Seleucus IV, to plunder the Jerusalem temple, an attempt the author describes as having been deterred by angelic beings (2 Macc. 3:1–40). Contrary to 1 Maccabees, the author includes Antiochus IV's vow to make a full restitution to the Jews, promising to become a Jew himself (9:11–17). His deathbed repentance urges Jews to be loyal to his successor, Antiochus V (9:18–27).

The two books of Maccabees are independent of one another, the unknown author of 2 Maccabees writing in an artificial style called "pathetic history," popular in Alexandria during the first century BCE. His book, rhetorical and melodramatic, is historically less reliable than 1 Maccabees.

The episode of Heliodorus in Jerusalem proved an ill omen of future Seleucid policy, aided by corruption in the Oniad family of priests in Jerusalem. The Oniads belonged to a family led by a certain Yohanan (Honi; Greek form, Onias), father of the high priest Simon, fervently praised in Sirach 50:1–21. Simon's son, Onias III (probably the "anointed prince" of whom Daniel speaks in 9:25–26), was high priest when Antiochus IV ascended the throne. However, Onias became the victim of his brother Jason, a Hellenist who set out to buy the office of high priesthood from the Seleucid authorities. Taking the bait, Antiochus IV deposed Onias in favor of Jason. During Jason's term as high priest (174–171), a full-scale Hellenization of Jerusalem was begun, despite the opposition of many Jews, who remained loyal to the tradition, especially the Hasidim, a group of super patriots called the "wise" in Daniel 12:3 and 12:10.

In 171, Jason, the brilliant conniver, was in turn outwitted by a certain Menelaus, to whom Antiochus gave the office of high priest, forcing Jason to flee to the Transjordan. Menelaus, pushing forward the Hellenization program, conspired to have Onias III murdered in Syria, where he had fled (according to 2 Maccabees 4, this happened in Daphne, near Antioch). These events provoked a civil war in Judea, the majority of Jews supporting Jason over Menelaus.

Of course, the situation is often more complicated than it seems, for by the seventies of the second century, those in power in Jerusalem were noted for their strong adherence to Hellenism. While the lower classes and rural priests were mostly traditionalist, the upper stratum of the priestly class (including the high priesthood), the Jerusalem aristocracy (members of the *gerousia*), and the wealthy elite, were all pro-Seleucid.

The important Tobiad family exemplified the ties that bound many Jews to the new ways. Descendants of the enemy of Nehemiah (Neh. 2:10), the Tobiads resided in splendor in the Transjordan region. Already in the third century BCE, they served as governors over the region. A Tobiad named Joseph won the favor of the ruling Ptolemies, and was appointed tax collector. Ruthless in his post, he became very wealthy. Through marriage, the Tobiads maintained close ties with the Oniads. For example, Joseph, son of Tobiah, became the nephew of Onias II by marriage. In his *Antiquities*, Josephus relates the biographies of Joseph and his son Hyrcanus in detail. Hyrcanus is mentioned as possessing treasure in the temple at Jerusalem (2 Macc. 3:11), which served the banking needs of the Jewish elite. The Tobiads lost their power and influence by the start of the Maccabean revolt, when Antiochus IV confiscated their possessions.

Under Antiochus IV, the Jewish Hellenizers converted Jerusalem into a Greek *polis* called Antioch-at-Jerusalem. In 169 a regular Greek city, surrounded by walls and fortified by towers, was built on one of the hills of Jerusalem, opposite the Temple Mount (see Dan. 11:39). The name of the city became Akra, that is, Citadel. As the center of the *polis* of Antioch-at-Jerusalem, the Akra ended in 162; however, as a fortress, the Akra continued to be an important Syrian outpost during the Maccabean period until 142, serving as the final refuge of the Hellenizers. During this period, the Jewish Hellenizers introduced Greek customs into Jewish life, built a gymnasium, and did not oppose the spread of the Greek gods in Jerusalem. This group allied with Antiochus IV, who intervened in the affairs of Judea, and backed their agenda with his military might. With his aid, the Hellenizers temporarily retained control of Jerusalem, until 168, when the Hasidim, combining religious and military might, put an end to their aspirations and restored the traditional form of national life.

With the death of Onias III and the unseating of Jason by Menelaus, the fortunes of the Oniads were dealt a crippling, though not a final, blow. In his *Antiquities*, Josephus tells us that the youngest Oniad (Onias IV) went to Egypt after the death of Menelaus in 162, when the high priesthood was officially transferred to Alcimus, a known Hellenizer.[3] In Egypt, Onias IV joined a Jewish military community in the remote village of Leontopolis, located in the Nile Delta between Alexandria and the ancient Egyptian city of Memphis. In his journey to Egypt, Onias was accompanied by priests, relatives, and supporters of the lawful dynasty of the House of Onias. In Leontopolis, later known as "Onias's territory," Onias established a reputation as a warrior loyal to the Ptolemies, founding a *katoikia*, a military colony where the troops dwelt when they were not needed for a campaign. In his role, Onias emerged as an Egyptian *strategoi*, that is, as a person of great influence in the Egyptian state.

At the death of Ptolemy VI Philometor (181-145), the latter's widow, Cleopatra, faced two foes, the future ruler, Ptolemy VIII Euergetes, who throughout his life had fought against his brother Philometor, and the Alexandrian populace, bent on uprising. Onias remained loyal to Cleopatra, entering Alexandria at the head of a military unit, intent on suppressing the revolt. Thus, the Jews took part in the political affairs of the Egyptian state, demonstrating the growing esteem given, at least officially, to the Jewish

---

3. According to Josephus, Alcimus did not belong to the Oniads. 2 Maccabees, on the other hand, says that Alcimus considered the high priesthood an ancestral inheritance, suggesting that he belonged to the Oniad family. In any case, the ruling Maccabean leaders, viewing Alcimus as a Seleucid pawn, did not accept his legitimacy. After Alcimus's death, the post of Jewish high priest remained vacant for seven years.

population of Egypt, and its flourishing condition in the middle of the second century BCE.

The intervention of the Jews in the life of the Egyptian state did not go well under Euergetes, however, a harsh and brutal individual who ruled Egypt from 145 to 116. Viewing the Jews unfavorably on account of the alliance with his deceased brother, Euergetes is known as the first person in history to attempt to perpetrate pogroms on the Jews. Thankfully, the persecution under Euergetes was short-lived. Later, in the time of Julius Caesar, the Jews at Leontopolis were charged with guarding the strategic route from Pelusium to Memphis, and when Antipater, Herod the Great's father, was hastening to Caesar's help, he entered into diplomatic negotiations with these Jewish warriors in order to bring them to his side.

About 145 BCE, when Onias IV founded the Jewish *katoikia* at Leontopolis, he built a temple, not so much to rival the Jerusalem temple, as many later interpreters suggest, but to meet the needs of the colonists there. His object was not to provide Egyptian Jewry with a temple of its own, a need the earlier temple at Elephantine had not intended to meet either, for Egyptian Jewry never officially recognized either shrine, so long as the temple of Jerusalem remained intact.

However, if the temple was built to meet only local needs, why not erect a synagogue instead? Two answers are normally given. The first, by Josephus, is related to Onias's personal ambition: he built a temple "to acquire a reputation and in order that his memory might be perpetuated." In other words, Onias sought to create for himself the atmosphere of high priesthood, a theocracy modeled upon the traditional Jerusalem aristocracy.

The second answer is more convincing, for it has to do with Egyptian ambitions in Palestine. Egypt had never given up its claims to southern Syria, a region annexed to Egypt during the preceding century and strategic to its military designs. Thus, when signs of decay appeared in the Seleucid dynast, Egypt was ready to intervene. Philometor had waged a prolonged war with Syria and even succeeded in having the crown offered him by the people of Antioch, had he not died in battle against Syrian forces.

The political situation of Palestine was unclear now, for the Hasmonean kingdom had not yet crystallized by 145, and the high priest Jonathan was still a Seleucid official representing Syria in a southern province of Syria. A rival candidate for the position of high priest, with legitimate rights to govern Jerusalem and dependent on Egyptian royal favor, would have been highly desirable to Philometor.

THE MACCABEAN ERA

The Seleucid king Antiochus IV Epiphanes (ruled 175–164) was eager to coerce his subjects, including the Jews, into conformity with Hellenism. However, Antiochus's enthusiasm for Hellenism was not the only reason for his intervention in Jewish affairs. He needed money, for protracted wars with the Ptolemies and the staggering expense of keeping his vast kingdom under control had drained his treasury. Jewish resentment against Antiochus was first felt on the economic level, in the form of higher taxes. However, it rose to a revolutionary pitch when the most sacred office, that of high priest, was auctioned off to the highest bidder.

After an unsuccessful attempt in 169 to conquer Egypt, Antiochus returned through Palestine in a spirit of vindictiveness. Treating the Jews and Jerusalem as though they had been the cause of his defeat, he gained possession of the city by treachery, sacking it and, with help from Menelaus, plundered the temple, destroying many sites. In 168, on his return from a second Egyptian campaign and angered by an ultimatum from Rome to leave Egypt immediately, Antiochus took further retaliatory measures. Faced with mounting opposition from Jews who called themselves Hasidim, he outlawed Jewish religion and issued orders intended to Hellenize Jewish life. The observance of the Sabbath, the rite of circumcision, and possession of the Hebrew scriptures were made crimes punishable by death. Jewish worship was abolished, pagan altars were erected across Judea, and Jews were forced to eat pork and make sacrifices to Zeus. The climax came when Antiochus erected an altar to Zeus (the "abomination of desolation" or "desolating sacrilege" of Daniel 9:27; 11:31; 12:11; see Mark 13:14), sacrificing swine—the most unclean animal, according to Jewish law—on the temple altar.

During the reign of terror, many Jews yielded to these decrees; others, refusing to surrender their faith, went to their deaths or fled into hiding. The tinder for revolt needed only a spark to ignite it. The spark was struck several months later in Modein, a town in the hill country a few miles northwest of Jerusalem. Mattathias, an elderly local priest, refused when a Syrian officer demanded that citizens make a pagan sacrifice. Then, seeing another Jew come forward to make sacrifice, Mattathias became enraged and killed both the Jew and the Syrian officer. He and his five sons fled to the hills, where they were joined by a band of loyal Jews. Using guerrilla tactics and, above all, their zeal, they organized opposition to Hellenistic rule.

On his deathbed, Mattathias commissioned his eldest son, Judas, a vigorous fighter nicknamed Maccabee ("hammer"), as leader of the nationalistic movement. Despite overwhelming odds, Judas and his band achieved astonishing results, soon winning a surprising victory over Antiochus's forces. By 165, the Maccabees had gained military control of much of the land. In 164, hearing of the death of Antiochus fighting against the Parthians on his eastern frontier, the Syrian general Lysius agreed to an accord with Judas and his party. The temple in Jerusalem was to be purified and restored to its original purpose, and the Jews were guaranteed religious freedom. In December, 164, three and a half years after its defilement by Antiochus (three and a half years is the "half week" of years of which Daniel speaks in 9:27 and the 1150 days of 8:14), Judas rebuilt the altar of the temple and restored Jewish worship, thereby inaugurating the festival of Hanukkah ("Rededication") that Jews still celebrate today.

About 165, after the outbreak of the Maccabean revolt and shortly before the death of Antiochus, an unknown author composed the book of Daniel, the last book of the Hebrew Bible to be written. Undoubtedly, the author was one of the Hasidim, a pious Jew who opposed Hellenistic ways and the tyranny by which it was imposed. The book is said to set forth the theology of the Maccabean revolution, and is rightly called "the Manifesto of the Hasidim."

The book of Daniel consists of two evenly divided halves. The first six chapters contain six accounts of Jewish heroes exiled to the Babylonian court in the sixth century BCE. The function of those chapters is to provide role models for the Hasidim. The last six chapters contain four visions, designed to provide assurance to the Hasidim that the future was in God's hands and that all would end well for God's faithful remnant. The book contains some historical errors, particularly concerning the Babylonian and Persian empires, events that had occurred much earlier, many of them hazy in the author's mind. Paradoxically, though the author was intimately acquainted with the career of Antiochus Epiphanes, he was incorrect about the details of Antiochus's death (11:45). Antiochus did not die, as the author says, between Jerusalem and the Mediterranean Sea, but in Persia. And the eschatological end did not arrive with the death of Antiochus, or even three and a half years later, as Daniel imagined (see 12:11–12, which lengthens the time before the culmination to 1290 days and then extends it to 1335 days, perhaps an anxious adjustment by a later editor when the expected end did not materialize).

What began as a resistance movement eventually exploded into a war of independence, carried on successively by the brothers of Judas, Jonathan and Simon (whose family name was Hasmonean), who acquired the dual roles of priestly and royal leadership. Favored by international developments, especially by Rome's increasing interferences in Near Eastern affairs, the zealous Maccabees achieved nearly a century of independence, from

142 to 63 BCE, by which time Palestinian Jewry grew disillusioned with a dynasty of kings who had not descended from David's royal line and who lacked the proper high-priestly pedigree. Failing to unify the Jewish nation or to inspire its people, the Maccabean rulers and their successors became increasingly secular and oppressive. Finally, out of desperation, the last of the Maccabees turned for support to Rome, the rising power in the west. In 63, Roman forces under Pompey, claiming to assist their ally, invaded Palestine, taking over control and establishing the region as a Roman province.

As far back as the pre-Maccabean period, the conflict between the major priestly and political factions in Palestine was not primarily over Hellenization, for the leaders of both sides were positively inclined toward Hellenism. Rather, the conflict was political, a conflict over whether to align with the Seleucids or the Ptolemies. As a result of the Maccabean revolt, Jonathan eventually took control, only to do what Jason and Menelaus had done, allied with one of the Seleucids (Alexander Ballas), accepting from him the title of high priest, of which he was less qualified than Jason. The Hasmoneans retained the title throughout their reign.

The later Hasmoneans proved to be quite Hellenized, in conflict with more traditionally inclined Jews, as the Jewish ruling class found Hellenism attractive. The Maccabean revolt was essentially against Seleucid domination, not a crusade against Greek culture in general. The Maccabean propaganda, especially as found in 1 and 2 Maccabees, made the revolt about Hellenism, and that accusation became a powerful rhetorical weapon in the hands of the Maccabees. However, the Maccabean literature was pro-Hasmonean and therefore biased. For example, Judas Maccabeus, unlike other Hasidim, decided to fight on the Sabbath, breaking with traditional Judaism. This proved to be a pragmatic (Hellenistic?) decision. Other Palestinian Jews of the time took Greek names, sent their children to Hellenistic schools, attended theaters and sporting events, and otherwise adopted the philosophical concepts of the Hellenistic culture. Some Jewish males went so far as to have the marks of circumcision surgically removed, so they could take part without embarrassment in the nude gymnastics of the contemporary Hellenistic culture.

During this period and into the first century CE, the Jewish nation lacked leaders who could weld the people into a strong unit. The leaders themselves were divided into various sectarian parties. Though these groups tolerated one another, each saw itself as the most authentic expression of Jewish identity. Likewise, each took a distinguishable stance toward pagan ruling authorities and the Hellenistic world.

On the one hand, there were the supporters of the Maccabean priest-rulers, their first concern being political power. Eventually this party came to be known as the Sadducees. The elite of Jewish society, they controlled the priesthood and the banking establishment. As members of the aristocracy, they appear to have been conciliatory toward the ruling Roman authorities, and it is likely through them that many Hellenistic ideas entered Judaism. They disappeared from history following the destruction of Jerusalem and the temple in 70 CE.

Over against them, and regarding them at times with bitter hatred, were the descendants of those who had supported Judas Maccabeus from the first days of the revolt to the rededication of the temple in 164, but who then withdrew their aid, on the basis that religious freedom was all they needed. From this group of Hasidim arose the party known as the Pharisees, a pietistic movement composed largely of laity. Recruited from the middle orders of society, they had a large following among the masses. Concerned with maintaining the distinctive practices and beliefs of Judaism, they could be faulted for being legalistic and for their rigid interpretation of the Sabbath laws. During the first century CE, both Jesus and Paul would be identified as closer to the Pharisees than to any other religious grouping. Significantly, it was through the Pharisaic wing, primarily as espoused by Paul, that many distinctive Christian doctrines emerged, including divine inspiration of scripture, election and predestination of believers, bodily resurrection of the dead, and belief in spirit beings. Combining conservative and progressive elements, this group alone, of the chief religious Jewish sects, survived the destruction of Jerusalem in 70 CE, becoming the basis for Rabbinic Judaism.

For the group known as the Essenes, however, even the distinctives observed by the Pharisees were not enough to keep them from cultural pollution. Concerned with purity, they left ordinary society and set up separate communities, with their own literature and traditions (believed to be the writers of the Dead Sea Scrolls, they are the subject of great scholarly interest). Believing that matter and pleasure are evil, they focused on ritual baptisms, stated periods of prayer, and the continuous reading and study of the Hebrew scriptures, all preparatory for an eschatological war with Rome, which they believed would usher God's long-awaited messianic kingdom. In 68 CE, because of the destruction of Qumran, their Dead Sea community, by the Roman armies, they joined the Zealots in active combat.

The Zealots, heirs of the Maccabees, emerged as a definite party by 6 CE, when the Romans took a census in Palestine for the sake of taxation. The movement grew in response to ongoing acts of Roman aggression. The Zealots held a militant version of the Essene theme of separation, feeling the only solution to severe Roman rule was to fight fire with fire, replicating the Maccabean tradition of violent resistance. It was they who gave impetus to the disastrous Jewish revolts against Rome (in 70 and in 132–135 CE) that would shatter Jewish life in Palestine. Out of that destruction emerged the Jewish sect that became Christianity, a world religion in its own right, inspired by the Jew, Jesus of Nazareth.

Political power remained with the Sadducees. In 142, Palestinian leadership fell to Simon, the last remaining son of Mattathias. In the same years Demetrius II, king of Syria, granted the Jews complete independence. This period of national freedom lasted about eighty years (until 63 BCE), the only such period of political independence the Jews knew from 586 BCE until the establishment of the modern nation of Israel by act of the United Nations in 1948. After Simon and his two sons were assassinated in 134 by Simon's ruthless son-in-law Ptolemy, the only surviving son who escaped, John, assumed the power and became known as John Hyrcanus (134–104).

Embarking on a career of expansion, John Hyrcanus subjugated the Transjordan, compelling the Idumean Arabs there to adopt Judaism as their faith, a step that involved forcibly circumcising male adults and male offspring, an act that produced momentous consequences for Palestinian Jews a century later, when Herod the Great, a descendant of these Idumeans, began a dynasty of local rulers, serving under Rome as client "King of the Jews." Hyrcanus also overran Samaria to the north, capturing the city of Shechem and destroying the temple on Mt. Gerizim.

After a long reign, Hyrcanus was succeeded by his son Aristobulus, who became known as a Philhellene—a friend of Greeks. A cruel and tyrannical individual, he changed the theocracy into a kingdom, calling himself a king but retaining the title of high priest. During his brief reign of one year, Galilee to the north of Samaria was conquered, and the Galileans, most of whom were Gentiles, were forcibly converted to Judaism.

THE HERODIAN DYNASTY AND THE JEWISH WARS AGAINST ROME

At the conclusion of the Hasmonean era, after Palestine was torn by dissensions between the Sadducees and the Pharisees, civil war broke out. Weakened by internal strife, the country became an easy prey to foreign domination. After attempting to negotiate with both Jewish factions, Pompey, the able Roman general, took possession of Jerusalem in 63, abolishing the Jewish kingdom and converting Palestine into the Roman province of Judea. As a result, Palestinian Jews were required to pay tribute, but they remained for a time under native rulers. In time, they came under rule by Herod, who, after subjugating the unwilling inhabitants of Judea, became client king with the capture of Jerusalem in 37 BCE. Herod's dynasty ruled over Judea until the fateful war of the Jews against Rome (66–70 CE), that ended with the siege and destruction of Jerusalem and the razing of the temple. Captives and spoils were carried to Rome for Titus's triumphal procession, and Roman coins were minted bearing the legend *Iudea Capta*.

Untold numbers of Jews perished during the four years of warfare, many thousands were sold into slavery or kept for gladiatorial games, and only a remnant remained in Judea. The country was made into an imperial province and renamed Palestine (Land of the Philistines) to symbolize the extinction of the Jewish nation. The cessation of temple worship required a rethinking of Judaism—and to some extent also of Christianity, by now more than a Jewish sect. Greater importance came to belong to the Jews of the Diaspora[4] and the predominantly Gentile character of Christianity became increasingly more pronounced.

A final attempt at restoring an independent Jewish nation took place under the reign of Emperor Hadrian (117–138 CE). In 132, when Hadrian issued a decree changing Jerusalem into a Roman colony, a second Jewish revolt took place, under the leadership of the messianic figure, Simon bar Coseba, nicknamed Bar Cochba ("Son of the Star"). After a bitter struggle lasting three years, the Romans ended the revolt in 135, at which time Hadrian instituted his plan. The devastated city of Jerusalem was rebuilt, laid out according to a Roman grid, and renamed Aelia Capitolina (*Aelia* after the family name of Hadrian, *Capitolina* in honor of Jupiter Capitolinus, the Roman God as worshiped in his great temple on the Capitoline Hill in Rome). On the site of the ancient Jewish temple Hadrian erected a pagan temple to Jupiter, and for some time thereafter, Jerusalem was off limits to Jews. All that remained of Jerusalem's ancient fortifications was the Western wall of the Temple Mount, a site Jews would visit on penalty of death as the Wailing Wall.

THE EMERGENCE OF RABBINIC JUDAISM

Despite the complete defeat of Zealots and other Jewish nationalists by the Romans in 70 and 135 CE, the continuity of Jewish identity and commitment was effectively carried out through the emergent rabbinic pattern of interpretation and practice of the Jewish tradition. Up to the fall of Jerusalem in 70, Jewish life was administered by a governing council called the Sanhedrin, a body in Jerusalem composed of seventy persons, presided

---

4. Scholars often call dispersed Jews of the period "Hellenistic Jews," in distinction from their counterparts in Palestine, appropriately named "Palestinian Jews."

over by the high priest, making seventy-one members. In New Testament times, the Sanhedrin included two types of members: the elders (the current high priest, previous high priests, and representatives of the lay aristocracy, chiefly from the Sadducean party), and the scribes (legal experts chiefly from the Pharisaic party). Under Herod the Great, the Sanhedrin possessed only limited powers, whereas under the Roman governors, it was the chief governing body in the land, regulating religious matters in complete freedom and civil matters within limits set by Rome. It was before this body that Jesus and later Peter and John, Stephen, and Paul were tried. The Sanhedrin was abolished at the destruction of Jerusalem in 70 CE.

Toward the end of the first century CE, Judaism began to undergo a major transformation. Schools came to be attached to synagogues. Instead of the earlier haphazard and unstructured exposition of the scriptures, conducted by individual teachers, methods of interpretation came to be specified and written down. After the fall of Jerusalem, scribes continued to exposit and codify Jewish law. These developments resulted in a weighty literature produced through the synagogue movement from the second to the sixth centuries. Included in the ancient documents were records of teachings and debates between representatives of various points of view among the rabbis. The title rabbi narrowed in meaning from a teacher of Torah to specialized leaders who focused their time and energy on interpreting the literature and its oral developments.

By about 100 CE, this tradition became institutionalized in an academy, established by an exile from Jerusalem named Johanan ben Zakkai. He received permission from the Roman authorities to establish a Jewish center in the coastal town of Javneh (Jamnia), where he worked to finalize the canonical process begun by Ezra. After Jamnia, the center of Palestinian Judaism moved to Galilee. About 200 CE, the initial legal collection of oral and institutional traditions was codified by Rabbi Judah ha-Nasi ("the Prince"). This material, in Hebrew, called the Mishnah ("learning"), comprises sixty-three tractates grouped in six major divisions.

Reducing the traditional law to writing did not end the matter. The ongoing oral traditions were collected at two great rabbinical schools, one in Palestine and the other in Babylonia. Called the Gemara ("study"), each of these commentaries on the Mishnah, embracing wide-ranging topics from jurisprudence, history, philosophy, and ethics to legend and folklore, soon imposed such a strain on the memory that in the fourth century the Gemara was reduced to writing in a multi-volume library known as the Palestinian Talmud ("teaching"). In the sixth century (about 500 CE) the much longer Babylonian Talmud was compiled. Consisting of Halakah (directions for everyday life) and Haggadah (inspiring and instructive tales), the Mishnah and the two Talmuds provide guidance for observant Jews. Supplementing these texts are the Targums, collections of paraphrases of the Hebrew Bible in Aramaic, the lingua franca throughout the Middle East in the ancient world. The emergence in the second to sixth centuries of these teachings made possible Jewish re-appropriation of the biblical traditions in a way that would ensure continuity for Jewish identity.

QUESTIONS FOR DISCUSSION AND REFLECTION

Select one or more of the following questions and write your answer(s) in a journal. If you are in a group study, be prepared to share your answers with those in the group.

1. Explain the term "Hellenism," and its impact on Second Temple Judaism.
2. In your estimation, were Palestinian Jews of the third and second centuries BCE better off siding with the Ptolemies (Egypt) or with the Seleucids (Syria)? Explain your answer.
3. Explain and assess the role and message of the Hasidim.
4. Explain and assess the role and message of Ecclesiasticus (Sirach).
5. Explain and assess the role and message of the Wisdom of Solomon.
6. Explain and assess the role and message of the book of Daniel.
7. Explain and assess the role and message of 1 and 2 Maccabees.
8. Describe the differences between Sadducees, Pharisees, Essenes, and Zealots. In your estimation, which best expressed Jewish identity? Explain your answer.

Chapter 7

The Pagan-Jewish Debate

DURING THE LAST THREE centuries BCE, all branches and forms of Judaism, whether in Palestine or the Diaspora, were affected to some degree by the prevailing Hellenistic environment. However, the greatest borrowing from Hellenism occurred among the Jews of the Mediterranean diaspora, especially among those living in the Egyptian metropolis of Alexandria. Alexandrian Jews produced an extensive body of literature in the Greek language, some texts surviving only in quotations, but other works preserved in complete form.

Apart from the Septuagint, Hellenistic-Jewish literature includes (1) epic poems and tragic dramas on biblical themes, of which only a few passages have been preserved; (2) historical works such as 1 and 2 Maccabees on the Maccabean revolt, 3 Maccabees on a supposed persecution of the Jews of Egypt in the mid-third century BCE, and the *Letter of Aristeas*, which contains the legend of how the Septuagint was translated; (3) imitations of pagan prophecies such as the Jewish Sibylline Oracles, which denounced idolatry and praised Jewish monotheism; and (4) several treatises showing the growing impact of Hellenistic philosophy on Jews, such as the Wisdom of Solomon, 4 Maccabees, and the writings of Philo of Alexandria.

ANTI-JUDAISM

With notable exceptions, Jews in the Hellenistic age were granted special privileges. In many localities, Jews long enjoyed freedom to pursue their unique customs and worship their God alone. Friendly Jews could be a source of military strength, and Jewish soldiers were notoriously loyal to their leaders. In Roman times, freedom of Jewish worship was guaranteed by Julius Caesar (about 48 BCE), through a decree of the Senate.

As to the nature of these privileges, Jews were not required to serve in the army or to provide an allotment of soldiers for service to Rome, as was required of other conquered peoples. Nor could Jewish soldiers be made to march or to fight on the Sabbath. Moreover, Jews were not required to worship Roman gods. While punishments followed any group or individual who failed to support emperor-worship, the Jews were exempt. For example, they were allowed to celebrate imperial festivals in their own way; instead of rendering offerings to the emperor and his family in pagan temples, Jews were allowed to substitute prayers on their behalf in their synagogues and in the temple in Jerusalem. Roman law also forbid placing imperial standards or other images in the synagogues. Furthermore, Jews were allowed to form associations and control the marital, financial, and judicial life of their members.

These and other privileges were granted Jews *en bloc*, that is, as a cohesive unit, for the various Jewish communities were viewed as a cohesive unity, legally part of one body. Culturally and religiously, Jewish communities were subordinate to central Jewish authority. Until the destruction of the temple in 70 CE, the high priest at Jerusalem was the chief of Jews everywhere, and Rome dealt with him on behalf of all Jews. However, in the Diaspora, as in Palestine, the synagogue, with its trained rabbi, was the center of the community.

Though Jews in the Greco-Roman age were privileged, they were not always safe. Privileges evoked protests, and attacks upon Jews then, as so often since, were common. It is probably erroneous to refer to these attacks as anti-Semitic, because that term presupposes the developed social theories of the nineteenth century. For that reason, the preferred term is "anti-Jewish."

The first contacts between Jews and Greeks were military and highly favorable. To the Greeks, Jews at first appeared as an admirable school of philosophers, and during the persecutions under Antiochus Epiphanes, it was to Sparta that many Jews turned. Spartan disciple and Jewish legalism were congenial.

Apart from the retaliatory attacks of Jews in Egypt by Euergetes II in the second century BCE, we do not hear of a specific pogrom until Roman times, when the first Roman emperor Caesar Augustus (ruled 19 BCE–14 CE) deprived the Greek inhabitants of Alexandria of their Senate, at the same time conferring the Jews all their rights. There were further outbreaks against Jews in the time of Caligula (37–41), when wealthy Jews of Alexandria were driven to the Delta region and four hundred of their houses were sacked. According to Josephus, in the late sixties, fifty thousand Jews were killed in Alexandria. During this period, even Roman Jews experienced uncertainty, undergoing expulsion under Tiberius (19 CE) and Claudius (49–50).

Anti-Judaism, even though it only erupted into open violence in the Roman period, had ancient roots. The Hellenistic age, syncretistic in nature, demanded religious pluralism that Jews could not fully support. However far Jews went toward assimilation, their cultural norms and religious commandments made final assimilation impossible. Thus, the Jews were accused of atheism, not because they rejected images (we have numerous examples of synagogue images in floor mosaics and wall paintings in Roman times, both in Palestine and in the Diaspora), but because they opposed worship of the "gods," an essential pillar of pagan life.

During the rule of Augustus, an important change took place in the situation of the Jews of Egypt, chiefly in Alexandria, when the question of Jewish citizenship provoked a decidedly practical problem. Augustus differentiated between the Greeks and other inhabitants of Egypt: the former enjoyed various privileges, while the latter were classed as simple subjects, and the whole burden of taxation fell upon them.

According to ancient sources, the most fateful year of the struggle for Jewish rights in Egypt was in 41 CE, when the "Jewish question" came up for arbitration at Rome before the Emperor Claudius, and delegations from both sides, representing non-Jewish citizens of Alexandria and Jewish residents of the city, appeared before him to defend their positions. One of the leaders of the Alexandrian opposition, Isidoros, uttered these words about the Jews of the city: "They are not like the Alexandrians, but in their way of life (they resemble) the Egyptians. Are they not like those who pay tribute (that is, the poll-tax)?" In a famous letter written to the Alexandrians in the year 41, Emperor Claudius addressed "the Alexandrians" and "the Jews" separately, thereby acknowledging that he did not consider Jews as citizens of the city. Claudius went on to prohibit Jews from participating in public (that is, in gymnasium) education, warning them not to aspire to additional rights but to be satisfied with the ordinary benefits of urban life. Claudius's letter agreed with the claims of the anti-Jewish faction, ending the struggle of Alexandrian Jews for emancipation.

However, Alexandrian Jews were not prepared so easily to accept defeat. All possible literary means were brought into play to prove to their antagonists the justness of their claims. This propaganda literature, primarily that written by Philo of Alexandria and later by the pro-Roman Palestinian historian, Josephus, like all literature created for political purposes, was one-sided and biased in nature.

PHILO OF ALEXANDRIA

According to ancient records, the Jewish community in Egypt was both sizeable and influential, an important percentage living in Alexandria, Egypt's great northern port city. Egypt's Ptolemaic rulers (332–30 BCE) assigned two of the city's five districts to the Jews, thereby allowing them to live according to their religious laws and cultural customs. Philo of Alexandria (c. 20 BCE–c. 50 CE) stood at the apex of the cultural activity of the Jewish-Alexandrian community, his literary work climaxing a long chain of Jewish-Hellenistic writings whose aim was to establish the validity and integrity of Jewish religious thought in the face of the counterclaims of the intellectually dominant Greek tradition. Educated primarily in a Hellenic environment, the son of a wealthy, aristocratic Jewish family, in his mature years Philo gained a profound interest in his Jewish heritage. His aim was to demonstrate that the truths discovered by Plato and other Greek philosophers had developed from the God-given teaching of Moses, and that it was the same truth as revealed in scripture.

Two of his works in particular, *Against Flaccus* and *The Delegation to Gaius*, written a short time after the riots against the Jews in the year 38, were apologetic in nature, denouncing to the Roman authorities those guilty of anti-Jewish persecution. Philo tells of attempts by Flaccus, the Roman governor of Egypt, to destroy the internal organization of the Jewish community of Alexandria and to deny its share of political rights.

From these writings we deduce that the Alexandrian Jews, in their claim to be citizens, could point to certain practices established during the Ptolemaic period designed to bridge the gap between Jews and Greeks. The new situation gave anti-Jews a pretext to call into question even those rights that had been the foundation of Jewish life in Alexandria from the start. Unfortunately, Philo's endeavors on behalf of the Alexandrian Jews did not end well.

Other than heading the Jewish delegation to the Roman Emperor Caligula in 39–40, following the violent pogrom against Jews in 38, little is known about Philo, aside from his voluminous religious writings, cast in the form of a commentary on the Pentateuch (the first five books of the Old Testament). He could have fashioned his synthesis of Judaism and Hellenism in the form of philosophical essays dealing with the major themes of biblical thought, but chose instead to pursue an exegetical approach, combining reverence for the text with the greatest possible freedom in interpreting it.

This he achieved by the method of allegory, a method he learned from the translators of the Septuagint, but also from Alexandrian Jews such as Aristobulus, who used allegory a century earlier to explain away the cruder anthropomorphisms of the Pentateuch. More importantly, Philo adapted his technique from the Greek allegorical tradition associated with the writings of Homer. In order to justify Homer against the detractors of his theology, this exegetical tradition attempted to demythologize the Homeric gods, employing ethical allegory to explain the Homeric epics as treatises on virtue and justice. Philosophical groups such as the Stoics later viewed the gods as personifications of natural substances useful to human life: bread becoming Demeter, wine Dionysus, water Poseidon, and fire Hephaestus.

Choosing the dramatic form of the philosophical dialogue, a form associated with Plato and characteristic of Middle Platonism (that is, a highly Stoicized form of Platonism accompanied by Neopythagorean concerns), Philo became convinced that it was possible to reconcile Judaism and Hellenism. He did so following a Neopythagorean ploy of "one-upmanship," which viewed Plato as a mere pupil of Pythagoras. This is a game in which Philo joined eagerly, putting forward Moses as the greatest authority of all, as being the teacher of Pythagoras and indeed of all Greek philosophers and lawgivers. Armed with Greek allegorical exegesis, which sought out the hidden meaning that lied beneath the surface of any particular text, and given the Middle Platonist and Neopythagorean penchant to read back new doctrines into the works of a venerable figure of the past, Philo was fully prepared to do battle for his ancestral tradition. Unfamiliar with the Hebrew language, he relied exclusively on the Septuagint translation, which he considered inspired.

FLAVIUS JOSEPHUS

Our best source of information about first-century Judaism is the Jewish historian Josephus (37–100 CE). While his information is not always reliable, due in part to a limited knowledge of the Greek language, he is valued for having lived in Palestine in the first century, having known many of the leading figures of his day and experienced first-hand the political and military crises faced by Palestinian Jews.

Like Philo, Josephus was a cosmopolitan and sophisticated individual, acquainted with Palestinian and Hellenistic Judaism. Born to an aristocratic priestly family, as a young man he was appointed to lead the Jewish troops in Galilee at the outset of the Jewish War against Rome (66–70). When his troops were surrounded by the Roman legions, he was taken prisoner. Brought before the Roman general Vespasian, Josephus declared that Vespasian would become the Roman emperor, a statement that became a reality

During the war, Vespasian and later his son and successor, Titus, used Josephus as an interpreter. At the conclusion of the war, Josephus was taken back to Rome, set free, and appointed by Vespasian as a kind of court historian. Josephus adopted Vespasian's family name, Flavius, and spent the next twenty-five years writing about the Jewish people, including a six-volume work on the *Jewish Wars*, a twenty-volume history of the Jewish people called the *Antiquities of the Jews*, and a defense of Judaism against pagan detractions entitled *Against Apion*. Using Stoic motifs to explain the Jews' loyalty to their traditions, Josephus contrasts the universalism of the Jews with the particularism of the Greeks. In his estimation, the Greek *polis* did not accept as citizens all who wished to share its way of life, whereas Judaism was open to all who wished to accept its principles and practices.

According to Josephus, Judaism, as based on the teachings of Moses, provided for the moral training of youth through intensive education and virtuous living. Indeed, Moses achieved what Plato had only dreamed of establishing in his famous *Republic*. Although obedience to the Jewish laws was voluntary, it inculcated fortitude, bravery, and self-sacrifice. In his description of Jewish ethics, Josephus emphasized industriousness, sobriety, mutual trust, sharing with the needy, and the value of strong family ties, which required Jewish parents to educate children in the traditions of their ancestors, and obligated Jewish children to honor their parents next to God.

Josephus wrote with two audiences in mind, wanting to show the Romans that Jews were loyal to the empire and to show the Jews that they could not resist the might of Rome. Despite his bias, Josephus's writings are extremely useful for historians and sociologists interested in the life, customs, society, politics, and culture of first-century Judaism, written by an eyewitness.

THE SEPTUAGINT

Under Ptolemy II Philadelphus (ruled 283–246), the Egyptian priest Manetho published his Egyptian history, which he wrote for the Greeks in their own language. In this work he touched on the Jews, writing what is justly considered as the first expression of literary anti-Judaism. His discussion regarding the Jews is not extensive but rather limited to the topic of the Exodus, which was of special interest to the Egyptians. In his remarks, he resorts to hearsay and legends that he seems to have collected from the Egyptian priesthood. He speaks of Jews as a race of lepers who turned against the gods of Egypt by slaughtering and eating animals sacred to the Egyptians. According to Manetho, in the second millennium BCE the Jews aided the Asiatic invaders known as the Hyksos in their conquest of Egypt. Eventually, however, the Pharaoh returned from exile and defeated the lepers who ruled his nation, pursuing the survivors as far as the frontiers of Syria. On their way, the Jews founded the city of Jerusalem in the land of Judea. Accounts such as these help explain why there was deep animosity against the Jews by the Greeks of Egypt. Greek citizens eventually took what the Egyptian priests had written, and the Egyptian version of the Exodus took deep root in Hellenistic literature.

We can assess the Jewish response to anti-Jewish sentiment in Alexandria by examining the extensive apologetic literature Jews produced, beginning with the Septuagint. Since Greek became the language of Jews in the Mediterranean diaspora, it became necessary to translate their sacred scriptures into Greek, a translation known as the Septuagint, from the Latin for "seventy." A legend preserved in the *Letter of Aristeas* indicates that the Greek translation of the Hebrew Torah was the work of seventy-two divinely inspired scholars (in time the figure was rounded to seventy). According to Aristeas, when Ptolemy II decided to expand his royal library to 500,000 volumes and wished to include the world's most important literature, he learned from his head librarian that one missing volume was the sacred laws of the Jews. Ptolemy then sent a letter to the Jewish high priest in Jerusalem requesting assistance in securing a copy in Greek. In response, the high priest sent seventy-two translators, six from each of the twelve tribes, to Egypt, where, secluded from one another, each completed an identical translation. Aristeas's account, however, only refers to the translation of the Pentateuch.

The books of the Torah were the first to be translated, about 250 BCE, and the Prophets and Writings in the following century. Because the Hebrew canon was still partly in flux, the Septuagint contains books and sections of books eventually not included in the Jewish Bible. These books, known as the Apocrypha, include works originally written in Hebrew and other works composed directly in Greek by Hellenistic-Jewish writers.

In light of the considerable differences between Greek and Hebrew grammar and vocabulary, the Septuagint was a remarkable achievement. For several centuries it was the biblical text used and expounded by Greek-speaking Jews throughout the Mediterranean. The Septuagint became the Bible for the early Christians as well, who came to regard it as authoritative. It is the Septuagint, not the Hebrew Bible, that is quoted by the authors of the New Testament, most of whom did not know Hebrew, but were fluent in Greek. The Septuagint facilitated Jewish and Christian proselytism and has been called one of the most important translations ever made, because through it the Bible first became an essential element of the Western tradition.

The Septuagint was primarily intended for synagogue worship. The aim of the authors was not to produce a work of literary excellence, but one faithful to the original. Because of this, it lacks elegance and unity. Experts note that the translations vary from one book to the next, and sometimes even within a single book. For example, the Pentateuch translation, though idiomatic, is generally faithful and competent. It is not the work of one translator or even of one group of translators, for differences in translational style reveal at least six distinct translations. The translations of the remaining portions of the Septuagint vary in quality and accuracy. Some sections, such as the book of Jeremiah, are considerably shorter than those later used for the authorized Hebrew test (known as the Masoretic Text), suggesting the existence of various competing textual traditions of the biblical texts at this time, an inference later supported by the biblical texts at Qumran, known as the Dead Sea Scrolls and dated to the first centuries BCE and CE.

Due in part to the success of the Septuagint in bringing converts to Christianity, in the second century CE the Jewish authorities abandoned this translation in favor of other translations, more literal and faithful to the Hebrew. Since the Septuagint was used extensively in Christian circles and frequently did not correspond exactly to the later standardized Hebrew text, about 130 CE a recension of the Septuagint made by the Jewish proselyte Aquila replaced the Septuagint as the accepted Greek version of the Hebrew Bible for Jews of the later Roman and Byzantine periods. Because Aquila's revision rendered the Hebrew *almah* in Isaiah 7:14 by *neanis* ("young woman") rather than by the Septuagint word *parthenos* ("virgin"), this and other textual incongruities intensified Jewish-Christian dispute.

While the Septuagint was made initially by Jews for Jews, according to the *Letter of Aristeas*, a further aim of this translation was to enable the Greeks to become acquainted with the Jewish scriptures. This is made clear by placing the initiative for the translational project upon Ptolemy and his courtiers. Believing that the gulf between Jews and Greeks could be bridged, Aristeas finds no internal antagonism between Judaism and Hellenism. For Aristeas, Judaism is conceived as identical with Greek philosophy, subject only to the addition of belief in one God. The Jewish God is the same as the God of the Greeks, only known to different people by different names (pars. 15–16).

In everyday life, the author of Aristeas encouraged Jews and Greeks to draw closer to one another. In Aristeas's account, King Ptolemy invites the elders to a symposium, and the conversation, though revealing the deep wisdom of the Jews, is taken from Greek ethics and politics. For Aristeas, the way to the cultural emancipation of the Jews leads through the Greek Bible; not through neglect of its precepts, but through studying and keeping its vital message. With the Septuagint, the Jews were preparing to ensure that Jews and Greeks should meet on friendly ground. From the literary standpoint, the Greek Bible, especially the Greek Torah, served as the basis for the rise and development of a rich Jewish Alexandrian literature, which received its climax and its most profound argument in the greatest Jewish philosopher of the early Roman period, Philo.

The desire to live with the Greeks and to discover a synthesis between Hellenism and Judaism appears to have brought about certain compromises, even on the central question that divided the two cultures, that of monotheism and polytheism. The Septuagint itself made the first step towards harmony with Greeks by translating Exodus 22:27, "Thou shalt not revile *the gods*," intentionally emphasizing the Hebrew plural in Elohim, as though it referred to pagan deities instead of as a title for the singular God of the Jews. The Jewish author Artapanos (believed to have lived in Alexandria around 200 BCE) went further when he made Jacob and his sons the builders of pagan temples and attributed to Moses the foundation of pagan cults in Egypt, including the cult of sacred animals.

Whatever its origin, the Septuagint had enormous influence and importance. It was widely used not only by Jews across the Roman empire, but was also read by intelligent pagans who wanted to know more about the Jewish faith. It also became the Bible of the first Christians, and its availability greatly assisted Christians in sharing their faith throughout the Hellenistic world.

JEWISH SYBYLLINE ORACLES

The detestation revealed in Manetho's *History of Egypt* had been unknown to Greeks previously. In the second century BCE certain Greek writers, like Lysimachus and Mnaseas, took what the Egyptian priest had written and added further slander. However, such literary slander was evidence only of local antagonism and did not yet point to the widespread anti-Judaism of the Roman period. The first century BCE saw a flourishing of anti-Jewish literature and attitudes throughout the Greco-Roman world, summarized in the statement of Cicero, who defined Jewish religion as a "barbarous superstition."

In the face of slanderous charges of atheism and misanthropy, the Jews did not stand by idly. The strongest weapon was literature and religious propaganda, and this avenue was pursued vigorously by Alexandrian Jews, particularly at the beginning of the Roman period, as anti-Jewish attacks became more intense and varied. The writings of Philo and Josephus reflect, in part, this apologetic trend. This Jewish literature was intended primarily for Jewish circulation. It contained polemics against polytheism and pagan customs, but also included elements that would appeal to Gentiles, should these books fall into their hands. These writings served the purpose of strengthening Jews in their faith, as they stood surrounded by the attractions and temptations of Hellenism, as well as training Jews in defense and propaganda methods. Perhaps indirectly, this literature also helped to create a better understanding of Jewish thought and religion among interested Gentiles.

Important evidence for the existence of a well-planned, enthusiastic, propaganda in Judaism was the literature Jews wrote under the name of the pagan Sibyl. In pagan antiquity, the Sibyl was a semi-divine prophetess who gave oracles concerning the fate of cities and kingdoms. These oracles enjoyed a high reputation among those who were religiously disposed. It was probably during the second century BCE that Jews adopted this medium to defend themselves and to propagate their faith, thus creating the Jewish Sibyl. Eventually, an extensive Jewish Sibylline literature was put into circulation in Alexandria. Through this literature, pagan poets were made to bear witness to the sublimity of the Jewish faith and pagan oracles were made to predict a mighty destiny for the Jewish race.

Alexandrian Jews believed the true Sibyl to be a Jewess, or a convert to Judaism. The Sibyl extended hope to all humanity, picturing an eschatological procession to Jerusalem and the universal worship of the one God. The purpose of these writings was less to convert Gentiles than to prepare their minds for a favorable reception of the Jewish teaching that was delivered orally in the synagogues.

THE SYNAGOGUE

Despite pagan hostility to Jews throughout the Greco-Roman period, Judaism was popular in the Hellenistic world. There were a number of reasons for this, not least the fact that large numbers of Jews lived in most of the major towns and cities of the Roman empire. Wherever they went, they took their distinctive beliefs and lifestyle with them. Generally speaking, wherever they gathered, they erected a synagogue, a place of worship requiring only a copy of the scriptures and ten adult Jewish males to constitute a quorum for worship. Over time, in addition to its function as a religious center, the synagogue also served as a place of instruction and a community center, where traditions were maintained and festivals celebrated.

In a period of decline in the classic Olympian religion, many Gentiles became dissatisfied with pagan alternatives, embarking in a religious quest for a truth that could satisfy them emotionally and intellectually. The Jewish concept of God and the synagogue emphasis on instruction made a considerable impression on many Greeks. Here was a religion that appeared much like a philosophy. Furthermore, the decline of classical religion was accompanied by a general weakening of morality. Judaism, with its emphasis on ethical living, offered a significant alternative. Significantly, inquirers could read the Jewish scriptures in the Greek language, deciding for themselves before making further commitments. There was never any pressure or coercion to join or convert.

Surprisingly, distinguished Roman writers of the era spoke positively, even fondly, of the synagogue. In his *Satires*, Horace, a leading lyric poet during the reign of Augustus, speaks of attending the Jewish synagogue as a natural thing. Likewise the late first- and early second-century CE Roman poet Juvenal, speaking of the decadence of Roman customs and of entire families embracing Jewish observance, asks his friend, "In what synagogue may I find you?" The first century CE Stoic philosopher Seneca also mentions the popular and widespread observance of the Jewish Sabbath by non-Jews.

The shifting of the center of worship from the temple to the synagogue revolutionized the Jewish religion. As a center for worship and instruction, the synagogue was a means of proselytizing. Jewish teachers were not slow to exploit the openness to Judaism current among those not ethnically Jewish. When Christianity emerged, the enthusiasm of Jewish rabbis in sharing their faith with others was legendary, or so it seems from Matthew 23:15, where we are told that Jewish teachers would "cross sea and land to make a single convert." It is significant to note that this idea regarding zealous Jewish missionaries appears only in Matthew, probably written in Antioch, Syria about 80 CE, shortly after the destruction of Jerusalem and around the time that Judaism and Christianity were in the throes of final separation from one another. The context is obviously polemical, written no doubt by a faction within Christianity engaging vigorously with Jews in apologetic and proselytizing endeavors. The comment in 23:15 is likely a Christian response to a Jewish community intent on apologetic and counter-proselytizing activities. In this setting, isolated Jews might have taken the initiative, but this would have been the exception rather than the rule.

The degree to which Judaism in the first century CE was missionary-minded is much debated, and it is a question to which I devoted my PhD dissertation in 1977. While I discovered evidence of a proselytizing tendency among some Jews of this period, I found no direct evidence of Judaism as a missionary religion. I concluded that Judaism in general displays an attitude of openness and availability to Gentiles, being only passively rather than actively missionary-minded,[1] for what is decisive for Jews is not that Gentiles convert to Judaism, but rather that Gentiles acknowledge the one God and follow the fundamental ethical demands of scripture.

While one of the factors explaining the remarkable size of the Diaspora population is the presence of converts, a distinction must be made among those attracted to Judaism. First, there were proselytes, that is, Gentiles who were so drawn to the Jewish faith that they undertook all the steps necessary to become fully Jewish, including circumcision for males and baptism. Circumcision, of course, was a chief obstacle to Gentiles who would become Jews, especially for Greeks who resented all mutilations of the body. Not surprisingly, there were more female proselytes than male. In addition to proselytes, those who were attracted to Judaism—particularly to its worship, traditions, and ethics—and were dissatisfied with the permissiveness of their own culture, were given a lesser status as "God-fearers."

These groups played a significant role in the growth and development of early Christianity. As the first Christian missionaries took their message across the Roman empire, they often found an enthusiastic response among such people. Thus Paul, the early Christian missionary to the Gentiles, made it a policy to go first to the local synagogue in every town he visited, where not only Jews but also proselytes and God-fearers congregated.

JEWISH INTERTESTAMENTAL LITERATURE

During the centuries between the close of the Hebrew Bible (the Old Testament period) and the emergence of Christianity, the Jews produced a vast religious literature. Much of this was on a lower level than that included in the Old Testament, and was never regarded by Palestinian Jews as possessing

---

1. In my dissertation, I distinguish between a centripetal and a centrifugal missionary consciousness in Judaism. The former demonstrates a welcoming attitude toward those who wish to join voluntarily (for example, by living exemplary lives, thus exemplifying what Isaiah 49:6 calls "a light to the nations), whereas in the latter, individuals pursue aggressively a policy designed to persuade outsiders to enter.

the same religious authority as the books of the Old Testament. At the same time, many of these "intertestamental" books were widely read, and exerted a lasting influence on religious life and thought.

In contrast to the authoritative or canonical literature of the Hebrew Bible, these books are often called apocryphal (meaning "hidden"). Traditionally, fifteen such books, or parts of books, belong to the Apocrypha, but besides these, there are other similar works that are also apocryphal. The intertestamental literature falls into several literary categories and may be classed as (1) historical; (2) legendary or novelistic; (3) sapiential or didactic; and (4) apocalyptic.

The books of 1 and 2 Maccabees, discussed earlier, are representative examples of the historical category. Among the purely legendary or novelistic books are the stories of Tobit and Judith. The former, an entertaining and moralizing narrative, was written in the early second century, about 190 to 170 BCE. It tells the story of Tobit, a devout Jew of Nineveh, who has the misfortune of losing his eyesight after having performed a pious act by providing burial for Jews who had been the victims of persecution. The book then relates the adventures of his son Tobias, who is accompanied on his journey by the angel Raphael, who is disguised as a traveling companion and guide. On his return, Tobias effects a cure on his father's blindness. It is not surprising that a book that manages to combine religious and ethical teaching with an entertaining story and a happy conclusion had a wide circulation.

Like 1 and 2 Maccabees, the apocryphal book of Judith is a response to the Maccabean crisis, but unlike the Maccabean books, which use the literary genre of history to recount the narrative, Judith is a response to the crisis through fiction. Another adventure story that attained wide circulation, at first glance the book appears to be historical, but the first sentence corrects that impression, describing Nebuchadrezzar as ruler of the Assyrians, rather than of the Babylonians. From the start, the reader knows this book, though inspiring, is not to be read literally. Written by a Palestinian Jew around the middle of the second century BCE, perhaps shortly after the book of Daniel, the author encourages Jews to resist their enemies while exhorting them to a strict observance of Torah. Teaching that Jewish patriotism and religion are one, the book affirms that God defends those who observe the Torah; the rest will perish.

This action-packed tale, one of the best examples of early Jewish storytelling, is the story of all Jews under duress, frequently threatened by foreign foes. The heroine is a Jewess who combines scrupulous observance of the Mosaic laws with a cunning bravery in the face of great personal danger. In the midst of war between the Assyrians and the Jews, the city of Bethulia (not the name of an actual town but a play on the Hebrew word for virgin, *betulah*, a term used in the Bible of Jerusalem or of the nation of Israel) is in grave danger of being destroyed. When it seems that all hope must be abandoned, Judith undertakes to outwit Holofernes, the general of the Assyrian forces, cutting off his head and producing victory for the Israelites. The victory of Judith over powerful enemies provides encouragement to vulnerable Jews living in dangerous times: what seems impossible from a human perspective is possible with God, who can do more through one individual than he or she might ask or imagine.

Two books of the Apocrypha, already discussed—the book of Ecclesiasticus (Sirach) and the Wisdom of Solomon—belong to that genre of ancient Jewish literature known as sapiential or wisdom literature. The authors of this type of literature were called wise men or sages, and they exercised almost as much influence in personal and national life as did the priests and the prophets.

Apocalyptic is the name given to that type of literature that purports to reveal the future. The book known as 2 Esdras, written late in the first century CE though attributed to the ancient Israelite leader Ezra, makes a valiant attempt to reconcile the earthly calamities of the Jews with the righteous rule of God. In common with Daniel and the New Testament book of Revelation, 2 Esdras includes symbols involving mysterious numbers, strange beasts, and the disclosure of hidden truths through angelic messengers.

Another apocalyptic work, though not included among the fifteen books traditionally called the Apocrypha, is the book of Enoch, a long, rambling work produced by several authors who lived from about 200 BCE to 100 CE. It, too, embodies a series of revelations, of which the antediluvian figure Enoch is the professed recipient, on such matters as the origin of evil, angels and their destinies, the nature of Gehenna and Paradise, and the preexistent Messiah.

Besides Enoch, several other Jewish pseudepigrapha (that is, writings circulating under false titles), were produced during the period just before and shortly after the emergence of Christianity. These include the Assumption of Moses, the Sibylline Oracles, the Psalms of Solomon, the Testaments of the Twelve Patriarchs, the Book of Jubilees, and the Ascension of Isaiah.

The importance of the intertestamental literature lies in the information it supplies concerning the development of Jewish life and thought prior to or during the emergence of Christianity. The political fortunes of the Jews; the emergence of groups such as the Pharisees; the growth of popular beliefs in the activities of angels and demons; the growing preoccupation with the origin and presence of evil; the blossoming of apocalyptic hope relating to the coming Messiah, the resurrection of the body, and the vindication of the righteous—all these subjects and many others come to light in the intertestamental literature.

HEIGHTENED INTEREST IN ANGELS AND ITS IMPACT ON JUDEO-CHRISTIAN THEOLOGY

Two features of later Palestinian Judaism, evident in the Intertestamental Literature and then in Hellenistic Judaism, are its conception of divine "hypostases" and its heightened interest in angels. Certainly the former, and likely the latter also, helped to create an atmosphere of thought conducive to the development of the Christian conception of God as three-personal—Father, Son, and Holy Spirit—and the Neoplatonic conception of the One—Being, Mind, and Soul—as a hierarchy of hypostases, which, understood as emanations of Being, leave the One undiminished and unchanged.

Student of the Hebrew scriptures are familiar with the growing tendency there to personify Wisdom and to assign it creative functions (Prov. 8:22–31; Wis. 7:22—8:21; Sir. 24:1–29). Likewise, New Testament authors such as Paul avail themselves of this idea to explain the status of Christ. In Late Judaism[2] we come across a multitude of such figures: Wisdom itself, God's "glory" or "Presence" (Shekinah), God's Logos,[3] and the Angel of the Lord (understood as a preexistent being who is divine; this figure can be called God, and is God's manifestation on earth in human flesh).

At the same time, there is an extensive fascination and sharpening in later Judaism of the belief in angels, frequently, and until Daniel (see 8:16; 10:13; 12:1) in the Hebrew Bible, mentioned only anonymously. In the Intertestamental Literature, several of these angels are named, and we encounter at least six archangels. Ministers of God, they are understood to be the means by which God's will is executed in the world; one angel, Uriel, is appointed to regulate the stars (1 Enoch 75:3). Of particular interest is the notion, found in several of the sources, that in the heavenly court two angelic powers, sometimes identified as Michael and Gabriel, stand before God's throne interceding for humans.

In Jewish literature of the first and second centuries CE, we find a proliferation of angelic intercessors and intermediaries, to the extent that they constitute practically an obsession. The foundation for such speculation and fascination seems to be biblical. Passages about divine beings who beget semidivine beings (such as the reference to Nephilim in Genesis 6:2–4), and

---

2. A term scholars use to refer to Judaism in the Greco-Roman period.

3. The Jewish philosopher Philo took functions assigned to Wisdom, both as creating and ordering all things, and attributed them to the Logos.

fascination with mysterious individuals such as Enoch, Abraham, Moses, Jacob, Elijah, and the quasi-human/quasi-divine "son of man" figure in Daniel 7, to whom God gives the kingdoms of the earth, led to a vast literature that told of humans who became angels and angels who became human.

In apocalyptic circles, the natural world is characterized not only as transient, but also by the fact that angels and demons exercise power in it. In general, the view of Jewish eschatology is that the evil of the world comes from demonic powers, and that angelic beings have, with God's permission, established themselves between God and humanity. Among them is the Angel of Death, who despite a sinister office, is thought of as standing in the service of God. In its simplest form, the conception of redemption is that the messianic kingdom puts an end to demonic power. The New Testament is written against this background.

In ancient Judaism, angels were widely understood to be superhuman messengers of God, standing between God and humans and mediating God's will on earth. In the Hebrew Bible it is striking that various angels sometimes appear on earth in human guise. This includes the Angel of the Lord, regarded as the chief angel. In some passages he is identified as God, while in others he appears as a human. An example appears in Genesis 16, where the Lord speaks to Hagar, servant of Sarah, who has been exiled to the wilderness, pregnant with Abraham's child. The Angel of the Lord appears to her and tells her to return to her mistress. The author then surprises us by indicating that the angel is none other than Yahweh, the Lord. Hagar, of course, is astonished that she had "seen God and remained alive after seeing him" (Gen. 16:13).

A similar ambiguity occurs in Genesis 18, this time with Abraham. In 18:1 we are told that "the Lord" appeared to Abraham, but when the episode is narrated, we learn that "three men" come to him. One of these three is later identified explicitly as "the Lord" (Gen. 18:13). Such ambiguity continues in the famous episode of Moses and the burning bush in Exodus 3. In 3:2 we are told that the Angel of the Lord appears to Moses, yet later we are told it is "God" who calls to him out of the bush. There are numerous other texts that describe angels as God and, equally important, as human.

From this evidence New Testament scholar Larry Hurtado formulates a key thesis: "I propose the view that the principal angel speculation and other types of divine agency thinking . . . provided the earliest Christians with a basic scheme for accommodating the resurrected Christ next to God without having to depart from their monotheistic tradition."[4] In other words, if humans could be angels, and angels humans, and if angels could

---

4. Hurtado, *One God, One Lord*, 82.

be gods, and if the chief angel could be Yahweh, then to make Jesus divine, one simply needs to think of him as an angel in human form.

QUESTIONS FOR DISCUSSION AND REFLECTION

Select one or more of the following questions and write your answer(s) in a journal. If you are in a group study, be prepared to share your answers with those in the group.

1. Explain the difference between "anti-Judaism" and "anti-Semitism." Why is it preferable to speak of Greco-Roman hostility to Jews as anti-Jewish rather than anti-Semitic?
2. In antiquity (as in the current period), Jews were valued as military combatants. Was this why most native Egyptian rulers viewed them favorably?
3. Explain the origin and development of anti-Jewish sentiment in Hellenistic Egypt.
4. Explain the statement, "Though Jews in the Greco-Roman age were privileged, they were not always safe."
5. Explain and assess the role and message of Philo of Alexandria.
6. Explain and assess the role and message of Flavius Josephus.
7. Explain and assess the impact of the Septuagint on Diaspora Jews.
8. Explain and assess the role and message of the Jewish Sibylline Oracles.
9. Explain and assess the role and message of the Jewish Intertestamental Literature.

PART III

The Christian Experience

Chapter 8

The Emergence of Christianity

CHRISTIANITY HAD ITS ORIGINS in first-century Palestine, a region of the Mediterranean on the eastern fringes of the Roman empire. This strategic corridor was vital to the empire, during a time of heightened cultural and religious unrest, exacerbated by economic and political factors. Christianity saw itself as a both a continuation and development of Judaism, initially flourishing in regions associated with Judaism, beginning with Palestine and rapidly expanding to Syria in the north, Egypt in the south, and Asia Minor in the west.

The first Christians also lived in a Greek world, dominated by alien values and beliefs. As Jews, they drew on Hebraic customs and beliefs, themselves shaped by alien cultural influences: Sumerian, Amorite, Egyptian, Hittite, Phoenician, Aramean, Assyrian, Babylonian, and Greek. Over time, these and other ancient neighbors in the eastern Mediterranean world had supplied beliefs and practices that resulted in views of God grouped variously under the rubric called "ethical monotheism." Like their forebears, the first Christians tried to reconcile diverse visions of deity, and the results, far from uniform, elicited unstable answers to unending questions.

Judaism was the cradle in which Christianity was nurtured, a source to which it was uniquely indebted. Judaism left a deep imprint on the church's liturgy and ministry, and an even deeper influence on its teaching. Until the middle of the second century, when Hellenistic ideas began to come to the fore, Christian theology was taking shape in predominantly Judaic molds, and the categories of thought used by almost all early Christian writers were largely Jewish. This "Judeo-Christian" theology continued to exercise a powerful influence well beyond the second century.

The first Christians, particularly those of Jewish descent, considered themselves as the "New Israel," for like ancient Israel, they believed they had a special role in history. Their relationship to Judaism was one of continuity and discontinuity. Like two partners joined in marriage, neither was a substitute for the other, nor were they independent of one another. Rather, there was relative independence, whereby they complemented one another. For Christians, the gulf between the church and the synagogue—between Christianity and Judaism—was bridged by Jesus Christ, whose person and work established discontinuity with Israel culturally and politically and, at the same time, deep continuity in the purpose of God. This continuity and discontinuity is further evident in the relationship between the Old and the New Testament scriptures, both ultimately necessary if Christians were to hear in the human words of the Bible the word of God.

Over the next several centuries, the "New Israel," no longer bound by ethnic or nationalistic limitations but open to all people, Jew and Gentile alike, expanded on the basis of faith. The new community did not establish a clean break with the people of Israel, whose life story is portrayed in the Hebrew Bible, but rather, as Paul puts it in Romans 11, became a "wild olive shoot" grafted onto the olive tree (Israel); a branch supported by roots that reach deeply into God's choice of Israel and God's faithful dealings with this people (Rom. 11:17–24).

Though the early church regarded itself as the true Israel, outwardly it differed little from the numerous synagogues that existed in Jerusalem. Like other members of the synagogues, its members took part in the regular worship of the temple (Luke 24:53; Acts 2:46; 3:1), observed the Jewish festivals, and in general kept the Mosaic law. Although some parallels can be drawn with the ancient Hebrew temple observances, the church in the New Testament was more similar to the Jewish synagogue (a learning center) than to the temple and its cultic activities. The first Christians, themselves Jews or proselytes to Judaism, modeled church worship after synagogue worship. This pattern included readings from scripture, prayer, preaching, and singing. The service closed with a distinctively Christian addition, the breaking of bread (the Lord's Supper or Eucharist), the central mystery at the heart of Christianity (see Acts 2:42). At first, homes of believers served as the places of worship; only later did Christians build church structures comparable to Jewish synagogues. The cross became the central cultic object, rather than the Ark of the Covenant or Torah scrolls. The cross served as a sign of Jesus' crucifixion and resurrection and symbolized the meaning of these events. The first day of the week (Sunday), which commemorated Jesus' resurrection, replaced the Jewish Sabbath as the primary cultic season. In addition to the regular activities of worship and education, which helped to unify the new Christian community, the basic cultic acts were baptism and the Lord's Supper.

Such worship and religious practices did not emerge without problems, however, and new leaders were required. Initially, the disciples of Jesus (the Twelve) became prominent leaders of the Jerusalem church, with a smaller number—consisting of Peter, John, and James "the Just"—exercising greater influence. A somewhat larger group, known as apostles, became the preeminent figures in the spread of Christianity. This group included the Twelve, but the total company of apostles was more numerous. What made a person an apostle was a personal commission by Jesus (the Greek word *apostolos* means "one sent"). Apostles were ambassadors of the risen Lord, understood to have extraordinary authority in the church.

In the world beyond Jerusalem, the church generally assumed the form of a synagogue, that is, a congregation. The Greek word for church (*ekklēsia*) means a group of people called together. It is one of the words used in the Septuagint to designate the assembly of the people of Israel. Because the Jews chose the word *synagogē* for their assemblies, it is quite likely that the first Christians deliberately, and to avoid confusion, rejected the term adopted by the Jews and chose the other.

From the start, one serious problem threatened the church's survival: the terms on which Gentiles could become Christians. At first, it was unclear whether Gentiles should be required to keep the Old Testament laws, either in whole or in part (Acts 10:1—11:18; 15:1-35; Gal. 2:1-10). In the end, however, Gentiles were accepted without such requirements, since Jew and Gentile had been reconciled to one another through the death of Christ (Eph. 2:13-18). Christ is the vine, Christians are the branches (John 15:1-11); the church is the olive tree, to which the natural branches (Israel) have been grafted and the wild branches (Gentiles) engrafted. God's work of election, as Paul and other early Christian writers stressed, is not based on ethnicity, gender, or merit, but on grace.

THE CHURCH SEPARATES FROM JUDAISM

While Christianity initially may have functioned like an appendage of Judaism, by the year 70 it was moving out on its own. The move to independence from Judaism was accelerated by Roman destruction of the Jewish temple and the cessation of the sacrifices that had played such a large role in Jewish worship.

Prior to the fateful year 70, Judaism tolerated varieties of opinions within its fold. Between the years 30 and 70, Jewish followers of Jesus continued worshiping in the synagogues. During that period, it was quite clear that Jewish people began incorporating Jesus into their faith story. Within the synagogues, Jewish Christians were at best an enriching new tradition and at worst a minor irritation. However, when the survival of the Jewish faith tradition was at stake, their level of toleration dissipated perceptibly. Acrimony grew between Jews committed to Jesus and traditional Jews who claimed orthodoxy for their convictions, tying their claims to the belief that the God they worshiped could be found only in the unchanging completeness of the Torah. The shift to a survival mentality set the stage for heightened negativity to develop. After the fall of Jerusalem, many followers of Jesus, both Jewish and Gentile, began to interpret the Roman defeat of the Jews and the loss of the temple as God's punishment of traditional Jews for their rejection of Jesus. Thus, the stage was set for hostility. Echoes of this rising hostility can be found overtly in the Gospels, particularly in Matthew (21:43; 23:31–38; 27:25). As rhetoric heightened, the lines around what Jews could tolerate within Judaism tightened considerably so that Jewish Christians, offended by this increasing hostility, began to move more and more into Gentile circles.

From that point on, fewer Christians wished to identify with the rigidly orthodox survival mentality that began to characterize Judaism, while fewer Jews wanted to see any aspect of the Jesus tradition left within their faith traditions. Somewhere in the late 80s a split occurred between the synagogue and the followers of Jesus. We can sense the pain of that split in John 9:22, which states "the Jews had already agreed that anyone who confessed Jesus to be the Messiah would be put out of the synagogue."

Once that split had occurred, Christianity began to move more and more into the Gentile world. Because the Gospel of Matthew was written during this separation and the Gospel of John shortly thereafter, the Fourth Gospel's blatant negativity toward orthodox Jews (John 8:44) and its descriptions of exclusion from the synagogues reflect that final fracture (John 9:22; 12:42). By the start of the second century, Jewish Christians faded into increasingly Hellenized and Gentile circles, and thereafter Jewish Christians ceased even to think of themselves as Jews, while those who claimed Jewish identity became more firmly entrenched in their tradition. By the middle of the second century there were hardly any Jews left in the Christian movement. "The common ground between Jews and Christians, once so powerful, became nonexistent. This hostile negativity toward Jews and all things Jewish has remained dominant in Christianity to this day."[1]

THE EPISTLE OF BARNABAS

As patristic[2] scholars note, the central debate in the Christian second century centered on the position of Judaism and the Old Testament in Christianity. This should come as no surprise, since in the second century Christianity was marked by a predominantly Gentile constituency, following the destruction of Jerusalem in 70 CE and the expulsion of Jewish Christians from Jewish synagogues during the ninth and tenth decades of the first century.

The beginnings of this apologetic are found already in the letters of Paul, who argued that the Old Testament law had an intermediary and custodial role, applicable only until the coming of Jesus Christ (see Gal. 3:19–26), at which time faith in Jesus replaced works of the law. By way of support, Paul appeals to Hagar and Sarah as representing two divine covenants (Gal. 4:21—5:1), the offspring of one corresponding to slavery (Judaism) and that of the other corresponding to responsible freedom and adulthood (Christianity). The apologetic continued in the second century with the proto-orthodox theologians Justin Martyr (c. 100–c. 165) and Irenaeus (c. 130–c. 200). Using typology, Justin argued that Leah and Rachel, wives of the patriarch Jacob, prefigured Jewish (synagogue) and Christian (church) worship, whereas the fuller statement of proto-orthodoxy is found in Irenaeus, who, countering the Marcionites, stressed that the one and same God bestowed both the Law of Moses and the grace of the New Testament, both adopted to different sets of conditions, yet both for the benefit of the human race. Like Paul, Irenaeus argued that, due to progressive human development, the Old Testament legislation was designed for humanity's earlier stages. In dealing with vindictive, ritualistic, or unethical passages, particularly those that seemed an impediment to Marcionites, Irenaeus suggested that believers look for their deeper significance, of which they were figures or types.

---

1. Spong, *Liberating the Gospels*, 53.

2. The term "patristic period" comes from the Latin word *pater*, meaning "father," a reference to the early Christian centuries, when bishops and theologians, collectively called Church Fathers, led proto-orthodox Christianity. The dates of this period are debated, but it begins with the close of the apostolic period toward the end of the first century and lasts through the fifth-century Council of Chalcedon (451), extending possibly to the seventh and last ecumenical council (the Second Council of Nicaea) in 787.

From the late second century, affirmation of both Testaments became common in proto-orthodox writers, for such belief was grounded in the view that Jewish prophets and Christian evangelists were inspired by the same divine Spirit. Affirmation of the oneness of God became the indispensable premise for any attempt to separate the Testaments, and to demonstrate this oneness became the principal task of Irenaeus and his proto-orthodox contemporaries. As a result of their efforts, later theologians such as Tertullian (c. 160–c. 225) and Origen (185–254) could speak of the harmony between the Testaments. In Origen's view, the dogmas common to both Testaments form a symphony, the Jewish scriptures preceding and the Christian scriptures following. This emphasis paved the way for the classic doctrine formulated in Augustine's maxim, "In the Old Testament the New is concealed; in the New Testament the Old is revealed."

Included among the Christian writings of the early second century is a document known as the Epistle of Barnabas, written around 130–135 CE. This text, later attributed to Paul's traveling companion Barnabas, was highly regarded by early Christians, to the extent that it hovered for some time on the fringe of the Christian canon, appearing in Codex Sinaiticus, the earliest complete manuscript of the New Testament, dated paleographically to the mid-fourth century (c. 330–360), about the time of the Roman emperor Constantine the Great, the first Christian emperor. In the end, Barnabas failed to secure admission to the canon, perhaps due to its uncertain authorship. This document is significant in that it portrays the relationship of Jews and Christians in the early decades of the second century. As one of the most hostile anti-Jewish treatises of Christian antiquity, it may well have damaged irreparably Jewish-Christian relations had it been included in the Christian canon, fanning further the flames of anti-Semitism that arose in late antiquity and continued through the Middle Ages to modern times.

In order to understand the polemic evident in this work, it is helpful to underscore features of early Jewish-Christian relations with which we are already familiar. Jesus and his first followers were all Jews. Jesus appears not to have been interested in establishing a new religion in opposition to Judaism, but rather, like the first Protestant Reformers, was primarily concerned to give the correct interpretation of the parent religion. When Jesus went to Jerusalem to celebrate the Jewish Passover, his opponents handed him over to the Romans, who had him crucified. Soon after his death, his followers claimed he had been raised from the dead, and this completely changed their conception of him. Rather than seeing Jesus as a rabbi or teacher of the Jewish Law, they came to see him as the long awaited Messiah of the Jews, whose death could bring salvation. The resurrection came to be viewed as God's stamp of approval on Jesus and on his message of repentance.

From that point, Paul and other Christian missionaries began preaching the importance of Jesus' death for salvation, and particularly in Paul's case, for the salvation of all humanity, Jews and Gentiles alike. Unlike the Judaizers—ardent Jewish Christians—Paul insisted that Gentiles need not convert to Judaism in order to benefit from Jesus' death. By the end of the first century, most people converting to Christianity were non-Jewish. This led to natural tensions between Christians—whether Jewish or Gentile—and non-Christian Jews, because both claimed to be the true heirs of the promises given by God to the Jewish people. In so doing, Christians claimed that non-Christian Jews had forfeited the blessings of God, now intended for Christians alone. Non-Christian Jews rejected this line of thinking altogether.

This ironic development, that non-Jews are heirs of the salvation promised to the people of Israel, is reflected in the Epistle of Barnabas. It is Christians, according to this tractate, who are the true Israel, not Jews. The Hebrew scriptures now belong to the Christians and no longer to the Jews. Such arguments, however, required a new way of thinking about scripture, a new way of interpreting its demands. According to this author, whom we call Barnabas, the Jews rejected God, and thus, God rejected them. According to the polemic in this text, Jews are said to have been deceived by an evil angel, forced to interpret literally laws that were meant to be taken figuratively. The God of Israel, Barnabas contends, never intended baby boys to be circumcised physically, never intended that people follow kosher food laws literally or observe Sabbath rest literally. As Israel's history demonstrated, such laws were not meant to be taken literally. From the beginning, while still on Mount Sinai, the Israelites violated the covenant they had with God, and continued throughout their history to disobey their laws, as witnessed by the prophets of Israel, who regularly pointed out Israel's unfaithfulness to their own laws and traditions.

If God's covenant with Israel had been abrogated and therefore annulled, how then were these laws intended by God, and who are God's people now? According to Barnabas, God's laws are not about precepts but about principles, not about exotic commandments to keep but about behavior toward God and others. Kosher food laws, for example, are not about foods to eat and avoid, but rather about not associating with certain types of people or being like them, people who behave like pigs when they eat, caring only about themselves and their pleasure instead of about God and the needs of others. Thus, when Moses commanded the people not to eat pork, what he meant was, don't be piggish. The same holds true for the other "food" laws. These are not to be taken literally, for they are not about food, but rather about behavior.

The same interpretation applies to the laws conserving Sabbath observance. The pattern they reflect, about working six days and resting on the Sabbath, is not about the workweek but rather about history. Creation is an ongoing process, according to Barnabas, not about what to do with one's weekend. For Barnabas, each day of creation is an age, not a day, and each age represents a millennium, that is, a thousand yeas (see Ps. 90:4; 1 Pet. 3:8). Thus, Barnabas becomes the first in a long line of speculative thinkers who thinks that history will last six thousand years, to be followed by a millennial kingdom of rest on earth.[3] This sort of speculation, propagated by Bishop Ussher's famous calculation dating creation to the year 4004 BCE, recently convinced many apocalyptically minded fundamentalist Christians to imagine that the end of history might come in their lifetime, perhaps around the year 2000 CE. In this respect, recall the Y2K computer "bug," viewed by some Christians as a sure sign of the "Great Tribulation" predicted in the Bible, an event believed to confirm their vision of the "End Times" and of the Second Coming of Christ.

As kosher food laws and the Sabbath observance should be interpreted symbolically, so, too, the law of circumcision. Rather than interpreting it as sexual mutilation, Barnabas indicates that it should be understood as a God-given prediction of the crucifixion of Jesus. Barnabas supports his interpretation by applying a numerological method of interpretation known as *gematria*, an ancient Jewish technique that takes the numerical equivalence of the letters of a word and interprets them accordingly.[4]

Recognizing Abraham as the first biblical person to receive the law of circumcision (Gen. 17:24–27), Barnabas turns to Genesis 14:14, where Abraham takes 318 servants and uses them to rescue his nephew Lot. Noting that the first reference to circumcision in the Bible is associated with the number 318, Barnabas points out that in the Greek language, the first letter associated with the number 318 is *tau* (which stands for the number "300"), a letter that looks like our letter T, which resembles a cross. The letters for "18" are *iota* and *eta*, the first two letters of the Greek name for Jesus. Using *gematria*, Barnabas sees the number 318 not as a literal number, but as a symbol foreshadowing the cross of Jesus. Hence, for Barnabas, circumcision predicts the crucifixion of Jesus.

---

3. This way of thinking may be seen in Revelation 20:2, which some Christians view as a symbolic reference to the church age, others to a literal millennial kingdom on earth at the end of history, and still others as a reference to a heavenly afterlife.

4. In the Hebrew language, as in most ancient languages, numerals are not used. Rather, each letter of the Hebrew alphabet has a numerical equivalent. Likewise, each word has a numerical value.

For Barnabas, the Jews are not and never were God's covenantal people. From the start, they violated their covenant with God, a covenant they broke by worshipping idols and through licentious behavior. That covenant, according to Barnabas, was never restored, and the Jews pursued their laws blindly, interpreting them literally rather than figuratively. As a result, God had called a new people—Christianity—to replace the disobedient Jews.

This supersessionist point of view became increasingly commonplace in the second century, as evidenced in the writings of prominent Christian thinkers such as the philosopher Justin Martyr. Writing around 150 CE, Justin claimed that God had given the Jews the law of circumcision so that Jews might be identifiable by those wishing to persecute them. In the late second century, Bishop Melito of Sardis preached a sermon in which he claimed that by killing Jesus, Jews were guilty of killing their own God, thereby charging Jews with deicide. Likewise, the apologist Tertullian, writing around 200, claimed that Jerusalem had been destroyed by the Romans as punishment for the Jewish rejection of Jesus. Such polemic must have been common in non-Jewish Christian circles after the apostolic period, but to have them placed into writing by prominent proto-orthodox Christian leaders was extreme.

In addition to the Epistle of Barnabas, another non-canonical work known for its anti-Jewish stance is the Gospel of Peter. Unlike Barnabas, this work was excluded from the canon because it was suspected of being heretical, possibly Gnostic. This gospel was known to exist as early as the second century, particularly from a reference in the fourth-century church historian Eusebius, who wrote about Serapion, a second-century proto-orthodox bishop in the Syrian city of Antioch, then one of the principal centers of Christianity. According to Eusebius's account, the Gospel of Peter was being used in worship services in a local church under Serapion's jurisdiction. Since there was yet no canon of Christian scripture, and since the gospel claimed to have been written by Peter, Jesus' closest disciple, Serapion saw no harm in its liturgical use.

One day, however, Serapion received an anonymous tip indicating that the gospel could be used for heretical purposes, and after reading the gospel, Serapion agreed. Fearing it might be a heretical forgery, he forbid its use. In his estimation, the gospel had a docetic Christology, for in addition to its legendary expansion of the death and resurrection of Jesus, it depicted Jesus as unable to suffer pain on the cross. Furthermore, it taught a separationist view, namely, that the divine presence departed from Jesus prior to his death.

While Eusebius created context for the gospel, even quoting Serapion's letter to the congregation, he failed to quote from the gospel itself.

Fortunately, a fragment of the gospel was discovered in 1886 by a French archaeological team in Akhmin, Egypt. While uncovering a monk's tomb, the team found buried with the monk a manuscript that contained several writings, including a fragmentary copy of a gospel. The surviving portion consisted of an account of Jesus' trial, death, and resurrection. The gospel was written in the first person, in the name of Simon Peter. While scholars cannot be certain that it is the lost Gospel of Peter mentioned by Eusebius, most scholars conclude that it is. While this gospel contains numerous similarities to the accounts of the New Testament Gospels, far more significant are the differences, including a heightened emphasis on the guilt of the Jews in the death of Jesus, indicative of an incipient anti-Semitism.

To understand such a polemic, we need to recall that Christianity was a Jewish religion at the beginning. All religions in the Roman empire were tolerated because all, except Judaism and later Christianity, were polytheistic. Judaism was an exception, but because of its antiquity, it, too, was tolerated. When Judaism and Christianity parted ways, Christianity emerged as a new religion, no longer having an ancient tradition to support its doctrines and forms of worship. Furthermore, Christianity was exclusivistic, refusing to worship the state gods.

To defend themselves against pagan persecution, Christians claimed that they were the true representatives of Judaism. This put the Jews on the defensive, and it widened the rift between the two religions, particularly between Jewish Christians and non-Jewish Christians. Using the argument that non-Christian Jews were responsible for the death of Jesus, their own Messiah, Gentile Christians concluded that God had forsaken the Jews fully and finally. This debate was particularly contentious in the second century, evident in such works as the Epistle of Barnabas and the Gospel of Peter.

Consider what happens at the beginning of Peter's fragmentary account of the trial of Jesus. Pilate washes his hands, absolving himself of all responsibility for the crucifixion of Jesus. Unlike Pilate, Herod (the King of the Jews) and the Jewish judges refuse to wash their hands, thereby admitting responsibility for Jesus' death (in this respect, see also Matthew 27:24–25, a narrative canonically exclusive to Matthew's Gospel.) In the Gospel of Peter, it is Herod, the Jewish king, not Pilate, the Roman governor, who condemns Jesus to death. Unlike Matthew's account, in the Gospel of Peter the Jewish leaders and the Jewish people as a whole are said to realize the evil they have done and to fear the wrath of God as a result. This emphasis is clearly associated with the common second-century Christian polemic that the destruction of Jerusalem in 70 CE came about as God's judgment against the Jews for having executed Jesus. Such a polemic intensified in the Middle Ages, when Christians accused Jews of being "Christ-killers."

While viewing Judaism and observant Jews with disdain is morally repulsive to most Christians today, this anti-Jewish polemic makes historical sense, for it was one of the few means available to Gentile Christians in support of their claim to stand in a special relationship with the God who created the world and who chose Israel to be his people. The second-century Christians making these claims were a persecuted minority that felt defenseless against overwhelming social odds in the larger Roman society. Wishing to shed pagan accusations of being a new and therefore a dangerous religious sect, they claimed to be the true heirs of the ancient traditions of Judaism. Such claims led to a counterattack from Jews, who rightfully claimed these religious traditions for themselves.

While apologetic attacks like these may have been defensive posturing by Christians early on, over time, as Christianity acquired more converts and eventually complete dominance religiously, culturally, and politically, deeper problems arose. After the conversion of Emperor Constantine to Christianity early in the fourth century, when Christians were able to claim social, economic, and military control, they took the anti-Jewish claims they had developed in Barnabas and Peter and applied them literally, maintaining the view that Jews were the enemies of the Christian God and, therefore, had to be punished and destroyed. Clearly, such polemic cannot be justified today or ever, certainly not in an age of Christian cultural dominance in the West.

The ugly history of Christian anti-Semitism is in many ways a direct result of writings such as these. One can only imagine how much worse it would have been had the Epistle of Barnabas or the Gospel of Peter made it into the Christian canon.

DETERMINING TRUTH: TO THE VICTORS GO THE SPOILS

For the standard account of how proto-orthodox Christianity emerged as victorious in the fourth century, we turn to Eusebius (265–339), one of the most important authors of Christian antiquity. Known as the "father of church history," Eusebius wrote his ten-volume *Ecclesiastical History* around 324, shortly before Emperor Constantine convened the Nicene Council in 325. As Bishop of Caesarea from 314 to 339, Eusebius was invited as a presenter at that council, despite (or perhaps because of) his pro-Arian views.

An important theologian and an even more prominent historian, Eusebius was the first Christian author to attempt a history of the Christian church, following the book of Acts, which covers the birth of the church up to and including the ministry of Paul, a thirty-year period. However, no church history covered the chronology of the church from that point onward, including such topics as opposition by Jewish authorities, the spread of Christianity, the rise of important churches and prominent locations, the internal conflicts among Christian, the persecutions of the church by government officials, the rise of monasticism, the conversion of Emperor Constantine, and significant Christian leaders and authors. For centuries, Eusebius was viewed as the primary authority for understanding Christianity in the first four centuries, particularly in citing at length many primary documents. Even today, many of these documents remain our only knowledge of early heterodox views.

It is to Eusebius that we owe what would become the classical perspective of the relationship of specific Christian groups to orthodoxy, whether deviant or authoritative. According to Eusebius, the doctrines espoused by orthodoxy were taught by Jesus to his immediate followers, who then taught them to bishops and other church leaders, who handed them down orally before putting them into writing, thereby ensuring that they would be the majority view from then on. Consistent with this view, orthodoxy is and always has been the view advocated by Jesus and his apostles, and thus the perspective held by the vast majority of Christians throughout history.

Heresy, in this view, is always a corruption of the truth, fabricated by a malevolent apostate and perpetuated by a troublesome yet devoted minority. In other words, heresy is a late, derivative, corrupt view. Orthodoxy involves certain lasting truths: that there is one God, who is the creator of the world; that Jesus—who is both human and divine—is God's only Son; that Jesus died for the sins of the world and was physically raised by God from the dead; that there is also a Holy Spirit, who with the Father and Jesus forms one God; and that these views are taught by the books authentically written by Jesus' apostles. Heresies deny or corrupt one or more of these views. This view of the emergence of Christianity held the field for the next sixteen centuries, and continues to be held widely by Christians to this day. A major shift in thinking came only in modern times, with the discovery of other early Christian writings and with a critical scholarly appraisal of the biases at work in Eusebius's account.

Perhaps the most significant critique of Eusebius's thesis appeared in 1934, in Walter Bauer's probing study, *Orthodoxy and Heresy in Earliest Christianity*. In this original study, Bauer maintained that Eusebius had rewritten church history to validate the victory of the orthodox party that he represented. Rather than being the original view consistently shared by the majority of Christians, what later came to be known as orthodoxy was simply one of many forms of Christianity in the early centuries. While it did eventually end up acquiring the majority of converts over time, it had not always been the majority view. It arose through coercion and by systematically eliminating competing views from the historical record. However, traces of the earlier conflict managed to survive.

Bauer's book proceeds region by region, showing that virtually everywhere one looks—Egypt, Syria, Asia Minor—the earliest attested forms of Christianity were non-orthodox, such as Gnostics in Egypt and Marcionites in Asia Minor. There were, of course, pockets of believers who held proto-orthodox views, but these were not the majority everywhere.

As we now see from the New Testament documents, early Christianity was widely diverse and not monolithic, as Eusebius maintains. While this diversity may be observed in the book of Acts, it is also reflected in the earliest Christian sources, namely, in the letters of Paul, which depict Paul as fighting Christian opponents in virtually all of his letters, in most cases addressed to churches that he founded. In every case, Paul thought he was right and his opponents wrong, while his opponents thought they were right and Paul was wrong. Furthermore, we only have Paul's side of the argument. If we had his opponents' views in writing, whose side might Christianity have taken? As scholars now detect, using non-biased hermeneutical techniques, the New Testament documents contain multiple theological perspectives, often differing significantly with one another. Even the four canonical Gospels have diverse emphases and points of view, written to different audiences with alternative views and practices.

Proto-orthodoxy proved to be dominant in one very important location, however, in the capital of Rome. That proved significant, because this church was able to use its vast wealth and administrative skill to exert influence on churches across the empire and, eventually, throughout the world. Literary evidence exists to support this view, including the epistle of 1 Clement, probably the earliest Christian writing we have outside of the New Testament. This letter was written by the church in Rome to the church in Corinth. It is a long letter, written to resolve a dispute over the leadership of the Corinthian church, and the Roman congregation wrote this letter to reverse the situation, which they were able to accomplish. The gist of the argument builds upon the notion of apostolic succession, that the displaced elders of the church had been appointed legitimately by those who had been appointed by apostles, who had been appointed by Jesus, who had come from God. Using this argument, the church of Rome managed to suppress the revolt in Corinth, and from that point, the influence of the Roman church grew exponentially. In time, the authority of the bishop of Rome became decisive, further substantiating the notion that bishops, like kings, ruled by divine right and choice. To oppose one's bishop, the proto-orthodox argued, was to disobey God. Conversely, to obey the bishop was to honor God.

According to Bauer, the Roman church intervened unsolicited in the internal affairs of other churches, and in the end, became successful in its influence and dominance. Its reputation enhanced, this church exerted influence not only literarily but also politically and economically. For example, Roman Christians were able to manumit slaves with their wealth, causing such individuals to attend recommended proto-orthodox congregations rather than heterodox ones. In this manner, churches agreeing with Rome's point of view grew numerically and influentially.

Roman Christians began asserting their influence as early as the end of the first century and continued doing so, ensuring that Roman Christianity spread across the empire. By the beginning of the fourth century, the Roman form of Christianity became dominant. When the emperor converted to Christianity, that changed everything, and there was an immediate explosion in the growth of Christianity, particularly the Roman form of Christianity, for that became the form of Christianity maintained by Emperor Constantine and his immediate successors. For the near future, it was the Roman church, or more precisely, the Roman Catholic Church, that determined the course of Western Christianity.

This understanding of the development of Christianity is quite different from that of Eusebius, who viewed Christianity as monolithic, rather than as it truly was, widely diverse from the start. In places such as Egypt and Asia Minor, heterodoxy rather than proto-orthodoxy was dominant, a topic we explore in the next chapter. Recent archaeological finds, such as the library discovered at Nag Hammadi, Egypt in the late 1940s, seem to confirm Bauer's thesis. Even these documents, discovered purely by happenstance, represent a range of beliefs. Each form of Christianity, then, even proto-orthodoxy, is typified more by diversity than by uniformity. Christianity, it appears, began not as one large, unified movement, but rather as many small groups in various parts of the ancient world, different geographical regions displaying different forms of Christianity, only one of which emerged victorious. This form called itself orthodox, and as part of its triumph, it rewrote the history of the engagement.

Christians on all sides wrote tractates supporting their perspective and attacking that of others, the proto-orthodox accusing opponents of heresy, and non-proto-orthodox accusing proto-orthodox of heresy. Each of these groups appear to have had its own books, allegedly written by apostles of Jesus, authorizing the theological views of the group. Furthermore, Christians of all sorts began compiling lists of books they accepted as authoritative, excluding books of differing perspective as heretical forgeries. Curiously, some of these forged writings, such as 2 Thessalonians, made it into the official canon, and some potentially authentic writings, such as 3 Corinthians, did not. Some Christian scribes, copying earlier texts, including books later accepted into the orthodox canon, changed certain passages to make them appear more orthodox, making potentially controversial passages say what they wanted them to mean.

Eventually, the group that won these battles ended up deciding which books were apostolic and therefore authoritative, and which books were forgeries and therefore unworthy of canonical status. This led to the next step, namely, declaring which doctrines were orthodox and therefore true, and which were heretical and therefore false.

As Bauer recognized, the production and dissemination of literature was extremely important in the struggles between various Christian groups. Christianity, unlike other religions in the world, was a literary religion. While Christians tended to belong to the lower classes, meaning they were not particularly literate, nevertheless, as a religion, Christianity relied on religious texts for its worship and practice, and Christians used literature primarily in their debates between heresy and orthodoxy.

As Christian theology developed, particularly from the middle of the first century, beginning with the letters of Paul, to the middle of the fifth century, with the formulations of the Council of Chalcedon (451), the church underwent its first great doctrinally creative period. However, even after its final four ecumenical councils, discussion was far from over. For example, the Christological issue, which Chalcedon seemed to settle, continued as a subject of controversy for centuries. Nevertheless, as far as the theological mainstream was concerned, the surge of fresh ideas that characterized the earlier centuries had run its course, ending in the establishment of orthodoxy.

QUESTIONS FOR DISCUSSION AND REFLECTION

Select one or more of the following questions and write your answer(s) in a journal. If you are in a group study, be prepared to share your answers with those in the group.

1. Assess the role of Christianity as both a continuation and development of Judaism.
2. Explain the process of the separation of Christianity from Judaism.
3. Explain and assess the role and message of the Epistle of Barnabas.

4. Explain and assess Barnabas's use of *gematria* as an interpretative technique.

5. Explain and assess the supersessionist point of view as it arose in the second century CE.

6. Explain and assess the role of the Christian historian Eusebius.

7. After reading this chapter, what did you learn about the emergence of Christianity?

Chapter 9

Early Christianities

DESPITE WHAT WE MIGHT think, Christianity is not monolithic. It is not so in the present, and never has been. While modern Christianity is widely diverse—in terms of ecclesiastical polity, social structure, belief, and practice—this diversity pales in comparison with Christianity in the first three centuries. During that period, people claiming to be Christian disagreed on most issues, including the nature of God (whether personal or impersonal, and whether one, two, three, or many); the nature of Jesus (whether human, divine, both, or neither); the resurrection of Jesus (whether physical or spiritual); the nature of salvation (whether temporal or eternal, and whether based on belief or knowledge); the death of Jesus (whether redemptive or symbolic, and whether actual or illusory); the nature of the afterlife (whether physical or spiritual, and whether this-worldly or other-worldly); the creation of the world (whether by a good God or a malevolent false god); the authority of the Hebrew scriptures (whether sacred or inspired by an inferior or evil deity); the status of Paul (whether a true or apostate Christian); and the makeup of the Christian canon (which books should be authoritative for all Christians). Furthermore, this summation is but a start to the endless list of items debated and disputed by early Christians.

The variety of early Christian beliefs raises an important question: Why didn't early Christians who held divergent beliefs simply read the New Testament and come to consensus? The answer, as noted earlier, is that Christians of the first several centuries did not read the New Testament because this authoritative collection did not yet exist. While most of the canonical books had been written by the end of the first century, they had not yet been collected into a sacred canon of scripture, a process that would take nearly four centuries to complete. Not surprisingly, even after the completion of the canon, Christians continued to debate its meaning and to disagree on its interpretation.

The canon consists of four types of books: gospels (four accounts of Jesus' life, death, and teachings); historical accounts (one book of the Acts of the apostles); epistles (numerous letters written for Christian individuals or groups); and apocalypses (one book about spiritual and earthly realities leading to the end of history). Additional such books were written thereafter, many of them claiming to be written by Jesus' apostles or by other prominent early followers of Jesus and his apostles: forged *gospels*, for example, attributed to Thomas, Peter, Philip, and Mary Magdalene; forged *letters* attributed to Paul, Barnabas, and other followers of Jesus and the apostles; additional "*acts*," purportedly about Paul, John, Thomas, Peter, and others; and *apocalypses* attributed to Peter, Paul, James, and even the Virgin Mary.

The authors of these apocryphal works derived not solely from deviant, minority, or heretical groups, but from Jewish-Christian and even proto-orthodox groups. All, however, are late and legendary, and many were forged in the name of apostolic authority. In this chapter we focus attention on three Christian groups we know to have existed in the second and third centuries: Ebionites, Marcionites, and Valentinians.

EBIONITES: AN EXTREME FORM OF JEWISH CHRISTIANITY

One of the earliest groups within the emerging Christian movement is the Ebionites, Jewish Christians who maintained their Jewish beliefs, practices, and identities while adhering to Jesus as their messiah. Heterodox in belief and practice, the Ebionites came to be branded heretics by the proto-orthodox, though ironically, their beliefs may have been closer to those of Jesus' own disciples than the views eventually adopted by mainline (catholic) Christians.

The meaning of their name is obscure, possibly deriving from an early Jewish-Christian leader named Ebion but more likely from the Hebrew word *ebyon*, meaning "the poor" (probably a reference to voluntary poverty, no doubt engendered by the purity and simplicity of lifestyle they advocated rather than by involuntary economic deprivation). It is unfortunate that we have no writings from any Ebionite author. To understand their views, we must rely on the words of their opponents—specifically the writings of

Irenaeus, a second-century bishop of Gaul (modern-day France), who wrote the five-volume work, *Against Heresies*, around 180 CE, and of Epiphanius, a bishop in Greece who wrote a book against heresies around 360 CE—who mentioned their views precisely to attack them. Occasionally, these authors quote from Ebionite writings available to them at the time. Later labeled adoptionists or simply Jewish Christians, the Ebionites were strict Jews who either were born Jewish or converted to Judaism prior to adopting Jesus as their messiah. In addition to faith in Jesus, the Ebionites kept Jewish laws and customs such as circumcision, Sabbath observance, and kosher diets. Viewing Jesus as a human messiah, they held to an adoptionist Christology, meaning that though born a human, Jesus achieved such righteousness that he was "adopted" by God to be his son at his baptism by John the Baptist. As God's adopted son, Jesus was appointed to fulfill the Jewish expectations of the messiah by dying for the sins of the world. As a reward for fulfilling his mission, God raised him from the dead.

Because they believed that Jesus was the Jewish messiah, they felt that anyone who wanted to be right with God had to become Jewish, keeping strictly the requirements of the Jewish law. Consequently, they tried to convert other Jews to their faith in Jesus, and if they converted Gentiles, they insisted that they also convert to Judaism. For the Ebionites, Christianity was a Jewish religion. Despite their commitment to Judaism, the Ebionites differed from most Jews in two ways: (a) they did not offer animal sacrifices to God, believing that through his sacrifice on the cross, Jesus had performed the ultimate and final sacrifice for sin; in addition, (b) they were vegetarian. In the Roman world, most people ate meat only after it had been sacrificed in a pagan ceremony.[1] As they spread across the ancient world and separated from orthodox Jewish communities, the Ebionites felt it was easier to avoid meat altogether, rather than rely on kosher butchers.

To understand their eventual rejection as heretical by both orthodox Jews and Christians, we must examine further their historical and theological context. Because of their views regarding Jesus, they were seen by their adversaries as neither Jewish nor Christian. By the second century, most Christian converts were former pagans who converted from polytheism (the worship of many gods) to monotheism. They believed in one God, but they were not interested in becoming Jews. Starting with the apostle Paul, proto-orthodox Christianity appealed to Gentiles by insisting that they did not have to become Jews in order to accept the salvation brought by the Jewish God. In addition, Paul taught that persons could be made right with

---

1. This concern is evident in the New Testament writings as well, especially in Paul's letters; see Paul's discussion in 1 Corinthians 8 and in Romans 14.

God by faith in Christ's death and resurrection alone, and not by keeping the ceremonial and ritual requirements of the Jewish law. To underscore the centrality of faith and grace, Paul believed that adherence to Jewish rituals prevented one from receiving grace and resulted in divine judgment (see Gal. 3:1–15; 4:8—5:15).

Not surprisingly, Ebionites rejected the teachings of Paul regarding the Jewish law, considering him to have apostatized from Judaism. Instead, they claimed loyalty to James the Just, the observant Jew who, as Jesus' blood brother, led the church in Jerusalem after Jesus' death. One of several early Jewish-Christian groups that disagreed with Paul and rejected his writings as scripture, the Ebionites established their own Christian canon, accepting as authoritative a version of Matthew's Gospel, sometimes called the Gospel of the Nazarenes, and a second gospel called the Gospel of the Ebionites. The Gospel of the Nazarenes may have been an Aramaic version of Matthew, excluding the birth narratives in chapters 1–2, since Ebionites denied that Jesus was divine and instead believed him to be fully human, the physical offspring of Joseph and Mary. Matthew appealed to this group because of its insistence that followers of Jesus keep the Jewish law fully (see Matt. 5:17–20). Their second gospel may have been a conflated version of the Gospels of Matthew, Mark, and Luke, with some interesting modifications, such as the omission of any references to Jesus' deity and the addition of the importance of vegetarianism. In their gospel, John the Baptist is said to have subsisted on a diet not of locusts and wild honey (see Matt. 3:4; Mark 1:6), but of pancakes and wild honey, something far more appealing. They arrived at this conclusion by emending the Greek word for "locusts," which differs by one letter from the Greek word for "pancakes."

It is ironic, of course, that the Ebionites, seemingly associated originally with James, the brother of Jesus, and with the Jewish understanding of Jesus by his first followers, should fall out of favor and be declared a heresy. However, as Christianity flourished in the Gentile world, it showed its resilience and openness to change. As a result, those who held to the original views were excluded, rejected, or merely left behind.

MARCIONITES: AN EXTREME FORM OF GENTILE CHRISTIANITY

The wide diversity of early Christianity can be seen by considering a second group of Christians proclaimed heretics by proto-orthodox thinkers. This group, named Marcionites for their adherence to the teachings of Marcion (c. 85–c. 160), the second-century Christian theologian, held views diametrically opposed to the Ebionites. If the Ebionites were "Judaizers"—Jewish Christians who stipulated that all Gentile converts to Christianity adhere to the traditions of ancient Judaism—the Marcionites were "Gentilizers"—Gentile Christians who sought to erase anything Jewish from the church's practice and identity.

Marcion was raised in a proto-Christian family in Sinope, a city in northern Asia Minor (modern-day Turkey), on the southern shore of the Black Sea. It is difficult to know what prompted him to turn against Judaism, but it was likely based on his study of the Hebrew scriptures, widely accepted as authoritative by early Christians. Unlike later Christians, who harmonized the Old and New Testaments by using the principles of allegory and typology, Marcion was a literalist. Finding numerous contradictions between the Hebrew scriptures and the Christian writings, Marcion's conclusions put him at odds with the views of Christians in the church at Sinope, particularly with his father, the church's bishop. When Marcion's views proved to be too extreme, his father excommunicated him from the local church and forced him to leave home.

Marcion seems to have been independently wealthy, possibly due to a successful career in shipping and merchandizing. As a result, he traveled to Rome, becoming involved in the city's thriving Christian community around the year 139. Eluding his heretical reputation, he made a large donation to the church in Rome, which heightened his status. Keeping a low profile, he devoted the next five years to research, producing two significant works, his *Antitheses*, a book that highlighted the contrast between the "Law" of Judaism and the "Gospel" of Christianity, and a work he edited, containing his version of the Christian scriptures. In his *Antitheses*, he attributed contradictory perspectives between the Jewish Law and the Christian Gospels to two distinct deities, viewing the God of the Old Testament and hence of Judaism as a God of wrath, and the God of Jesus and of Christianity as a God of love and mercy. His second book became the first canon of Christian scripture. It contained eleven writings: ten of Paul's letters (the same as those currently found in the New Testament, with the exception of 1 and 2 Timothy and Titus, books later attributed to Paul but possibly unknown to Marcion), and a gospel much like the New Testament Gospel of Luke. He excluded the Hebrew scriptures from his canon and felt it necessary to revise even his eleven selections. Like "Jefferson's Bible," Marcion removed all teachings he disputed from his scriptures, including any references to the Old Testament or to the God of Judaism, in addition to positive comments about creation, the merits of the natural order, and the physical birth of Jesus. In his opinion, such passages had been corrupted by Judaizing Christians, and he felt justified to remove all elements that seemed to contradict the gospel he believed came from Jesus and Paul, Jesus' one authoritative apostle. It was Paul who converted from Judaism to Christianity; it was Paul who contrasted law with gospel; and it was Paul who developed the idea that salvation comes through faith in Jesus, primarily through belief in Jesus' crucifixion and resurrection.

In Marcion's estimation, the God of the Old Testament is not the God of Jesus, but rather an inferior deity concerned not with salvation but with judgment. This God is fair, but wrathful. As a result, this God called the Israelites to be his people, providing laws they were to keep as their side of the covenant agreement. If they broke God's law, they would be condemned, and the ultimate punishment for sin is death, a condition inherited by every human being, for God also established standards for the rest of humanity. God is just, willing to reward the faithful, but since no one is righteous, all humans come under God's wrath.

In his *Antitheses*, Marcion highlighted the contrast between the God of the Old Testament, who commanded the Israelites to kill their enemies, and the God of Jesus, who told his followers to love their enemies. Likewise, the God of the Old Testament allowed the prophet Elisha to call a bear to attack and kill the children who taunted him, whereas Jesus welcomed and cared for all children. The God of the Old Testament proclaimed a curse upon anyone who hung upon a tree (whether by lynching or crucifixion), whereas the good God ordered Jesus to achieve blessing by being crucified on a cross. In Marcion's view, Jesus was sent to this world by the true, merciful God in order to save humans, not only from their sin, but also from the wrath of the Old Testament God, who created this world and established nearly impossible standards.

In his opposition to the God of the Old Testament and the scriptures of Judaism, Marcion held many views in common with early Gnostics, regarded by proto-orthodox Christians of the second and third centuries as their greatest threat. Like the Gnostics but contrary to the Ebionites, Marcion refused to accept the humanity of Jesus, over-emphasizing his divinity. Since creation was the product of a lesser God, Jesus, as the agent of the true God and the redeemer of humanity, had no physical attributes. He was fully divine and not actually human. Though he appeared to be human, he was not born physically but remained external to the material world.

This point of view, that Jesus was not human but only appeared to be human, is called Docetism, from the Greek word *dokeo* meaning "to seem" or "to appear." This, too, was a cherished view of the heretical Gnostics, another point of commonality between Marcionites and Gnostics. Docetic views would be roundly condemned by proto-orthodox and orthodox bishops and theologians, on the basis of anti-docetic Christian texts, written in the late first century and found in biblical passages such as Colossians 1:22; 2:9; 1 John 1:1–3; 4:1–3, and 2 John 7. Marcion possibly found support for his view in Romans 8:3, where Paul indicates that God sent "his own Son in the *likeness* of sinful flesh," to do what the law "could not do."

Like the Ebionites, none of the writings of Marcion or of the Marcionites survived, and thus for knowledge of Marcion's beliefs, we must rely on the critical and disparaging comments of his antagonists. His views are discussed at length in writings of the early third-century theologian Tertullian (c. 160–c. 225), a pagan convert to Christianity from the North African city of Carthage. Often regarded as the Father of Latin or Western theology, he defended the unity of the Old and New Testaments against Marcion. In so doing, he laid the foundation for a doctrine of the Trinity. An apologist for the sufficiency of scriptures, Tertullian opposed making theology dependent upon extra-scriptural sources such as secular or natural philosophy. An important figure in the development of proto-orthodox theology, Tertullian maintained high ethical standards while opposing all Christian heresies. He wrote numerous books against heretics, particularly five volumes against Marcion and the Marcionites, which serve as our principle source on Marcionism. In these works he often quotes extensively from Marcion's writings, though not always to the satisfaction of neutral observers.

It is unfortunate that we do not have Marcion's own works to clarify his thought process, for on the surface, it does not make sense how a non-human could suffer and die on a cross, and even if this were possible, how a fully divine being could substitute for sinful humanity. It may be, as some scholars suggest, that Marcion was more concerned to show how one who seemed perfectly human and therefore a suitable substitute could fulfill the creator God's need for justice. Marcion may have been an early advocate of what became known as the "ransom theory," an explanation widely held by orthodox Christians for centuries, by which a bargain was struck between the good God and a fallen or lesser earthly deity, whereby the latter was tricked into accepting as payment the substitute (Jesus), so cleverly disguised as a human that the lesser divine god, whether viewed as just, malevolent, or simply as Satan, accepted the arrangement.

In 144 CE, after fully developing his theology, Marcion called a council of the leaders of the churches of Rome—the first such church council since the so-called Apostolic Council met in Jerusalem in 49 CE to address problems raised by the success of the early Christian mission to Gentiles (see Acts 15:1–35)—in hopes that they would endorse his views. Instead, the Roman church found Marcion's views unacceptable, excommunicating him from their church and returning his donation. This decision proved to have unfortunate consequences for proto-orthodox Christianity, for Marcion returned to Asia Minor and began establishing churches of like-minded Christians in major urban areas, proving remarkably successful. The churches he established multiplied, many in areas where Paul had labored with equal success less than a century earlier, and became quite a challenge to proto-orthodoxy. His success is why Tertullian and other heresiologists devoted so much time and energy to Marcionism, for Marcion's churches spread rapidly and widely, lasting for centuries. In some parts of Asia Minor, their presence outnumbered proto-orthodox churches, placing in question the future nature of Christianity.

The following contrasts between Marcionites and Ebionites highlight the wide diversity of early Christianity:

1. Ebionite Christians were strict monotheists; Marcionite Christians were ditheists.
2. Ebionite Christians accepted the Jewish law completely; Marcionite Christians rejected it completely.
3. Ebionite Christians insisted that Jesus was fully human and not divine; Marcionite Christians insisted Jesus was fully divine and not human.
4. Ebionite Christians rejected Paul as arch-heretic; Marcionite Christians revered Paul as the one who best understood Jesus' teachings, viewing him as second founder of Christianity.
5. Ebionite Christians accepted an edited form of Matthew's Gospel as scripture; Marcionite Christians accepted only an edited form of Luke's Gospel as scripture.

For historians, it is important to note the positive effect both Marcionites and Ebionites had on the development of orthodox Christianity. The Ebionites led orthodox Christians to stress monotheism and the canonical authority of the Hebrew scriptures. Marcion, of course, understood the importance of having a Christian canon, and his initial canonical attempt led to the establishment of the New Testament as Christian scripture.

In many ways, Marcion and his teachings continue today among Christians who have never heard his name. Many Christians continue to contrast the Old Testament God of wrath and the New Testament God of mercy. Likewise, many Christians also relegate the Law of Moses to the Jews, interpreting it messianically, typologically, and allegorically rather than literalistically.

VALENTINIANS: AN EXTREME FORM OF GNOSTIC CHRISTIANITY

Despite the concerns of proto-orthodox Christians with groups such as the Ebionites and Marcionites, they were even more apprehensive of the religious movement that historians call Gnostic, as evidenced by their frequent appearance in the writings of proto-orthodox apologists.

Before the mid-twentieth century, virtually our only source of knowledge about these widespread and influential sectarian groups came from the writings of heresiologists, namely, the late second- and early third-century Church Fathers Irenaeus (c. 120–c. 200), Tertullian (c. 160–c. 225), and Hippolytus (170–235). That changed in 1945 with the remarkable discovery of fifty-two tractates unearthed by Bedouin in Upper Egypt near the village of Nag Hammadi. Those tractates, written principally for and by Gnostics, have increased significantly our knowledge of ancient Gnosticism.

As is commonly known, the word Gnostic comes from the Greek word *gnosis*, meaning personal, direct, and immediate knowledge. The adjective and noun "gnostic" comes from the Greek adjective *gnostikos*, invented by the Greek philosopher Plato to describe fields of study or parts of the human intellect having to do with higher knowledge, that is, knowledge that can make us wiser or more virtuous, as opposed to practical knowledge used to accomplish ordinary projects or trades such as carpentry or baking. When ancient Gnostics spoke of *gnosis*, they referred not only to revealed yet hidden knowledge of God, but also to secret knowledge about the physical world, namely, that all materiality, including earth and heavens, planets and stars, is an evil prison for human souls or spirits, which originated within the Pleroma,[2] the spiritual world beyond space and time and to which they must return. For Gnostics, salvation involves knowing the distinction between spiritual and material reality, including the makeup, origin, and destiny of human beings.

While ancient Gnostics shared beliefs and common mythologies, they were divided into numerous sects, even numerous religions, each with its own literature, beliefs, and practice. Because gnostic literature was written by Gnostics for Gnostics, their views were not thoroughly explained in their writings, and certain beliefs, including knowledge necessary for the salvation of the soul remained secret, hidden from outsiders. The essential

---

2. For Gnostics, the word *"pleroma,"* often translated as "fullness," refers to the spiritual world beyond space and time. This term is found seventeen times in the New Testament, particularly in the Deutero-Pauline writings of Ephesians and Colossians (see Eph. 1:10, 23; 3:19; Col. 1:19; 2:9).

gnostic worldview, however, particularly as it affected Christianity, revolved around four factors:

1. *Cosmological element.* Most gnostic systems are dualistic, understanding the cosmos as divided into two opposing realms: the divine realm of light (the Pleroma) and the demonic realm of darkness. According to some Gnostics, the physical world originated from a disruption in the Pleroma, when Sophia or Wisdom, the lowest deity (*aeon*) in the Pleroma, chose to create a material copy or image from the spiritual prototype, acting autonomously. That disruption in the Pleroma resulted in a qualitative difference between matter (viewed as evil) and spirit (viewed as good). Thus, life and death, truth and falsehood, salvation and the ruin of human life, are anchored in the cosmos. The world and all things visible in the universe are characterized as darkness and as under the control of evil spirits (often called rulers or *archons*). The *archons* are planetary deities (see Eph. 2:2), evil powers in the heavens whose task is to block the soul's escape from this world after death.

2. *Theological element.* Gnostics had many deities, some good (called *aeons*) and others evil (the *archons*). The primary God, who dwells in the abode of light and is Light, is unknown and unknowable. A lesser craftsman or demiurge, created by Sophia's indiscretion, fashioned this world, trapping particles of light in the darkness of matter.

3. *Anthropological element.* Humans consist of body (flesh) and soul (soul and spirit are sometimes further distinguished), two elements in conflict with one another. Within (some) humans is a spark or particle of light, placed into humanity during the primeval period by the demiurge. Apart from enlightenment, humans remain ignorant of their true (godlike) inner nature. Once redeemed, the spark must escape back to its source, the unknown God.

4. *Christological element.* Christ, an *aeon* sent into this world to bring saving knowledge of the world above—the Pleroma—is understood to be a divine emissary, for knowledge of liberation cannot come by natural means but only through divine revelation. Jesus is a redeemer (Savior) who provides knowledge (*gnosis*) about the unknown God and the divine element to those who by origin are divine. Because matter is evil, Christ is never really embodied. Either he dwells in the man Jesus temporarily or else his body is an illusion. In Jesus, Christ only appears human in order to deceive the forces of evil and to penetrate the realm of darkness with secret insight and saving knowledge.

According to Gnostics, elements in the physical realm such as matter, soul, and spirit exist proportionately in various beings and things. These qualities make living beings such as angels and humans more or less spiritual (hence closer to deities and other higher beings), or more or less material (and closer to animals and other lower beings). For Valentinians, that is, followers of the influential second-century Gnostic Christian Valentinus (c. 100–c. 160), just as the three elements of matter, soul, and spirit are the building blocks of the cosmos, so, too, they are present in differing amounts and proportions in human beings. On this basis, humans can be divided into three categories, based on which element predominates in them: the "spiritual" (the pneumatics), the "psychic," (the animates) and the "sarkic" (the fleshly, earthly, or material humans).

The highest element, spirit, predominates in spiritual people. Depending on the group or sect, these are the Valentinians, Gnostics, or Christians, who possess *gnosis* of God and of themselves. Obviously, these people will be saved and enter the Pleroma. The lowest element, matter, predominates in material people. These are non-Christians or non-Gnostics, including pagans, Jews, and anyone who does not believe in Jesus or worship Christ. Like the material element to which they are oriented, these people will perish at the end of the world. Animate people (who possess the soul element) have the freedom to turn toward God, live righteous lives, and receive salvation, or to turn away from God, live sinful lives, and perish with the material people. The sources disagree on the destiny that awaits animate people.

According to Irenaeus, the Valentinians taught that the three categories are three different kinds of human beings, descended or derived from the three sons of Adam and Eve. Cain is the father of the material people, Abel the father of the animate people, and Seth the father of the spiritual people. As Irenaeus presents it, spiritual people will be saved no matter what, and material people will be destroyed no matter what. The only people whose destiny is uncertain are the animate people. They can choose to live righteous lives and gain limited salvation, or they can live sinful lives and be condemned.

Based on research, many modern scholars disagree with Irenaeus's depiction, finding in the original sources now available that Valentinians may not have been so deterministic. Valentinus seem to have taught that every person consists of all three elements, and that it is up to each individual to choose how to live and which to follow. Over time, these choices determine which element predominates and, thus, whether a person is spiritual, animate, or material.

Gnostics in general, together with some Valentinians and other early Christian groups, believed that humans have their origin in the spiritual world of the highest God. If so, this means that our True Self is not our body or ego and possibly not even our soul, for these substances are said to come from the lower universe and hence are not eternal. Our True Self is our spirit (Gnostics might call this our "mind" or "intellect"), which originated in the spiritual realm and is destined to return there. In this respect, knowledge of the *gnosis* that Gnostics offer is knowledge of one's True Self.

While gnostic ideas possibly preexist the birth of Christianity, having appeared initially in Jewish and Hellenistic contexts, the so-called gnostic school of thought flourished in the Roman empire during the second and third centuries CE. In works such as the Apocryphon (The Secret Book) of John and the Gospel of Judas, we find Gnostics combining the book of Genesis with Jewish, Platonic, and Christian traditions to create a strange myth that explains how the universe came into being through an ignorant and malevolent god. Christian Gnostics offered salvation from ignorance, fate, and the evil material world through knowledge of a higher God, who sent Jesus, and they claimed that people could have mystical contact with God now.

While gnostic sources are post-Christian, some scholars claim that gnostic beliefs predate Christianity and may have influenced Christianity, since Gnosticism flourished during the second century CE. Some Pauline scholars suggest that the central problem Paul dealt with after the Apostolic Council stemmed from Gnosticism. There is no question that some of the scandals that arose in Paul's Corinthian churches point to Gnostic-like behavior and belief.[3] There is little question that incipient Gnosticism was present in first-century churches, but full-blown Gnosticism did not appear until the second and third century. Valentinus and his disciples revised the original gnostic myth to make it even more Christ-centered, and they invited Christians to a deeper understanding of the Christian scriptures, sacraments, and doctrines. Valentinian forms of Christianity existed alongside of, and in competition with, orthodox Christianity for centuries.

Because many of the gnostic texts are permeated with Jewish thought, focusing on the nature of the Jewish God and his creation and interpreting figuratively such Jewish texts as the opening chapters of Genesis, scholars stress the likelihood that Gnosticism emerged from Judaism. If true, such an origin did not take place suddenly but gradually, after many centuries of speculation. One of the earliest theological beliefs attested in ancient Israel was that God had elected Israel to be his people by intervening on their

---

3. A partial list from 1 Corinthians includes (a) the presence of the "Christ-party" (see 1:12), (b) esteem of *gnosis* (1:17), (c) devaluing the earthly Jesus (12:3), (d) emphasizing glossolalia (speaking in tongues) over other gifts (13:1; 14:1–5), and (e) denying the resurrection of the body (15:12–19).

behalf during the Exodus, when they were rescued from slavery in the land of Egypt. This notion that Israel was God's chosen people was challenged in the course of historical realities, for Israel constantly had to fight for its survival against harsh natural conditions and powerful military and political enemies. The first and possibly the predominant answer to Israel's suffering was offered by the ancient Hebrew prophets as due to divine displeasure at individual and corporate sin. Suffering, they claimed, came as punishment from God. In the sixth century, during the Babylonian captivity, this traditional explanation for suffering came to be seen as unsatisfactory, at which time it became apparent that the righteous suffer disproportionately to the unrighteous, the wicked often prospering at the expense of the righteous. This led to the literary figures of Job and Isaiah's Suffering Servant, images of righteous Israel suffering vicariously on behalf of others.

Such thought led to a new religious understanding that emerged about two centuries before Christ in a movement that scholars call apocalypticism. Apocalypticism, seen in the biblical book of Daniel, in the later prophetic literature, and in some of the intertestamental writings such as the books of Enoch and the Dead Sea Scrolls, led to views of cosmic dualism, expressed in the notion that God's people suffer on account of temporal forces of evil, soon to be overthrown by the righteous, almighty God.

As Jews lived with this alternative, a nagging thought emerged: What if this cataclysmic act of God didn't occur? One result of such speculation might be a new religious perspective, in which God is thought not ultimately to be in charge of this world because God did not create this world and has nothing to do with it. The world is an evil place, created by a malevolent deity. If this is true, then, according to this way of thinking, when salvation comes, it is not salvation *to* this world (as traditional Judaism taught), but *from* it. This, ultimately, becomes the view of Gnosticism. It did not persuade most Jews, but it profoundly influenced Christian eschatology.

We know very little of Valentinus's early life, but he is believed to have spent his early years in Alexandria, Egypt. At this time, Alexandria was one of the leading centers of intellectual life in the ancient world. Two important institutions—the museum and the library—supported serious scholarship in the city. These institutions were a kind of think-tank, where scholars carried out research, led seminars, and gave lectures. People came to Alexandria from across the Roman empire to study with well-known scholars, some of whom were Jewish or Christian.

Some modern scholars argue that an early source for the biblical Gospel of John, the so-called "Signs Gospel" or "Signs Source," was written in Alexandria around the middle of the first century, predating the first version of John, itself possibly written in Alexandria. We know that Alexandrian

Christians had a high regard for the Gospel of John. In fact, the first commentary written on this Gospel was produced in Alexandria early in the second century by a Gnostic Christian named Heracleon, suggesting that John may have revised the so-called Signs Gospel in Alexandria.

It seems likely that the Gnostic school of thought originated in Alexandria. All of these teachers and groups used Greek wisdom, including philosophy, mathematics, and astronomy, to deepen their understanding of the Bible. And Christians like Valentinus believed that their teachings about Jesus continued this great tradition of Greek learning.

By around the year 140, Valentinus had moved to Rome, where he was a popular and effective teacher. Some of his students became important Christian theologians. According to Tertullian, Valentinus was a candidate to become bishop of the church of Rome, but when his bid failed, he turned his back on the church and went his own way. While this may be true, it is more likely that his bid failed because of unorthodox views he may already have espoused. In his lifetime, he was never declared a heretic, and while many Christian teachers considered his views wrong, he had a substantial following. Later church authorities condemned him as a heretic, and due to his condemnation, nearly all of his writings became lost.

One of the clearest expositions of early Christian Gnosticism is found in the Gospel of Truth, a text from Nag Hammadi. The sermon is an invitation to every Christian to experience the hope, joy, and security of knowing God the Father through Jesus Christ. The sermon defines sin—what separates us from God—as ignorance. Salvation—our return to God—is discovering the Father through the power of the Savior, Jesus Christ. The Gospel of Truth, one of the most intriguing documents from the Nag Hammadi collection, is believed to be a sermon by Valentinus. Because it is the only extant Valentinian writing, it is indispensable for understanding Valentinian theology.

The tractate's title, "Gospel of Truth," comes from its opening line, which reads, "The Gospel of Truth is joy for those who have received from the Father of Truth the grace of knowing him." The book is unlike the Gospels of the New Testament in that it does not relate stories about the life, death, and resurrection of Jesus. Instead, it celebrates the "good news" of the salvation he has brought by revealing the knowledge that can free the soul from its bondage to material things. Strikingly, the views of this text stand diametrically opposed to those that eventually became dominant in Christianity. Unlike Christian orthodoxy, which concluded that the world was the deliberate creation of the one true God, and, as such, was made good, the Gospel of Truth maintains that the material world came about by mistake, by a conflict in the divine realm, resulting in ignorance, suffering, and error.

While Christianity eventually claimed that Christ's death and resurrection brought salvation, the Gospel of Truth maintains that Jesus brought salvation by delivering the truth that alone can set the soul free. Whereas Christianity concluded that God would redeem this world and create it anew as a utopian place of eternal life, the Gospel of Truth claims that once saving knowledge comes to souls entrapped in this world, ignorance will vanish and with it all vestiges of the material world. The tractate concludes with an exhortation for its hearers to share the true knowledge of salvation with those who seek the truth, and not to return to their former (that is, their proto-orthodox) beliefs, which they have surpassed.

According to the Gospel of Truth, everything that exists is in God the Father, and all real beings are emanations from God. For all beings, joy and blessedness are to know and to be known by the Father. Jesus makes possible the *gnosis* that removes ignorance and brings joy. For Valentinus—and possibly for some Gnostics as well—the journey back to God commences with rituals such as worship and observance of the Eucharist, but these groups also added mystical rites such as the "bridal chamber," a ceremony whereby participants were consecrated ritually in a "spiritual marriage" in anticipation of the final union with the Pleroma (the fullness of God) at the end of time.

Valentinians and other early sectarian Christians envisioned heavenly perfection figuratively, symbolized by the sacred union between a man and a woman. Since the world and the fall of the spirit originated through the disruption of this original unity, the return of the spirit to its ideal prototype becomes the decisive event at the end of time. The Valentinian rite of the bridal chamber symbolized the Pleroma ideal of the eventual unity of separated elements. According to Gnostic teaching, the Gnostics or "pneumatics" (spiritual persons who possess the perfect knowledge of God and undergo the proper rituals) are said to become "brides of the angels," and their entrance into the world beyond is likened to a wedding feast, when the saved enter the bridal chamber within the Pleroma and attain to a vision of the Father, at which time they become spiritual *aeons*, united with Infinite Reality.

Perhaps the most famous of Valentinius's pupils was Ptolemy, who, in a letter he wrote about 160 CE to a proto-Christian woman named Flora, explained his views regarding the Old Testament, which, in his estimation, is deeply flawed, as evident by a study of its teachings. It includes, for example, commands that are not appropriate to God, such as when God tells the Israelites to murder the Canaanites. However, the Old Testament could not have been inspired by Satan either, because it contains laws that are just and good. The Old Testament, he concluded, contains three different kinds of laws, which originate from different sources. Some laws, like the Ten Commandments, were inspired by a divine being, but it was neither the one true perfect God nor his nemesis, the Devil, but some deity between the two. Other laws were given by Moses, such as the law of divorce (see Deut. 24:1–4), which Jesus indicates did not come from God (see Mark 10:11–12; Luke 16:18). And there are laws obviously given by the elders around Moses, such as the laws setting aside honoring one's father and mother,[4] which Jesus attributed to ungodly traditions. Some laws are honorable, such as the Ten Commandments; others are tainted by injustice, such as the law of retaliation ("an eye for an eye"), and others are purely symbolic and not to be taken literally, such as laws about circumcision, Sabbath observance, and fasting. Ptolemy assumed that Jesus' teaching regarding the Jewish law presupposed another god, a just divine being who is not the one true perfect God.

Unlike other heterodox texts we have considered, Ptolemy's *Letter to Flora* does not come from the Nag Hammadi library but is preserved in the writings of the fourth-century bishop and heresiologist Epiphanius (c. 310–403), a vigorous apologist of Christian orthodoxy. Epiphanius is best known for a book called the *Panarion*, a compendium of eighty heresies up to the time of its composition around 360, twenty of which are pre-Christian—of either Jewish or Greek origin—and sixty of which he considers to be Christian heresies. Many of these heresies would be unknown to us, had Epiphanius not catalogued and described them. His compendium contains many quotations that are often the only surviving copies or fragments of suppressed texts, as is the case with Ptolemy's letter, which promises a sequel that did not survive.

Concluding that the gnostic Christian understanding of the divine realm is correct, Ptolemy disagreed, like Valentinus, Marcion, and the Ebionites, with proto-orthodox Christians on essential Christian belief. Interestingly, ancient heterodox groups considered themselves true Christians, and for a while, Christians on both sides of the dehate polemicized against the other, each arguing for their brand of Christianity. In the end, it became a debate only one side could win.

CONCLUSION

Despite Christianity's fragile foothold in the ancient pagan world, its existence questioned by pagan authorities, the Christian movement remained undaunted, its fervor and resilience unstoppable. Because there was yet no church magisterium—no central office or authority to provide guidance for belief and practice—diversity flourished.

---

4. In Matthew 15:2–6, Jesus calls ungodly a tradition whereby one takes money or a gift due one's parents and presents it instead as a votive gift to the temple.

While Ebionites believed in one God, Marcionites believed in two gods and gnostic Christians in many divine beings, some good and others evil. Moreover, Ebionites thought that Jesus was a human being—a righteous man adopted as Son of God at his baptism—whereas Christian gnostics thought that Jesus was human but Christ was divine. Many Christian gnostics held to a separationist Christology, believing that Christ—a divine *aeon*—indwelt Jesus at his baptism (see Mark 1:9–11) and left Jesus prior to his crucifixion, compelling Jesus to declare from the cross, "My God, my God, why have you forsaken me?" The proto-orthodox agreed with the Ebionites that Jesus was human, but disagreed with them when they rejected Jesus' divinity. Furthermore, the proto-orthodox agreed with Marcionites that Jesus was divine, but disagreed with them for teaching that Jesus was not human. The proto-orthodox also disagreed with Gnostics and separationists, affirming that Jesus was both human and divine, but they disagreed that these were two separate beings. For the proto-orthodox, there was one being—Jesus Christ—simultaneously God and man.

As we can now see, the proto-orthodox Christology emerged, at least in part, in response to the various views it opposed. The many Christian groups contending for orthodoxy differed in theology, Christology, anthropology, and cosmology. In fact, they disagreed on most religious issues.

Each group had authoritative books that claimed to represent the views of Jesus and his apostles, books they could use to support their various perspectives. The Ebionites used a version of the Gospel of Matthew, viewed as the most Jewish of the four canonical Gospels and therefore as appropriate to Jewish Christianity. Those who separated Jesus from the Christ used the Gospel of Mark, which concentrates on Jesus' ministry from his baptism to his crucifixion, eliminating accounts of his birth and of his post-resurrection appearances. Marcionites used a version of the Gospel of Luke, viewed as the most Gentile of the four Gospels. Gnostic Christians such as the Valentinians favored the Gospel of John, viewed to be the most spiritual and mystical of the four canonical Gospels, finding in its pages a Christology of Jesus as a preexistent divine being who came to earth to give his followers truths that would set them free (see John 8:32).

Unlike sectarian Christians, many selecting favorite passages and favoring one Gospel, the proto-orthodox affirmed all four Gospels together, finding commonality and divine guidance in their unity and diversity. In their estimation, only the four Gospels, read together, provided a correct and complete understanding of Jesus and his message.

Other groups had other gospels—the Gospel of Thomas, the Gospel of Truth, the Gospel of Philip, and so forth. Because books in antiquity were rare and costly, available only in handwritten copies, some churches and groups had one or at most two Gospels, some only canonical Gospels, others only apocryphal gospels, and some a combination of both types. It was difficult for most groups to have all four canonical Gospels at their disposal.

Only one of these groups emerged as victorious in the struggle to win converts and to establish the "true" nature of Christianity. This victorious group—Christian orthodoxy—shaped for all time what Christians would believe and which scriptures they would accept, eliminating virtually all traces of competing scriptures in the process.

As we have seen, the study of church history during the second and third Christian centuries reveals a wide range of early Christian beliefs and practices. While consensus was attained by the fourth and fifth centuries, it came about mostly through a combination of compromise and coercion. Diverse views would continue, however, for the next millennium. The medieval consensus ended around 1500 CE, when forces emerged in Europe that further challenged the concept of Christendom, fragmenting Christianity into multiple sects and denominations, eventually threatening the very foundation upon which Christianity had been erected.

During the Enlightenment, skepticism and secularism threatened Christianity's core principles, replacing its theological and ecclesiastical supremacy with the "rights of men," including freedom of religion and from religion. Into this vacuum flowed Eastern religions, vying for allegiance with the monotheisms of Judaism, Christianity, and Islam and heralding the ideological fluidity and diversity of the second and third centuries, this time in the guise of modernity and postmodernity.

QUESTIONS FOR DISCUSSION AND REFLECTION

Select one or more of the following questions and write your answer(s) in a journal. If you are in a group study, be prepared to share your answers with those in the group.

1. After reading this chapter, what did you learn about diversity in early Christianity?
2. After reading this chapter, what did you learn about the Ebionites?
3. After reading this chapter, what did you learn about the Marcionites?
4. After reading this chapter, what did you learn about Valentinus?
5. After reading this chapter, what did you learn about Gnosticism?
6. In your estimation, which came first in Christianity, heterodoxy or proto-orthodoxy? Explain your answer.

Chapter 10

The Pagan-Christian Debate

DURING THE SECOND HALF of the first century, most people converting to Christianity had been pagans, that is, non-Jewish, and it is these people who helped transmit and record the "Jesus material," at first orally, and then literarily. What these people believed about religion prior to their conversion certainly influenced their understanding and interpretation of Jesus, including how they might have modified the tradition they inherited from Jewish Christians.

Pagan religions, as we learned earlier, focused on sacrifices to the gods, a gesture believed to placate or please such powers, but also to result in benefits or blessings. Pagan religions focused on the needs of the gods rather than on affirming specific teachings or truths. Of course, worshippers believed in the gods, that is, in their existence and power, but there were no creeds or doctrines to affirm, and being religious did not require adherence to prescribed ethical standards. While religion presupposed general ethical principles, specific norms were personal, as were matters of lifestyle, more subjects of philosophical debate than of religious practice.

Unlike Christianity, pagan religions were not exclusive; people worshiped many different gods, and did so in traditional or in non-traditional ways. Because such religions were highly diversified, pagans did not consider their gods as jealous or in competition with one another. They understood the realm of the gods as hierarchically ordered, ranging from the great gods of Greek and Roman mythology to local gods of one's city or town, from gods of specific functions to those of rivers, forests, and homes.[1]

For most pagans, certainly the most literate or best educated, the top of the pyramid was held by one supreme deity, whether Zeus, Jupiter, or some unnamed god. Below this deity were the great gods, such as those comprising the pantheon on Mount Olympus.[2] Below these great gods were various kinds of local deities, who were still mighty, by comparison with humans, but who were not as powerful as the great gods. Below these local gods were family and personal deities, minor in the grand scheme of things, but nonetheless important to individual people, for they were actively involved in human affairs. Below these divinities were lesser beings known as *daimonia*, not necessarily evil spirits but lower-level divinities involved more intimately with human life.

The next level of this divine pyramid comprised a group of demi-gods, that is, humans who were half-mortal and half-divine. Included in this group were people of superhuman strength, like Hercules, or individuals of superhuman wisdom, like Pythagoras, or of superior influence, like the Roman emperors. Hence, imperial rulers were believed to be partly divine. They may have been low on the sacred totem pole, but still supremely powerful on the human scale and therefore worthy of worship. On this lower tier were human representatives of the divine such as Apollonius of Tyana (c. 15–c. 100 CE), the famous neo-Pythagorean philosopher of the first century CE, said to have had a miraculous birth, to perform miracles, and to gather disciples. Even after his death, his followers believed he had ascended to heaven, and they claimed they had seen him alive afterward.

Some pagans might have viewed Jesus of Nazareth in this way, treating him as a kind of "divine person," one worthy of allegiance and even of worship. Perhaps among those who converted to Christianity were some who contributed to the canonical Gospels, for in them we note progression in the treatment of Jesus, beginning with Mark and concluding with John. Mark's Gospel contains no birth narrative and only hints at a resurrection, whereas Luke's Gospel tells of Jesus' miraculous birth and ends with a description of Jesus' ascent into heaven. John's Gospel, the latest of the four, portrays Jesus more in line with what pagans typically thought about "divine persons." Is it

---

1. On this topic, see the discussion in Ehrman, *Brief Introduction to the New Testament*, 19–21.

2. Though ancient pagans read the mythological accounts, saw them portrayed on stage or at festivals, or heard them recited by troubadours, most people did not accept these accounts as literally true, that is, as portraying events that had occurred historically. Rather, they viewed such accounts as ways of speaking of traits or aspects of deities, deities that truly existed.

an accident that the earliest canonical Gospel portrays Jesus as human and the latest as divine?

RELIGIOUS TRENDS IN THE ROMAN WORLD

The world in which Christianity emerged, if somewhat painfully, was hungry for religion. Facing hardship, uncertainty, and deprivation at every turn, people in antiquity, in all social classes, displayed a deep need for assurance that life was worth living. In that regard, they longed for assurance against death and fate, protection from evil, spiritual renewal, and union with the divine. To meet this need, the old classical religions had little to offer. Despite periodic attempts to revive ancient piety, the gods of Greece and Rome had lost whatever power they possessed to inspire. The worship of the emperor or his *genius*,[3] fostered by Rome, became increasingly prominent and had official backing. At best, however, emperor worship provided a means for corporate loyalty and the sense that Providence watched over the empire.

In this welter of superstition and genuine piety, two phenomena became prominent. One was the extraordinary appeal of the so-called mystery religions that from the first century BCE spread rapidly across the Greco-Roman world. This is the name given to those close-knit religious groups or associations into which newcomers had to be initiated by sacred ceremonies ("mysteries") not communicable to outsiders. In classical times, the mysteries held at Eleusis in honor of Demeter and Persephone were the most famous. In the first three or four centuries CE, the most popular were Oriental in origin. There were mysteries of Serapis and Isis, of Egyptian origin, and of the great Anatolian mother-goddess Cybele and her youthful lover, the vegetation god Attis. These divinities gained masses of devotees, having temples erected to them at public expense. Perhaps the most widespread of these mysteries was that of Mithras, the Persian god popular with soldiers as an ally of the Sun and thus the champion of light against darkness.

In the second century, during the reign of the Nerva-Antonine dynasty (a dynasty of seven Roman emperors who ruled from 96 to 192 CE), these cults received imperial sanction, particularly when the emperors Hadrian and Marcus Aurelius became initiates of the Eleusinian mysteries and Antonius Pius legalized the cult of Cybele. As a result, senatorial participation in non-Roman (Mithras, Dionysius) or Greco-Roman (Isis/Diana, Serapis/Jupiter) cults increased markedly.

---

3. In Greco-Roman times, each family had a personal deity, a kind of guardian angel called a *"genius,"* thought to reside in the head of the household.

These mystery religions had much in common, including sacred meals, preparatory stages, and occultist rituals, which imparted revelation to the initiates and secured mystic union with the deity. In the rites of Mithra or of Cybele and Attis, for example, initiates underwent a kind of baptism in the blood of a bull or a ram, resulting in the experience of rebirth and the sense of divine protection and eternal security. The appeal of these mystery religions undoubtedly lay in the satisfaction they gave to the craving for an intense personal experience of the divine, with an accompanying sense of release from guilt and fear.

This proliferation of religions achieved a profound syncretism in Greco-Roman times, the gods of one country or region being identified with those of another, and the various cults fusing with and borrowing from one another indiscriminately. In addition, there was widespread belief in the immortality of the soul, sometimes linked with the idea of the transmigration of souls taught by the ancient Greek philosopher Pythagoras (c. 570-c. 490 BCE), and in a future judgment leading either to punishment or to a blessed life with the gods in the afterlife.

The second phenomenon to emerge at this time was a growing attraction, for educated and uneducated people alike, of a monotheistic interpretation of the conventional polytheism. A growing number of deities of the pagan pantheon were coming to be understood either as personified attributes of one supreme God, or as manifestations of the singular Power governing the universe. The current syncretism made this process simple and natural, and at a higher level, it coincided with the trend of enlightened philosophical opinion. An instructive example is Aelius Aristides (117-189), the pagan orator who lectured in Asia Minor and Rome in the middle of the second century CE. Many of his speeches survive, celebrating Asclepius, the god of healing who exemplifies the personal concern of the gods for the wellbeing of the individual. Aristides's *Sacred Tales* reveals that, although a worshiper of one god, in his view all the gods represent cosmic forces emanating from the one universal Father.

The same holds true for Plutarch (46-c. 120), the biographer, essayist, and Middle Platonist philosopher who, while, adhering to ancestral religious practices and admitting the existence of subordinate gods and demons (*daimonia*), combined this with belief in a single supreme and perfect God. When in 274 CE the Roman emperor Aurelian instituted the state cult of Sol Invictus, he was not merely honoring the sun as protector of the empire, but acknowledging the sole universal Godhead, which, recognized under many names, revealed itself most fully and splendidly in the heavens. Likewise Apuleius (c. 124-c. 170), the Platonist philosopher and rhetorician best known for his bawdy novel *Metamorphoses* (*The Golden Ass*), sums up the matter when he describes Isis as "the inclusive manifestation of gods and goddesses," a deity worshiped across the Greco-Roman world under many forms and names.

During the second century, the church stood at a crossroads. Could it draw clear lines between true worship of Jesus Christ and the era's multitude of Greek, Roman, and Middle Eastern philosophies and mystery religions that also featured revelations from a high God and appeals for dedicated moral life on earth? The answer is affirmative, but the journey was long and arduous before Christian orthodoxy prevailed.

An umbrella of protection was needed, broad enough to accommodate the masses, yet specific enough to deal with deviant belief and behavior. Many Gentiles, formerly pagan, began joining the church. Most were illiterate, in a state of spiritual infancy, and not yet ready for the freedom Paul spoke about in Galatians (see 3:23–26; 5:1). Like all adolescents, they needed guidance and protection. By the year 112, Ignatius, leader of the Christian church in Antioch of Syria, urged fellow believers to "follow the bishop as Jesus Christ followed the Father." On his way to martyrdom in Rome, he wrote letters to the churches of Asia Minor and to Rome. In each letter, he calls for submission by the members to the bishop and the elders and urges respect for the deacons. In his letter to Polycarp, bishop of Smyrna, Ignatius declares, "Let nothing be done without your approval." His injunction reveals the emergence of a system of church organization constructed around locally powerful bishops.

By the time of Ignatius there circulated among the expanding Christian congregations two collections of Christian documents, one consisting of the four gospel accounts of the life of Jesus as attributed to Matthew, Mark, Luke, and John, and the other containing copies of the letters credited to the apostle Paul. Soon Christians would add to these the Acts of the Apostles and other sacred writings, set alongside the Hebrew Bible to provide written guidance for the church.

In roughly the same period that witnessed the evolution of an episcopal system of church organization and a scriptural record of Christ and the early church, there also appeared short, concise summaries of what it means to be an orthodox Christian. These creeds (from the Latin *credo*, "I believe"), proved immensely useful both as a way of marking out the boundaries of Christian faith and as an introduction for inquirers or the children of believers. Some creeds were baptismal, formulated as a way to teach catechumens (converts undergoing instruction). Together with the episcopate and the canon of scripture, the early creeds became the anchors that stabilized the church in its early subapostolic history. The importance of creed, canon, and episcopacy for the development of orthodox Christianity cannot be overestimated.

THE PAGAN SIDE OF THE DEBATE

Following the destruction of Jerusalem in the year 70 and its reconstitution as a Roman colony in 135, Christians continued their claim to be the New Israel, although the issue for Christians about obeying the Jewish cultic laws died out with the destruction of the Jerusalem temple and the emergence of Rabbinic Judaism. Although Jerusalem continued to be an important center of the church in the eastern Mediterranean, it was at Caesarea on the Palestinian coast and at Alexandria in Egypt that the vitality of the cultural life of the church was most evident. These cities were centers of Greco-Roman culture and learning, and in both cities Christians took on the task of coming to terms with the challenges from culture. In each place, Christians developed schools for the instruction of their leaders that helped shape the life and thought of Christianity for centuries. By 180, a school existed in Alexandria for the intellectual training of leaders of the church, headed by two of the early church's greatest scholars, Clement and Origen. There they pursued the claim that through Jesus, God had brought to fruition the fuller and final disclosure of the divine plan for the human race.

In Rome and Carthage, the major centers of Roman culture in the western Mediterranean world, the issues that dominated the thought of the church differed. For them, the central concern involved the identity of the church, specifically, defining Christian orthodoxy. Important for the church was the developing attitude toward the Christian movement on the part of both the political and the intellectual leaders of the Roman world. Speaking for Christianity were some who had been trained in the best methods of the Greco-Roman intellectual tradition, providing reasoned explanations for what Christians believed and taught. The Greeks called this strategy an *apologia*, which means a "rational defense" for one's position (the New Testament also encourages apologetic defense of one's beliefs; see 1 Pet. 3:15; Titus 1:9; Jude 3). Four Christian thinkers whose extensive writings provide the fullest picture of this effort are Justin Martyr, Origen, Irenaeus, and Tertullian.

The Gentilizing of Christianity and its encounter with pagan culture were two of the most important historical phenomena of the second century CE. By this time, as the Judaizing of Christianity ceased to be an issue, proto-orthodox Christians came to be seen as a threat to the social, political, and religious fortunes of the Greco-Roman world. As pagans began distinguishing Christianity from Judaism, philosophical Greeks and Romans initiated a systematic attack on Christianity, a debate that lasted into the fifth century and beyond.

The debate engaged some of the best philosophical minds, pagan and Christian alike, a debate conducted on many different intellectual and social levels. Besides the literary format, the debate must also have been conducted, frequently and bitterly, in the council-chambers and market places of many cities, as well as in thousands of homes. Our knowledge of the discussions at these levels is limited, but we know that the debate was not static. Both Christianity and pagan philosophy were in continuous process of change and development throughout this period, and the relationship between them changed accordingly. We can speak of four phases in the debate, associated with four pagan voices. The most substantial critics of Christianity (and Judaism) were the influential philosopher-physician Galen (129-c. 200), who served as personal physician to Emperor Marcus Aurelius; the second-century Middle Platonist philosopher Celsus (dates unknown); the Neoplatonist philosopher Porphyry (c. 234-c. 305); and the Emperor Julian, who ruled from 361 to 363. The most important works on the pagan side of the debate were Celsus's *The True Word* (c. 178), Porphyry's *Against the Christians* (c. 270), and Julian's *Against the Galileans* (c. 362). On the Christian side, the most important works were Origen's *Contra Celsum* (c. 248) and Augustine of Hippo's *City of God*, written after the sack of Rome in 410.

The first phase of the debate occurred during the Antonine age (from 138 to 192), notably in the reigns of Marcus Aurelius (161–180) and Commodus (180–192), when a renewed interest in various forms of Platonism as spiritual ways of life existed side by side with developing Christianity. This period began with the Christian apologists Justin Martyr (c. 100-c. 165) and included Irenaeus (c. 120–200), Clement of Alexandria (150-c. 211), and Tertullian (c. 160-c. 225). On the pagan side, this phase included the satirist Lucian of Samosota (c. 125-c. 180) and the physician Galen, and ended with Celsus's full-scale systematic critique of Christianity.

During the second century, neither paganism nor Christianity formed a closed or unified system. Greek philosophy only achieved a synthesis a century later under Plotinus (205–270), but there was yet little agreement, even among Platonists. Christians were divided into many competing sects, often having little or nothing in common save the name Christian, since there was no authoritative Christian creed or fixed canon at this time.

It is at this point that the debate began. The Christian writings of the first-century had been intended only for fellow-Christians. The Christian apologists who emerged in the second century for the first time stated the case for Christianity to the world of educated pagans—not so much in the expectation of converting them as in the hope of persuading them to call off the intermittent local persecutions aimed at Christians. It was in the latter part of the second century that Celsus responded to what he saw as a threat to the stability and security of the empire, namely, the continuing growth of Christianity that could disrupt the bonds of society and weaken Roman resolve in repelling the barbarian threat. He expressed his views in a book entitled *The True Word*, thought to be published under Marcus Aurelius's reign. Unfortunately, the book no longer exists, but only its reconstructed argument as preserved in Origen's *Contra Celsum*, written about 248, some two generations later.

Galen's basic critique, echoed by later pagans, is summed up in his idea that Jews and Christians substitute blind faith for a reasoned account of their beliefs. While praising the Christians for their way of life, moral and self-disciplined, he finds that, unlike the educated Greeks, they are overly reliant on parables and miracles and appear unable to follow philosophical arguments. When they use reason and intellectual argumentation, it is defective, substituting scriptural faith for logic.

Celsus continued Galen's argument, but, unlike Galen, he was not a friendly critic. He considered Christian faith to be pure superstition. It is clear that Celsus knew the New Testament writings, as well as the claims being made in the second century by various competing Christian groups, such as the Gnostics and the followers of Marcion. Using the tactic of a scornful critic, Celsus's attack featured a fivefold critique: (1) Christians rely on miracles, which can be equated with magic; (2) Christianity is a low-class movement, appealing to the ignorant and the gullible, who are obsessed with healing and prophecy rather than with wisdom and philosophical truth; (3) Jesus is not divine, but the illegitimate offspring of a Roman soldier. Claiming allegiance to a resurrected Lord, Christians actually worship a powerless corpse; (4) the Jewish-Christian view of God, revealed to a minor race of people and thereby excluding from participation the majority of the human race, is preposterous and unacceptable; (5) the Jewish-Christian scriptures, embarrassing when read literally, have to be interpreted allegorically to cover up their improbable teaching.

Celsus's alternative to the Jewish-Christian perspective was to disavow their doctrine of God, affirming that there is only one god behind the many names. He maintains that there is, and always has been, a single god accessible to humanity through reason. There are, Celsus acknowledges, some admirable moral truths affirmed by Jews and Christians, such as love of one's neighbor, but these insights were already present in the writings of the Greek philosophers, as are the teachings of other religions. Christians are foolish to employ the human, fleshly Jesus as their basis for understanding the divine purpose for the cosmos.

The second phase of the pagan-Christian debate began with the Christian philosopher Origen teaching in Alexandria in 203, and ended in 248, with the publication of *Contra Celsum*, his great defense of Christianity. For Christians, this was a time of relative freedom from persecution, of steady numerical growth, and of intellectual advance. Already, Clement of Alexandria had recognized that if Christianity was to be more than a religion for the uneducated, it must come to terms with Greek philosophy and science. In preparation for a teaching career, the youthful Origen studied under the pagan Platonist philosopher Ammonius Saccas, who later taught Plotinus, widely regarded as the founder of Neoplatonism.

Trained also in Christian learning, Origen developed special competence in the languages and contents of the Jewish and Christian scriptures, so that at the age of eighteen he began presiding over the Christian academy in his native city, Alexandria. By means of allegorical and figurative interpretation of the scriptures, Origen was able to show correlation, as he saw it, between Greek philosophy and the Bible. His instructed his pupils not only in philosophy but in mathematics and natural science, developing an educational plan based on Plato's and not differing in essentials from that of Plotinus. Henceforth, the Christian debate with paganism would be between intellectual equals.

On the pagan side, there were signs at this time of a desire to absorb Jesus Christ into Roman paganism, as so many earlier gods bad been absorbed, or at any rate to create terms on which peaceful coexistence might be considered. It might have been with that purpose that Julia Manaea, the Empress Mother, invited Origen to her court. It is known that her son, the Emperor Severus Alexander, who ruled from 222 to 235 as the last emperor of the Severan dynasty, kept in his private chapel statues of Abraham, Orpheus, Christ, and Apollonius of Tyana, four "prophets" to whom he paid equal reverence. He was not alone in this attitude; about the same date the Gnostic Carpocrates was promoting a similar comprehensive perspective, his followers worshiping images of Homer, Pythagoras, Plato, Aristotle, Christ, and the apostle Paul. Unfortunately, Severus's assassination in 235 marked the start of the Roman "crisis of the third century," nearly fifty years of civil wars, foreign invasions, and collapse of the monetary economy.

The third phase began with the Decian persecution of 249, the first systematic attempt to exterminate Christianity by depriving the church of its leaders, and one that might have succeeded had it not been cut short by Decius's death in battle in 251. Origen was one of those tortured under Decius, dying from those injuries in 254. The mixture of the astonishing courage of the martyrs' convictions coupled with the intellectually impressive defense of their faith offered by brilliant thinkers such as Justin, Irenaeus, Clement, Origen, Tertullian, and Cyprian forced many thoughtful Romans to reassess their attitudes toward the resilient Christian movement. By 250, however, Rome faced multiple problems: Persians on the east, Goths on the north, economic woes, and a plague swept across the empire. Emperor Decius felt he had an answer: Rome had lost its ancient spirit, nourished by ancient values. Rome needed a revival of "true" religion, and so Decius appointed a day on which all his subjects would be required to sacrifice to the ancestral gods, followed by a signed pledge of loyalty. A magistrate would attest the certificate. Under dire pressure, some Christians recanted their faith; others experienced torture and confiscation of property; some were exiled, and others martyred. Thankfully, Decius's reign ended a year later, but within six years, Emperor Valerian renewed the persecution, though he was soon captured by the Persians. The next emperor restored personal and church properties to the Christians, and for the next four decades, the church had relative peace.

The third phase ended with the great persecution under Diocletian and Galerius. A disturbance related to the army sparked the persecution under Diocletian, the final and most violent persecution of Christianity. While some Christians had served in the army, many attempted to leave, while others refused to serve in the military. Some church leaders discouraged combat, espousing love of enemies and other forms of pacifism. The conflict erupted in 303, when Diocletian issued a decree that prohibited Christians from meeting, required the demolition of all churches, the burning of all copies of the Christian scriptures, and the stripping of citizenship for Christians of high rank, forcing all others into slavery. Two fires broke out in the palace, and, as in the days of Nero, Christians were blamed. Prisons filled and stayed full even though pardon was offered to those who recanted. One observer recorded seeing nearly one hundred Christian men, women, and children on their way to slavery in the mines, their right eye gouged out and their left foot crippled. In Egypt alone, thousands of Christians submitted to death, after dreadful torture.

The martyrs who perished in this final persecution gave medieval Christians many edifying tales and legends. Martyrs include Pope Marcellinus; St. Sebastian, a Roman soldier who survived death by arrows only to be clubbed to death; St. Agnes; a gentle girl who refused to marry a pagan; and St. Lucia, a girl of Syracuse who came to be revered in Sweden. The persecutions under Galerius, who followed Diocletian, claimed as victims St. George, honored by soldiers and also by England as their patron saint, and St. Catherine of Alexandria, whose name is attached to the famous monastery at the base of Mount Sinai. All this changed in 312, when Constantine defeated his rival Maxentius at the battle of Milvian Bridge.

The mindset of this third phase was strikingly different from that of the preceding period. During this period, aided by the dismal social and economic conditions of the years 250 to 284, Christianity gained rapidly in numbers and influence. It was in this interval, probably about 270, that the Neoplatonist philosopher Porphyry produced his polemical book *Against the Christians*, which found numerous imitators in ensuing years but also provided many replies from the Christian side. In his book, Porphyry expresses the alarm that is now felt by all religiously minded pagans. He speaks of Christianity as an ideology being proclaimed universally, noting how in Rome the cult of Jesus is replacing that of Asclepius, Pythagoras, and Apollonius of Tyana. Christians, he adds, are prospering, to the point of building large churches everywhere. He does not call for persecution, a policy he abhors. However, his fellow pagan Hierocles was less empathetic. In his treatise *The Love of Truth*, he exalted Apollonius as a rival to Jesus, and as provincial governor he became one of the instigators and promulgators of the great persecution. He was one of the last Roman officials to promote paganism, helping to transform Neoplatonism into a religion with its own saints and miracle-workers. Both responses—those of Porphyry and Hierocles—were reactions against the advance of Christianity.

Similar responses were evident on an even larger scale in the fourth stage, the brief reign of Emperor Julian (361–363). Known by Christians as "the Apostate," Julian was raised Christian, but he converted to paganism and sought to restore the empire to its traditional polytheism. Elevated by Constantius to Caesar of the west in 355, he proved himself adept as a soldier. In 360, when he was acclaimed Augustus by his troops, he openly renounced Christianity. While he did not persecute Christians, he promoted a syncretistic form of religion, restoring pagan education and pagan temples while honoring Jesus among other sages and heroes of the past. One wonders what might have happened if Julian had not been cut down in battle after a brief reign.

Succeeding emperors quickly and decisively restored Christian privileges, some allowing freedom of worship while others rejected pagan worship and emperor worship. The decisive establishment of Christianity as the state religion of the empire took place under Theodosius the Great, who ruled the east from 379 to 392 and was sole ruler from 392 to 395. By 380, rewards for Christians gave way to penalties for non-Christians. In that year Theodosius issued an edict imposing Christianity on all inhabitants. He closed all pagan temples, where possible converting them to Christian worship. In 392, he declared sacrifice to the gods to be treason, punishable by death. Jews were allowed to assemble for worship, but were not allowed to proselytize or enter into marriage with Christians.

It is interesting to compare Julian's critique of Christianity with that of Celsus. Writing in 362, a century after Origen, when Christianity had become firmly entrenched in the empire, Julian entitled his work *Against the Galileans* to show that Christianity was a small, relatively unimportant sect. Nevertheless, he recognized the potential of the Christian message, seeing it as a major threat to his efforts to restore pagan culture. In one of his edicts, he forbids Christians to teach in the public schools. "How can the Galileans who openly despise the old gods rightly teach any of the literature and philosophy of the ancient Greeks?" he asks. "It is absurd that men should teach what they do not believe to be sound."[4]

In his diatribe, Julian claims that Christians have no single admirable or important doctrine, compared with those held by Greeks or Jews. Contrary to the biblical accounts of creation, he prefers the view of Plato, who in the *Timaeus* affirmed that the universe came into being as a living creature, possessing soul and intelligence by the providence of God. Julian also decries the scandalous particularity of both Jews and Christians. If the Creator chose the Hebrew nation alone, it looks as if God cared only for the Jews. He then asks why the God of the Jews should send Jesus and the prophets to the Greeks, having kept them in ignorance for a thousand years. "In our teaching," he writes, "the Creator is common Father of us all, while other functions are assigned to national gods and gods of the cities." He indicates that with the exception of the commandments forbidding the worship of other gods and requiring Sabbath observance, the Decalogue is common to every nation.

Citing the lack of culture and learning of Christians he asks, "Did you originate any science or philosophy?" Then he lists the achievements of the pagans in astronomy, geometry, arithmetic, music, and law. He also faults Christians for claiming to worship one God while worshiping a man (Jesus) as divine along with the Creator God. Furthermore, the Incarnation implies a belief in a change in God's nature, a view incompatible with the idea of divine perfection. In this regard, Christians are in disagreement with both Plato and Aristotle. In keeping with a longstanding pagan attack, Julian regards Christians as poor citizens, who do not honor or obey the emperor.

THE CHRISTIAN SIDE OF THE DEBATE

In addition to creed, canon, and episcopacy, essential for maintaining identity and unity, Christian orthodoxy developed a substantial apologetic literature to deal specifically with external challenges from paganism. Apologetic literature had its roots in Judaism. Such literature arose among Diaspora Jews like Philo of Alexandria and Josephus, who responded to

4. Head, Constance, *Emperor Julian*, 76.

anti-Semitic charges of misanthropy with historical and philosophical treatises that demonstrated how the Jewish law and the Jewish manner of life was actually philanthropic.

The essential elements of the Christian side of the debate are well summarized in the writings of Justin Martyr, Irenaeus, Origen, and Tertullian. A native of Palestine, Justin explored the major philosophical options of his day before turning to an investigation of Christianity. He wandered about the Mediterranean world as a Christian philosopher, finally settling in Rome, where he founded a Christian school. His two major writing that have survived are both apologies, the first addressed to a Jewish rabbi (*Dialogue with Trypho*), and the other to Gentiles (*Apology*). In his first work, Justin claims that the new covenant established by Jesus had displaced the covenant with Israel described in the Bible, supporting his contention that the church was now God's instrument to bring the light of God's knowledge to all nations. His *Apology*, addressed to Emperor Antoninus Pius (138–161) and to the Roman senate and people, describes Christianity as a rational search for truth and invites dialogue on philosophical grounds. In a third apology (actually an appendix to earlier ones), Justin counters the false charges that have been brought against the Christians. He notes that the bravery of the Christians in the face of persecution had been an important factor that originally attracted him to that faith.

A major figure among the Christians of the late second century was Irenaeus, who worked to consolidate Christian orthodoxy. Born at Smyrna around the year 130, he was ordained bishop of Lyons in Gaul in 178. Anxious to reconcile Christians in the eastern and western Roman worlds and to establish principles on which such unity might be affirmed and maintained, Irenaeus wrote *Against Heresies*. This major work not only attacks false teaching, but it also offers a full declaration of what Irenaeus considered the essence of authentic Christian faith. Like the philosophical insight of which Origen wrote, faith has an intellectual content that can be defined with increasing clarity. Nevertheless, false teachers who deny aspects of the faith that Irenaeus has identified as orthodox are threatening this unity of faith. Included among these heterodox groups are Gnostics, who deny that creation is good or that the God of Jesus is the creator of the universe. To support their heretical views, Gnostics produced rival writings to the New Testament, including gospels, apocalypses, acts, and letters attributed to various apostles.

In his definition of orthodoxy, Irenaeus claimed a threefold approach to tradition: the canon of scripture, the rule of faith, and the authority of bishops. In countering heresy, Irenaeus argued for the necessity of a literary canon, a standard by which books could be used to define Christian teaching and practice. He refuted Marcionites, Gnostics, and other sectarian teachers with specific citations from the Old and New Testament, indicating which compositions he was using and thus showing which are truly authoritative and which are rejected. Using this method, Irenaeus represents an important stage toward the final formation of the New Testament canon. Unlike the heretics, who take only one Gospel as their norm, Irenaeus insisted that there are four, just as there are four winds and four corners of the earth. The one gospel message rests on four pillars, "breathing immortality on every side and enkindling life anew in human beings."

Irenaeus also draws upon the developing tradition of a rule of faith—or creed—to provide a doctrinal framework for Christian belief. Irenaeus's rule of faith, like the Apostles' Creed, presents an epitome of the scriptural story. As such, it also provides a guide to the reading of the scriptures.

The notion of the bishops as the successors of the apostles, already found in Clement of Rome, was argued more fully by Irenaeus, with specific attention to the bishops of Rome. The institutional argument directly opposed the Gnostic position concerning secret teachings, secret teachers, and secret books. Christianity has a public creed, an apostolic tradition, and a clear canon of scripture. The consensus of the patristic period, already visible by the end of the second century, is that the unity and truth of the church, represented by the orthodox tradition, is to be maintained by the apostolic witness, the succession of leadership from the apostles through the bishops, and fidelity to an accepted collection of scriptures. These church standards will develop more fully during the conciliar age (the ecumenical councils of the fourth through seventh centuries).

Origen was one of the most brilliant thinkers in the history of Christianity. When he was ten years old, his father was killed during the persecution of the church by Emperor Severus (193–211). Origen wished to follow his father in martyrdom, but his mother kept him safe in the house by hiding his clothes. Trained in both secular and Christian learning, he quickly excelled, developing special competence in the languages and contents of the Jewish and Christian scriptures, so that at the age of eighteen he began to preside over the Christian school in his native city, Alexandria. By means of allegorical and figurative interpretation of the scriptures, Origen was able to show the correlation, as he saw it, between Greek philosophy and the Bible. In 232 he moved to Caesarea, where his program of teaching and writing was so colossal that he had stenographers on hand during his lectures to record his discourses.

Origen's greatest contributions were his detailed commentaries on the Bible and an extended apologetic response (*Contra Celsum* and *The First Doctrine*) to an earlier attack on Christianity by Celsus. As apologist, Origen was both a biblical theologian and a Neoplatonic philosopher. When Celsus based his criticism of Old Testaments accounts on a literal reading, Origen interpreted them allegorically, reminding Celsus that the Greeks also allegorized their myths. To Celsus's charge that Christianity appeals only to ignorant and superstitious rabble, Origen makes a strong case for the fact that both Testaments exhort wisdom, noting that this is the thrust of the Wisdom literature in the Old Testament. He also cites as fact that while Jesus taught in parables to the crowds, to the disciples he gave deeper, more spiritual meanings.

Significantly, Origen also used philosophy as part of his apologetics, utilizing Platonism as one of his main weapons in the counterattack. According to W. R. Inge, in *Contra Celsum* we find numerous references to classical authors such as Aristotle, Callimachus, Empedocles, Euripides, Heraclitus, Herodotus, Hesiod, Homer, Josephus, Numenius, Pindar, Thucydides, and Zeno. There are no less than thirty references to Homer and sixty-one references to Plato.[5] The Alexandrian school of Christian thought, of which Origen was a leading figure, was instrumental in enabling Christian thought to adapt to Greek philosophy.

Another kind of response to the mounting pressures on Christianity in the later second century was the promotion of the idea that God would intervene directly in current affairs to vindicate the church and destroy opposition. One Christian leader who came to share this point of view was Tertullian. Born of pagan parents in Carthage around 160 and trained as a lawyer, Tertullian converted in 193. Thereafter, he devoted his legal skills to the defense of Christianity. His writings were in Latin, which was a new feature in Christian literature. Until that time Greek had been the primary literary language of the Christians, and Latin the vernacular of the masses in the western Roman world. According to one analysis, Tertullian coined 509 new nouns, 284 adjectives, and 161 verbs in the Latin language. Of these, perhaps the most important is the word "Trinity" (*trinitas*).

In his *Apology*, Tertullian addressed the two major charges brought against the Christians of his day: that they do not worship the traditional gods (which is sacrilege) and that they do not offer the sacrifices for the emperor (which is treason). Instead of accepting the charge that Christians are morally and politically subversive, Tertullian argues that they follow Jesus, the embodiment of reason and power and the enlightener of the human race. As his followers, Christians are the enemies of human error, not the enemies of the human race. Defending Christians, Tertullian provides modern readers with a vivid picture of life in the churches of the second century.

---

5. Cited in Hovland, "Dialogue Between Origen and Celsus," 207.

They gather to pray to God for strength and guidance, for the welfare of the state and its rulers, and for the triumph of peace in the world. They live according to high moral principles, presided over by elders, sharing the modest resources of the members. They provide support for burial of the poor, for orphans, for the aged, and for victims of tragedy.

Concerned to affirm the continuity of the Christian tradition in the face of new interpretations that were arising, it is ironic that in his later years Tertullian was strongly influenced by the Montanists, a charismatic movement that claimed to have received prophetic revelations that supplemented and modified the New Testament writings.

QUESTIONS FOR DISCUSSION AND REFLECTION

Select one or more of the following questions and write your answer(s) in a journal. If you are in a group study, be prepared to share your answers with those in the group.

1. Explain and assess the notion of a hierarchical pyramid in ancient pagan polytheism.
2. In your estimation, how did pagan views latent in Gentile converts to Christianity influence their understanding and interpretation of Jesus?
3. Explain and assess the meaning of the statement, "The world in which Christianity emerged . . . was hungry for religion."
4. Explain the role and message of the mystery religions in pagan antiquity.
5. Explain the role of bishops, creeds, and the biblical canon in the development of orthodox Christianity.
6. Explain the role and message of Irenaeus in the pagan-Christian debate.
7. Explain the role and message of Celsus in the pagan-Christian debate.
8. Explain the role and message of Origen in the pagan-Christian debate.
9. Explain the role and message of Tertullian in the pagan-Christian debate.
10. Explain the role and message of the Emperor Julian in the pagan-Christian debate.

Epilogue

WHY WERE CHRISTIANS UNPOPULAR in late antiquity? As we have seen, the evidence points to a number of reasons, in addition to the generalized need in society for scapegoating, that is, needing someone to blame for the ills of the world. Initially, Christians shared the long-standing unpopularity of the Jews. One of the earliest references to Christianity in pagan records was as a dissident Jewish sect that, at the instigation of one "Chrestus," had disturbed the peace by engaging in faction-fights with fellow Jews in the city of Rome.[1] Like the Jews, Christians were accused of being a "godless" people who disrespected public images and temples. However, whereas the Jews constituted an ancient nation with an eminent tradition that entitled them legal protection, the Christians were an upstart sect; being of mixed nationality, they could claim no such privilege.

Furthermore, Christians appeared to constitute a secret society, and, like gypsies today, seemed bound by mysterious intimacy. Like the Dionysian societies suppressed in 186 BCE, Christians were viewed with intense suspicion, charged with indulging in incestuous orgies, a charge that persisted well into the second century. The Christian apologists all felt such charges needed defense. To such charges their antagonists added political accusations. Christians did not behave like loyal citizens. To the average pagan, their refusal to honor the emperor on his birthday by refusing to offer incense in public meant not only disrespect but also disloyalty. Hence the charge that they separated themselves from the rest of humanity, which Celsus brings against them. Celsus faults Christians for shirking their duty as citizens by refusing to serve in the army or even in civilian offices.

Origen's reply, that Christians by their prayers did more to help the empire than others did by fighting, would hardly have impressed patriotic

---

1. Suetonius, *The Lives of the Twelve Caesars*, published around 120 CE.

citizens. Of course, there were already Christians in the army by the beginning of the third century, and that situation changed so dramatically over time that by the end of that century Diocletian felt obliged to institute a purge. By Porphyry's time, the charge of lack of patriotism was obsolete, and was apparently dropped.

More persistent—and harder to dismiss because less rational—was the accusation that Christians were responsible for every natural calamity; their "atheism," pagans claimed, had offended the gods. Throughout the third century, when disasters were many and relief-measures inadequate or non-existent, Christians served as convenient scapegoats. In 235, a series of earthquakes in Asia Minor started a local persecution; in 248, a civil war was blamed on Christians. About 270, Porphyry associated the frequent epidemics at Rome with the decline of the cult of Asclepius, and in the early fifth century, the sack of Rome and other calamities were blamed on the Christianization of the empire, a charge Augustine attempted to refute in his *City of God*.

Another cause for resentment was the effect Christianity had on family life. Like all creeds claiming total allegiance, early Christianity was a divisive force. According to Eusebius, writing early in the fourth century, every town and house was divided by debates between Christians and pagans. Nevertheless, in the face of overwhelming prejudice and hostility, Christianity survived and thrived.

In his influential work, *Pagan & Christian in an Age of Anxiety*, the distinguished scholar of antiquity E. R. Dodds notes that the central thesis in the pagan-Christian debate began with the pagans claiming to represent reasoned conviction (*logismos*) against the blind faith (*pistis*) of the Christians.[2] To those reared in classical Greek philosophy, *pistis* meant the lowest level of knowing: it was the state of mind of the uneducated, who believe things on hearsay rather than on logical argumentation. Even the apostle Paul, following Jewish tradition, promoted *pistis* as foundational to Christianity. What astonished early pagan observers such as Lucian, Galen, Celsus, and Marcus Aurelius, was the Christians' total reliance on unproven faith—"their willingness to die for the indemonstrable."[3] According to Galen, Christians possessed three of the four cardinal virtues, exhibiting courage, self-control, and justice. But they lacked intellectual insight, the rational basis of the other three.

By the third and fourth centuries, the tables had turned, so much so that while Christians now made a reasoned case for their beliefs, pagans began replacing reason with their own forms of authority and revelation.

2. Dodds, *Pagan & Christian*, 120.
3. Ibid., 121.

Whereas Plotinus resisted *pistis* and gave his pupils the task of exposing intuitive hunches and subjective revelations, after Plotinus, Neoplatonism became less a philosophy and more a religion, its followers occupied, like their Christian counterparts, in expounding and reconciling sacred texts. If it were to fight Christianity on equal terms, Neoplatonism had to rely on *pistis*, something previously demanded in Hermeticism. As the Roman empire slowly Christianized, pagans began showing a lively interest in sacred texts and mystical practices. Plato and the obscure Chaldean Oracles became canonized. Theurgy, a type of pagan sacramentalism, became increasingly influential, until it superseded pure philosophy; in some pagan circles, theurgy became essential for salvation. As Christians developed a philosophical theology, pagans developed a theological philosophy.[4]

On the Christian side, the most impressive outcome of the debate was the magnificent attempts by Clement, Origen, and eventually Augustine to produce a synthesis of philosophy and religion, of *logismos* and *pistis*. For example, Origen, like the erudite Jewish Platonist Philo, made far-reaching concessions to pagan philosophy, incorporating both the substance of Plato's theology and the Platonic worldview. Greek philosophy was correct as far as it went, and Plato the closest pagan to Christian philosophy. *Logismos* began supporting *pistis*, allowing Christian theologians to acquire a deeper understanding of doctrine.

For Origen, the cosmos was a living creature, sustained by the Logos, which functions like the Platonic world soul. Within the cosmos are many living beings, including the stars, themselves ensouled, which may provide a future home for certain souls. The cosmos has a beginning and will have an end, but, for Origen, the end will be followed by a succession of other worlds. The grand finale to Origen's redemptive myth is the Apocatastasis (salvation by restoration, when all things return to their original state).

More striking than Origen's cosmology is his psychology, closer to Plotinus than to the apostle Paul. The soul is eternal; though created, its origin is outside of time. Every soul begins as pure intelligence, and every soul is eventually restored to that condition. However, in the interim, it must rise and fall many times, an idea similar to Plato's notion of reincarnation. Between incarnations, the soul's fate depends on the life it has lived in time. The bad will suffer purgation, but not eternally, since divine justice is remedial, not vindictive. Hell is not a place of torture but rather a state of mind. Heaven, like hell, is a future state of mind, a state of endless growth and wonder, and as physicality gradually changes to spirituality, bodies become increasingly subtle and less material, their final condition probably bodiless.

---

4. Bregman, "Logismos and Pistis," 225.

The spiritual body of which Paul spoke in 1 Corinthians 15:44 ("What is sown a physical body is raised a spiritual body") is, for Origen, a temporary concession, for no Christian doctrine was more offensive to pagan intellectuals than the resurrection of the body.

Origen's life reveals a complicated relationship with the organized church. On the one hand he was, like Irenaeus, faithful to the church, an opponent of heretics, and a member of the clergy. On the other hand, he was also like Clement and even Valentinus, dedicated to advanced learning, highly creative, eager to help people advance to higher *gnosis*, and always questioning, unwilling to settle for easy or customary answers.

Origen appealed to Christians who wanted a more intellectual, less close-minded approach to Christian truth. However, he understood that some people find the myths of the Gnostics and Greeks attractive. The stories they tell explain the nature of God, how and why this world comes to be, and where human beings come from and are going. The Gnostic myth is a compelling response to human suffering, oppression, and death, and it offers hope for serenity and equality in this life and in eternity. Thus, Origen realized that orthodox Christianity needed a better myth than that of the Gnostics and Greeks—a more complete story of creation, fall, and salvation than offered by a literal reading of the Bible. In his sermons, commentaries, and theological writings, Origen laid out his comprehensive vision of Christian truth, refining and elaborating on that vision for the many students and listeners that attended his services and lectures, some of them pagans.

Origen's mythological account of salvation resembled that of the Gnostics in that it was a story of a fall from a blessed existence in another world into life in this world, and then a return to union with God. However, Origen's story emphasized God's love for humanity and the freedom of human beings. God wants everyone to be saved, that is, to return to the original blissful existence, and it seems that this would happen. Origen's story did not make this universe a mistake, nor did an inferior or hostile God rule over it. Instead, this universe is a good creation, made by God to help us return to him.

Origen's bold rethinking of New Testament doctrine was rendered possible by an allegorical exposition of scripture. This art of textual interpretation, originally developed by Homeric scholars and later by Jewish and Gnostic exegetes, had long been practiced in Alexandria; from there it was taken and adapted first by Clement and then by Origen. Celsus and Porphyry both protested against abuses of this method, but both were on thin ground, for they used the same method to discover Platonism in Homer.

When Origen wrote *The First Doctrine*, Christian notions of eschatology were in flux, and they remained so for a long time. In 410, when the Platonist philosopher Synesius became a Christian bishop, he professed belief in the preexistence of the soul, doubting the resurrection of the body and the eventual destruction of the cosmos. More than a century after Origen, the Eastern Church Father Gregory of Nyssa (c. 335–c. 395), following Origen, could still reject eternal punishment, holding that all souls will eventually be restored to their original paradisiacal state.

Origen, like nearly all Christians of this period, believed in the reality and power of the pagan gods; he merely transformed them from gods into demons or fallen angels. Origen's world was inhabited by a vast multitude of supernatural beings: each nation, like each individual, has both a good and a bad angel. Porphyry's world had a similar mixed population; what Christians called angels, he called gods. Like Celsus, Porphyry defended the popular practice of offering sacrifice to such beings as a token of good will and gratitude, but this formed no part of his personal religion. For Porphyry, like for Paul and many early Christians, the only true sacrifice is the communion of the individual with the supreme God.

Nor is there any substantial difference between pagan and Christian Platonists about the nature of the supreme God. That God is incorporeal, passionless, unchanging, and beyond the reach of human thought was common ground to Celsus and Origen; both attacked popular anthropomorphic notions as vulgar. In antiquity as in the present, people may call this God by different names, but such distinctions are a quarrel about semantics.

That such a God should take human shape and suffer pain and humiliation was incomprehensible to pagans, as to many Christians. Origen and other early apologists dismissed this by treating Jesus less as an historical personality and more as a Hellenist "second God," the timeless Logos that was God's agent in creating and governing the universe. The human qualities and sufferings of Jesus played an inconspicuous role in the Christian propaganda of this period. They seemed more of a hindrance in the face of pagan criticism.

To many pagans and believers alike, it may seem a historical calamity that Origen failed to win ultimate acceptance by the church. However, literal reading of the Bible proved an attraction too strong to resist. After three centuries, virtually all of Origen's innovations were condemned as heretical by an edict of Byzantine emperor Justinian in 543. It was not Origen but Augustine who would determine the future pattern of Western Christianity.

PAGANISM'S DEMISE

Julian's attempt to resuscitate paganism by a mixture of occultism and sermonizing likely would have had little lasting success even if he had lived to enforce his program. Pagan vitality was gone. One reason for the success of Christianity was the weakness and weariness of the opposition: by the fourth century, paganism had lost faith in itself. Christianity, on the other hand, was judged worth living for because it was seen to be worth dying for; as Tertullian wrote, "The blood of martyrs is the seed of the Church." It is evident that all pagan apologists, in their polemic against Christianity, were inspired by the courage of Christians in face of torture and death. Such courage was a convincing catalyst for many conversions.

There were, of course, other reasons for Christianity's success, including its exclusiveness, nowadays seen as a weakness, but under duress it proved a source of strength. The religious tolerance that Greek and Roman pagans practiced led to a bewildering mass of alternatives, too many philosophies of life from which to choose. Orthodox Christianity presented one choice, *pistis*, and on the basis of faith in Christ, the road to salvation was clear.

Though exclusive in doctrine and conviction, Christianity was inclusive in that it was open to all. In principle, it made no social distinctions. While catechumens were taught the essentials of the faith, Christian indoctrination required no further education, unlike Neoplatonism. Furthermore, in a period of history when earthly life was increasingly devalued, Christianity held out hope for a better inheritance in the afterlife. Porphyry remarked, as others had done, that only sick souls stand in need of Christianity. However, sick souls were numerous in this age.

Lastly, the benefits of becoming a Christian were not confined to the next world. From the start, Christianity displayed a fellowship (*koinonia*) and community much fuller and more compelling than those of corresponding groups of philosophical clubs or Isis and Mithra devotees. Its members were bound by need but also by generosity and compassion. The church cared for widows and orphans as well as the elderly, disabled, and unemployed; it also provided a burial fund for the poor and a nursing service in time of plague. The love of Christians, not only for one another but also for strangers and people in need, even for enemies, may have been its greatest resource and perhaps the strongest single cause for its growth and endurance.

RELIGIOUS LIVES MATTER

In 1989, during a two-month sabbatical trip across the Mediterranean world, I visited the Yad Vashem Holocaust Memorial in Jerusalem.[5] I pondered the experience of Holocaust survivor Elie Wiesel, who in his heart-wrenching autobiographical account recalls his first night in the extermination camp

5. I narrate this experience in my 2010 book, *Into Thin Places*.

at Birkenau, the reception center for Auschwitz. Only fifteen years old at the time, he had just been separated from his little sister and his mother, who were headed to the ovens:

> Never shall I forget that night, the first night in camp, which has turned my life into one long night, seven times cursed and seven times sealed. Never shall I forget that smoke. Never shall I forget the little faces of the children, whose bodies I saw turned into wreaths of smoke beneath a silent blue sky. Never shall I forget those flames which consumed my Faith forever. Never shall I forget that nocturnal silence which deprived me, for all eternity, of the desire to live. Never shall I forget those moments which murdered my God and my soul and turned my dreams to dust. Never shall I forget these things, even if I am condemned to live as long as God Himself. Never.[6]

The late Jewish scholar Emil Fackenheim indicated that there can be no explanation for Auschwitz or the Holocaust. He maintained that no redeeming voice can ever be heard from the extermination camps because Auschwitz is "a unique descent into hell . . . It is an unprecedented celebration of evil. It is evil for evil's sake." To respond with despair or to merely forget, Fackenheim argued, would be further victories to Hitler, and thus impossible.

Fackenheim, called the philosopher of the Holocaust, very nearly became one of its victims. Born in Germany and ordained a rabbi in Berlin in 1939, he fled to Canada in 1940, where he had a long, illustrious scholarly career. He formulated the "614th commandment" (adding one to the 613 found in the Torah): there must be no slackening of Jewish faith because that would be to grant Hitler a posthumous victory.

As "Black Lives Matter" is teaching America and the world, survival matters. Black lives matter, and so do Jewish lives, Christian lives, and pagan lives. While the preceding study is primarily religious in nature, it is also about culture, history, and sociology. As Huston Smith, long the world's mentor on world religions, indicates in his classic gem, *Forgotten Truth*, anthropology is a microcosm of cosmology. As there are four tiers of reality—terrestrial, intermediate, celestial, and Infinite—so there are four corresponding tiers of selfhood—body, mind, soul, and Spirit. As black lives must survive and thrive, so must Jewish, Christian, and pagan lives. Each is beloved of God, chosen for its sensibility and contribution to progress and wellbeing. If pagans may be said to represent the divine body, Jews the divine mind, and Christians the divine soul, together they represent the divine Spirit.

6. Elie Wiesel, *Night*, 32.

Each group, Jewish, Christian, and pagan, has witnessed eras when it thrived, but also periods when it suffered and came close to extinction: Jews against pagans, pagans against Christians, and Christians against Jews and pagans. As there is a resurgence of paganism and Neopaganism in postmodernism—a mindset characterized as inclusive and as ecologically minded—so there must be a resurgence of Judaism and Christianity, in all their manifestations: conservative, moderate, progressive, secular, even fundamentalist. In this postmodern age, all must thrive and survive, not through competition or wars of attrition, but through cooperation, mutual respect, and mutual admiration. The world needs Jews, wise, industrious, and gifted—thank God, they survived! The world needs Christians—compassionate, faithful, progressive Christians. The world also needs pagans— ecologically conscious and socially and religiously aware, enhancing the causes of pluralism, diversity, justice, and multiculturalism.

Following America's Civil War, two colleges, located fifteen miles apart and separate since their log-college founding in 1781, joined to form Washington & Jefferson College. Washington College, considered the southernmost northern college in the United States (located in Washington, Pennsylvania) and Jefferson College, considered the northernmost southern college (located in Canonsburg, Pennsylvania), overcame their differences (during the Civil War, occasions arose in which brothers and roommates fought one another on opposing sides), uniting under the banner, *Juncta Juvant* ("together we thrive").

This Latin phrase serves today as motto to W&J College, one of America's oldest institutions of higher education, where the liberal arts represent the foundation for careers in law, medicine, business, education, science, and beyond. For some two hundred years, until becoming co-ed in 1970, the college was all-male. After their arrival, the female students quickly achieved near parity with their male counterparts, not only in number but also in accomplishment, their best students more than a match socially and intellectually with their male classmates. The college continues to emphasize inclusivity, creating a climate where female and male, black and white, Latino and Asian, northern and southern, religious and secular, can thrive, acknowledging that society cannot be united unless every citizen is healthy, vital, and valued. It is at W&J where I, too, thrived, teaching Religious Studies and serving as College Chaplain for nearly forty years.

As *Response to the Other* shows, Jewish lives matter; Christian lives matter; pagan lives matter. Locally and globally, each must survive, and in company with diverse cultures, faiths, races, and lifestyles . . . thrive!

Appendix

Chronological Timeline

Paganism

Pre-Socratic Period	
Homer	c.750 BCE
Pythagoras	c. 570–c. 490
Classical Greek Period	
Plato	427–347
Aristotle	384–322
Hellenistic Period	**334–31 BCE**
Alexander the Great	356–323
Battle of Issus	333
Epicurus	347–270
Zeno	c. 336–264
Posidonius	c. 135–c. 51
Roman Period	**31 BCE–476 CE**
Emperor Augustus's Reign	19 BCE–14 CE
Emperor Tiberius's Reign	14–37
Apollonius of Tyana	c. 15–c. 100
Emperor Caligula's Reign	37–41
Emperor Claudius's Reign	41–54
Emperor Nero's Reign	54–68

Emperor Vespasian's Reign	69–79
Emperor Titus's Reign	79–81
Emperor Domitian's Reign	81–96
Emperor Trajan's Reign	98–117
Emperor Hadrian's Reign	117–138
Galen	129–c. 200
Emperor Marcus Aurelius's Reign	161–180
Celsus	c. 178
Plotinus	205–270
Porphyry	c. 234–305
Sack of Rome	410
Fall of Rome	476

Judaism

Hebraic Period	**c. 2000–586 BCE**
Patriarchal Period	1850–1700
Egyptian Period	1700–1250
Exodus from Egypt	c. 1250
United Monarchy	1025–926
David's Reign	c. 1005–c. 965
Solomon's Reign	c. 965–c. 926
Northern Kingdom (Israel)	926–586
Southern Kingdom (Judah)	926–586
Neo-Babylonian Period	**586–539**
Nebuchadnezzar's Rule	605–562
Babylonian Exile	586–539
Edict of Cyrus	538
Persian Period	**539–334**
Nehemiah's Arrival in Jerusalem	445
Ezra's Arrival in Jerusalem	398
Hellenistic Period	**332–63**
Alexander the Great Conquers Jerusalem	332
Founding of Alexandria, Egypt	331
Ptolemaic Period	323–198
Ptolemy I's reign	323–283
Ptolemy II Philadelphus's Reign	283–246
Translation of Septuagint (Torah)	c. 250

Seleucid Period	198–142
Antiochus IV Epiphanes's Reign	175–164
Maccabean Revolt	167–142
Book of Daniel Published	165
Hasmonean Period (Home Rule)	**142–63**
Roman Period	**63 BCE–324 CE**
Herod the Great's Reign	40–4
Philo	c. 20 BCE–50 CE
Birth of Jesus	c. 6 CE
Flavius Josephus	37–100
First Jewish Revolt vs. Rome	66–70
Rabbinic Judaism	70–present
"Council" of Jamnia	c. 100
Second Jewish Revolt vs. Rome	132–135
Mishnah Codified	c. 200
Byzantine Period	**324–640**
Palestinian Talmud Codified	c. 350
Babylonian Talmud Codified	c. 500

Christianity

Roman Period	**63 BCE–324 CE**
Birth of Jesus	c. 6 BCE
Ministry of Jesus	c. 27–30
Crucifixion of Jesus	c. 30
Apostolic Period	30–100
Paul's Missionary Journeys	47–58
Fall of Jerusalem	70
Separation from Judaism	c. 80
Patristic Period	**100–451**
Marcion	c. 85–c. 160
Valentinus	c. 100–c. 160
Justin Martyr	c. 100–c. 165
Irenaeus	c. 130–c. 200
Clement of Alexandria	150–c. 211
Tertullian	c. 160–c. 225
Hippolytus	170–235
Origen	185–254

Decian Persecution	249–251
Eusebius	265–339
Diocletian Persecution	303–311
Emperor Constantine's Reign	306–337
Epiphanius	c. 310–403
Edict of Milan	313
Council of Nicaea	325
Augustine of Hippo	354–430
Emperor Julian's Reign	361–363
Athanasius's New Testament Canon	367
Emperor Theodosius's Reign	379–395
Christianity as Roman State Religion	380
Council of Chalcedon	451

Bibliography

Anderson, Bernhard W. *Understanding the Old Testament*. 5th ed. Upper Saddle River, NJ: Pearson, 2007.
Armstrong, Karen. *A History of God*. New York: Ballantine, 1993.
Bickerman, Elias. *From Ezra to the Last of the Maccabees*. New York: Schocken, 1962.
Brakke, David. *Gnosticism: From Nag Hammadi to the Gospel of Judas*. Transcript Book. Chantilly, VA: The Great Courses, 2015.

———. *The Gnostics: Myth, Ritual, and Diversity in Early Christianity*. Cambridge, MA: Harvard University Press, 2010.

Bregman, Jay. "Logismos and Pistis." In *Pagan and Christian Anxiety: A Response to E. R. Dodds*, edited by Robert C. Smith and John Lounibos, 217–31. New York, University Press of America, 1984.
Brown, Raymond, et al. *The New Jerome Biblical Commentary*. Upper Saddle River, NJ: Prentice Hall, 1990.
Coogan, Michael D. *A Brief Introduction to the Old Testament*. New York: Oxford University Press, 2009.
Dodds, E. R. *Pagan & Christian in an Age of Anxiety*. New York: Norton, 1970.
Ehrman, Bart D. *A Brief Introduction to the New Testament*. 3rd ed. New York: Oxford University Press, 2013.

———. *Lost Christianities: The Battle for Scripture and the Faith We Never Knew*. New York: Oxford University Press, 2003.

Fowden, Garth. *The Egyptian Hermes: A Historical Approach to the Late Pagan Mind*. Princeton: Princeton University Press, 1988.
Gager, John. *The Origin of Anti-Semitism: Attitudes toward Judaism in Pagan and Christian Antiquity*. New York: Oxford University Press, 1983.
Greer, Rowan A. *Origen: Translation and Introduction*. The Classics of Western Spirituality. Ramsey, NJ: Paulist, 1979.
Head, Constance. *The Emperor Julian*. Boston: G. K. Hall, 1976.
Heine, Ronald E. *Origen: Scholarship in the Service of the Church*. Oxford: Oxford University Press, 2010.
Hovland, C. Warren, "The Dialogue Between Origen and Celsus." In *Pagan and Christian Anxiety: A Response to E. R. Dodds*, edited by Robert C. Smith and John Lounibos, 191–216. New York, University Press of America, 1984.

Hurtado, Larry W. *One God, One Lord: Early Christian Devotion and Ancient Jewish Monotheism*. Philadelphia: Fortress, 1988.

Jonas, Hans. *The Gnostic Religion: The Message of the Alien God and the Beginnings of Christianity*. Boston: Beacon, 1958.

Kee, Howard Clark, et al. *Christianity: A Social and Cultural History*. 2nd ed. Upper Saddle River, NJ: Prentice Hall, 1998.

Klauck, Hans-Joseph. *The Religious Context of Early Christianity: A Guide to Greco-Roman Religions*. Philadelphia: Fortress, 2003.

Lane, Eugene, and Ramsey MacMullen. *Paganism and Christianity: 100–425 CE: A Sourcebook*. 3rd ed. Philadelphia: Fortress, 2005.

Lane Fox, Robin. *Pagan and Christian*. New York: Alfred A. Knopf, 1987.

Lee, A. D. *Pagans and Christians in Late Antiquity: A Sourcebook*. New York: Routledge, 2000.

Lounibos, John. "Plotinus: Pagan, Mystic, Philosopher." In *Pagan and Christian Anxiety: A Response to E. R. Dodds*, edited by Robert C. Smith and John Lounibos, 131–66. New York, University Press of America, 1984.

Maxwell, Jaclyn. *The Oxford Handbook of Late Antiquity*. New York: Oxford University Press, 2012.

McLynn, Neil. *Being Christian in Late Antiquity*. New York: Oxford University Press, 2014.

Metzger, Bruce M. *An Introduction to the Apocrypha*. New York: Oxford University Press, 1957.

———. *The New Testament: Its Background, Growth, and Content*. Nashville: TN, 1965.

O'Donnell, James J. *Pagans: The End of Traditional Religion and the Rise of Christianity*. New York: Ecco, 2016.

Pearson, Birger A. *Gnosticism, Judaism, and Egyptian Christianity*. Minneapolis, Fortress, 1990.

Rivers, James. *Religion in the Roman Empire*. Malden, MA: Wiley-Blackwell, 2006.

Robinson, James M. *Nag Hammadi Library in English*. New York: Harper & Row, 1977.

Royalty, Robert M. *The Origin of Heresy: A History of Discourse in Second Temple Judaism and Early Christianity*. London: Routledge, 2012.

Rudolph, Kurt. *Gnosis: The Nature and History of Gnosticism*. San Francisco: HarperOne, 1987.

Seltzer, Robert M. *Jewish People, Jewish Thought: The Jewish Experience in History*. Upper Saddle River, NJ: Prentice Hall, 1980.

Simon, Marcel. *Verus Israel: A Study of the Relation between Christians and Jews in the Roman Empire (135–425)*. Translated by H. McKeating. New York: Oxford University Press, 1986.

Smith, Robert C., and John Lounibos. *Pagan and Christian Anxiety: A Response to E. R. Dodds*. New York, University Press of America, 1984.

Spong, John Shelby. *Liberating the Gospels: Reading the Bible with Jewish Eyes*. San Francisco: HarperSanFrancisco, 1996.

Tcherikover, Victor. *Hellenistic Civilization and the Jews*. Translated by S. Applebaum. New York: Atheneum, 1970.

Trigg, Joseph W. *Origen*. Atlanta: John Knox, 1983.

Turner, John D., and Ruth Majercik. *Gnosticism and Later Platonism: Themes, Figures, and Texts*. Atlanta: Society of Biblical Literature, 2000.

Vande Kappelle, Robert. "Evidence of a Jewish Proselytizing Tendency in the Old Greek (Septuagint) Version of the Book of Isaiah." PhD diss., Princeton Theological Seminary, 1977.

———. *Into Thin Places: One Man's Search for the Center*. Eugene, OR: Resource, 2010.

———. *The New Creation: Church History Made Accessible, Relevant, and Personal*. Eugene, OR: Wipf & Stock, 2018

———. *The Second Journey: Visions and Voices on First- and Second-Half-of-Life Spirituality*. Eugene, OR: Wipf & Stock, 2020.

Wiesel, Elie. *Night*. New York: Bantam, 1982.

Winston, David. *Philo of Alexandria*. The Classics of Western Spirituality. Ramsey, NJ: Paulist, 1981.

Wright, Robert. *The Evolution of God*. New York: Little, Brown, 2009.

Index

Abraham (patriarch), 30, 31, 32, 34, 38, 106, 118
Albright, William, 35, 36
Alexander the Great, ix, 14, 55, 63, 69, 72–73, 74–75
Alexandria (Egypt), 48, 73, 75, 76, 78, 81, 91, 92–93, 94, 97, 100, 139–40, 150, 153, 164
   See also Diaspora, Alexandrian
Anat (goddess), 46
angels, 34, 105–7, 165
animism, 3, 31, 32
anti-Judaism, 91–94, 96, 97, 119, 120, 121, 155
Antiochus III (ruler), 76, 77, 78
Antiochus IV (ruler), 79–81, 83–84
anti-Semitism, 49, 67, 92, 99, 116, 120, 121
apatheia, 21
Apocalypse of Peter, 11
apocalyptic genre, 57, 64, 65, 103, 104, 106, 139
Apocrypha, apocryphal, 77, 97, 103, 104, 128, 144
Apollonius of Tyana, 146, 153, 155
Apuleius, 148
Aramaic, 9, 46, 47, 60, 67, 90, 130
Aristeas, 75
   Letter of, 91, 97, 98. 99
Aristides, Aelius, 148
Aristotle, Aristotelianism, 13, 16, 17, 20, 72, 156, 159
Armstrong, Karen, 30

Asclepius (god), 148, 155, 162
Asherah (goddess), 36
Athanasius (bishop), 11
atheist, atheism, 4, 14, 30, 93, 100, 162
Augustine (bishop), 30, 70, 116, 151, 162, 163, 165
Augustus (emperor), 92, 93, 101

Baal (god), 31, 32, 36, 37, 39, 46
Babylon, Babylonia, 43, 44, 54, 73
Babylonian Exile, 39, 42, 44, 45, 48–52, 68, 76
Barnabas, epistle of, 11, 115–21
Bauer, Walter, 122–24, 125
Beard, Charles A., 67
belief
   in paganism, 5
   See also Christianity, and belief

Caesarea (Palestine), 121, 150, 158
Caligula (emperor), 92, 94
canon, canonical, 10, 119, 127–28, 130, 131, 134, 149, 157–58
Carthage, 11, 133, 150, 159
Celsus, 151, 152, 158, 159, 161, 162, 164, 165
Chalcedon, Council of, 116n2, 125
Christianity, 87, 102, 115, 125, 127, 165, 166
   and belief, 5–7
   and canonical process, 10, 125, 127–28, 131
   early, 70, 88, 127–44

178 INDEX

Christianity (continued)
  emergence of, 102, 111–13, 121–25
  and happiness, 16
  and Hellenism, 113–15
  and Judaism, 5–6, 15, 120
  and pagan philosophy, 15, 22, 23, 24, 25, 153, 162–63
  and paganism, 145, 150–60, 161, 162, 166
  and scripture, 7–12
  separation from Judaism, 113–15
  and Septuagint, 96–99
Chronicles (1 and 2), 45, 46, 51, 61
Cicero, 100
circumcision, 58, 83, 85, 102, 118, 119, 129
Claudius (emperor), 93
Clement, first letter of, 11, 123
Clement of Alexandria, 21, 150, 151, 153, 163, 164
Clement of Rome, 158
Constantine (emperor), 116, 121, 122, 124, 154, 155
creeds, 149, 158
Cynicism, 14
Cyrus (ruler), 49, 55, 56, 74

Daniel, book of, 51, 64n6, 66, 74, 80, 83, 84, 103, 104, 105, 106, 139
David (king), 30, 40, 42, 43, 52, 61
Dead Sea Scrolls, 60, 86, 98, 139
Decian persecution, 153, 154
Deuteronomistic History, 50, 59, 60
Diaspora, 9, 45, 68, 69, 74–77, 92, 93, 102, 156
  See also Egypt, Diaspora in
  Alexandrian, 48, 76, 91, 92–93, 94–95, 97, 100
  Asia Minor, 76
  Babylonian, 64, 69, 74–75
  definition of, 9n2, 88n4
  Syrian, 76
diatribe, 14, 78, 156
Diocletian persecution, 154, 162
Docetism, 132–33
Dodds, E. R., 162

Ebionites, 128–30, 131, 134, 142, 143

Ecclesiasticus. *See* Sirach
Egypt
  Jewish diaspora in, 46–47, 69, 75–76, 81–82, 96–97
  See also Diaspora, Alexandrian
El, Elohim, 32, 34, 36, 37, 38, 99
Elephantine, 46, 47, 82
Elijah (prophet), 33, 39, 65, 106
Enlightenment, 144
Enoch, book of, 104, 105, 139
Epicurus, Epicureanism, 13, 14
Epiphanius, 129, 142
episcopacy, 149, 156, 157, 158
Esdras, book 2 of, 104
Essenes, 70, 86
Esther, book of, 67
Eusebius, 119, 120, 121–22, 123, 124, 162
Ezekiel (prophet), 50, 65
  book of, 44–45, 46, 49, 58
Ezra, 50–51, 55, 61, 62–63, 66, 89
  book of, 60–61, 64
Ezra-Nehemiah, 45, 51, 60

Fackenheim, Emil, 167

Galen, 151, 152, 162
gematria, 118
Gnostic, Gnosticism, 10, 15, 22–23, 123, 132, 135, 137–38, 141, 143, 152, 157, 158, 164
  and Judaism, 138–39
  worldview, 136
God, 132
  doctrine of, 29–41
  as material being, 21
  and pagan gods, 98, 99, 148, 165
  as reason, 20, 21
  as source of all, 23
  as three "hypostases," 23
Gospel of Peter, 10, 119–21
Gospel of Philip, 10, 143
Gospel of Thomas, 10, 143
Gospel of Truth, 140–41, 143
Gregory of Nyssa, 165

Hadrian (emperor), 88, 147
Haggai, book of, 56, 65

INDEX

happiness, 16
Hasidim, 77, 81, 83, 84, 85, 86
Hasmoneans, 84–85
Hebrew scriptures (Old Testament),
    7–8, 56, 97, 98, 102, 103, 105,
    106, 115, 117, 141–42
  allegorical interpretation of, 95,
    131, 134, 153, 158
  doctrine of God in, 29–41
  and New Testament, 112, 116
Hecateus of Abdera, 75
Hellenism, 9, 63, 69, 74, 78, 80, 83, 85,
    91, 93
  and Judaism, 98
Hellenization, 72, 77, 79, 80–81, 85, 114
henotheism, 32, 34
heresy, 122, 129, 130, 140–41, 142,
    157–58
Hermeticism, 22, 163
Herod the Great, 82, 87–88, 89, 120
Hippolytus, 135
Holocaust, 167
Homer, 95, 153, 159
Hurtado, Larry, 106
hypostasis, 105
  definition of, 23

Ignatius, 149
Inge, W. R., 159
Irenaeus, 115, 116, 129, 135, 137, 150,
    157–58, 164
Isaiah of Jerusalem (prophet), 46, 51, 57
  See also Second Isaiah; Third Isaiah
Ishtar (goddess), 44, 48
Isis (goddess), 147, 149, 166
Islam, 4, 30, 58, 144

James the Just, 130
Jason of Cyrene, 76, 79
Jeremiah (prophet), 33, 43, 44
  book of, 49, 58, 59, 98
Jerome (theologian), 67
Jerusalem, 45, 61–62, 150
  first fall of, 44, 50, 57, 58
  as Greek *polis*, 80–81
  second fall of, 55, 86, 87, 88, 89, 92,
    96, 114, 115, 119, 120, 150
  third fall of, 87, 88

Jesus, 86, 87, 112, 115, 116, 120, 127,
    136, 138, 143, 145, 146–47,
    149, 153, 159, 165
  as Angel of the Lord, 106–7
  belief in, 6–7
  as Messiah, 6, 52, 114, 116, 120, 129
  as rabbi, 8, 116
  Second Coming of, 118
Jew, Jewish, Judaism, 4, 7, 58, 88, 91,
    96, 114, 119
  and belief, 6
  and cultural assimilation, 63, 69, 93
  definition of, 45
  and Diaspora, 9, 74–77
  distinguishing marks of, 58
  emergence of, 42, 50, 57
  and emergence of Christianity,
    111–15
  exilic, 42–52
  and Hellenism, 85, 98, 100–101
  Hellenistic, 45, 88n4, 91, 92, 94–95
  Intertestamental Literature, 102–5
  and monotheism, 29–41
  and pagans, 161
  Palestinian, 45, 67, 77–82, 87,
    88n4, 89, 91, 92, 102, 105
  postexilic, 54–70
  privileges, 91–92
  proselytism, 69–70, 98, 101–2, 112
  Rabbinic, 86, 88–90, 150
  and scripture, 7
Joel, book of, 65
John Hyrcanus, 79, 87
Jonah, book of, 66
Josephus, 75, 76, 78, 81n3, 82, 93, 94,
    95–96, 100, 156
Judah. *See* Southern Kingdom
Judas Maccabeus, 83–84, 85, 86
Judea, 77, 80, 81, 83, 87–88, 97
Judith, book of, 103–4
Julian (emperor), 151, 155–56, 165
Julius Caesar, 82, 92
Jupiter (god), 88, 146, 147
Justin Martyr, 115, 119, 150, 151, 157

Kaufmann, Yehezkel, 44

Lamentations, book of, 59

Late Judaism. *See* Restoration
Leontopolis (Egypt), 81–82
Letter of Aristeas, 97, 98
Letter to Flora, 141–42
Lucian of Samosota, 151

Maccabees, Maccabean period, 66, 67, 80, 83–85, 86
  book 1 of, 66, 79, 85, 91, 103
  book 2 of, 76, 79, 80, 85, 91, 103
  book 3 of, 91
  book 4 of, 91
Malachi, book of, 65
Manetho, 96–97, 99
Marcion, Marcionites, 11, 115, 123, 130–34, 142, 143, 152
  view of canon, 131
  view of God, 132
  view of Jesus, 132
Marcus Aurelius (emperor), 15, 147, 151, 152, 162
materialism, 21
Mishnah, 70, 89
monotheism, 32, 51, 58, 91, 98, 129, 134, 144, 148
  doctrine of, 29–41
Montanism, 160
Moses, 33, 34, 36, 38, 70, 94, 95, 96, 99, 106, 117
mystery religions, 147–48, 149
Mythra(s), Mithraism, 147, 166

Nabateans, 59
Nebuchadrezzar (Nebuchadnezzar), 43, 55, 68, 103
Nehemiah, 61–62, 64, 66
  book of, 58, 60–61
Neoplatonism, 13, 22–25, 78, 105, 155, 159, 163, 166
New Testament, 46, 60, 98, 106, 115, 123, 127, 134, 160
  allegorical interpretation of, 164
Nicaea, Council of, 121
Northern Kingdom, 42, 46
  fall of, 42, 45, 74

Obadiah, book of, 59, 60, 64
Oniads, 80–81

Origen, 116, 150, 151, 152, 153, 155, 158–59, 161, 163–65
Orpheus (god), 153
orthodoxy, 17, 122, 124, 125, 134, 144, 150
  proto-, xin1, 6, 124, 130, 133, 134, 135, 141, 142, 143, 150, 156

pagan, paganism, 3–7, 70, 93, 145–47, 162, 165, 167, 168
  and belief, 5, 145
  and Christians, 150–60
  definition of, x–xi
  demise of, 165–66
  and ethics, 5, 145
  and monotheism, 148
  philosophy, 13–25
Palestine, 9n1, 48, 68, 73–74, 78, 83, 85, 86, 95, 111
  definition of, 88
Paul, 6, 9, 15, 16, 78, 86, 89, 102, 105, 112, 113, 115, 117, 122, 123, 125, 127, 129–30, 131, 132, 133, 134, 138, 149, 153, 162, 163, 165
Pentateuch. *See* Torah
Persia, 54–70, 72, 73, 84
Petra, 59
Pharisees, 7, 70, 86, 87, 89, 104
Philo, 15, 76, 78, 91, 94–95, 99, 100, 105n3, 156, 163
Plato, Platonism, 13, 15, 17–20, 23, 94, 95, 135, 153, 156, 159, 163
Plotinus, 13, 22–25, 78, 151, 153, 163
Plutarch, 148
polytheism, 31–32, 33, 99, 129
Pompey (general), 85, 87
Porphyry, 22, 25, 151, 155, 162, 165
Posidonius, 15
postmodernism, x, 144, 168
primal peoples, 3
prophecy, 65
proselytism. *See* Jew, proselytism
Ptolemies, 68, 74, 80, 81, 82, 85, 94
Ptolemy (Valentinian author), 141–42
Ptolemy I, 74, 75, 76
Ptolemy II, 75, 96, 97, 98
Ptolemy VI, 81, 82

Ptolemy VIII, 81, 92
Pythagoras, Pythagorean, 13, 95, 146, 148, 153, 155

Rabbinic Judaism. *See* Jews, Rabbinic
rabbis, 89, 92
religion, 29–30
    Greco-Roman, 3–7
Restoration (Second Temple) period, 45, 54, 56, 63, 66, 67, 68, 105
Revelation, book of, 9, 11, 45, 65, 104, 118n3
Roman empire, 68, 86–87, 92, 100, 138, 139, 147
    Christianization of, 162, 163, 166
Rome, 83, 84, 87, 89
    Christians in, 123–24, 131, 133, 139–40, 150, 157
    Jews in, 93
royal theology, 42, 43, 52

Sabbath, 58, 63, 83, 92, 101, 113, 118, 129, 156
Sadducees, 7, 70, 85–86, 87, 89
Samaria, 45, 46, 47, 61, 68, 73, 87
Sanhedrin, 89
Second Isaiah, 39, 45, 46, 49, 51, 57, 58, 64, 66, 70
Second Temple Judaism. *See* Restoration
Seleucids, 68, 74, 77–82, 85
Septuagint, 9, 67, 77, 91, 95, 96–99, 113
Shema, 33, 58
Sibylline Oracles (Jewish), 91, 99–100
Sirach, book of, 77–78, 104
Smith, Huston, 167
Smith, Morton, 40
Socrates, 18, 19
Solomon (king), 42, 51, 52, 78
Sophists, 18, 20
Southern Kingdom, 42, 43, 44, 45, 46, 57, 63, 64, 72, 73, 74

Stoic, Stoicism, 13, 14–15, 21–22, 78, 95
supersessionism, 119
synagogues, 50, 55, 89, 92, 98, 100–102, 112, 114

Talmud, 70, 74, 89–90
Targum, 60, 90
Tcherikover, Victor, 77
temple, first, 43, 48, 49, 50
temple, second, 54, 55, 56–57, 63, 150
Ten Commandments, 33, 141, 142, 156
Tertullian, 116, 119, 133, 134, 135, 140, 150, 151, 159–60, 166
Theodosius (emperor), 155
theurgy, 163
Third Isaiah, 58, 64, 65, 70
Tiberius (emperor), 76, 93
Titus (emperor), 96
Tobiads, 80
Torah, 7, 33, 46, 49, 51, 55, 56, 62, 68, 69, 70, 78, 97, 98, 103, 112, 167
totemism, 31
Trinity, doctrine of, 133, 159

Valentinus, Valentinians, 137–42, 143, 164
Vespasian (emperor), 96
Vulgate, the, 67

Wellhausen, Julius, 31, 32
Wiesel, Elie, 166–67
Wisdom literature, 51, 56, 67, 77–78, 104, 105, 159
Wisdom of Solomon, 11, 77, 78, 91, 104

Zealots, 86–87, 88
Zechariah, book of, 56, 64, 65
Zeno, 21, 159
Zerubbabel, 56, 65
Zeus (god), 83, 146

www.ingramcontent.com/pod-product-compliance
Lightning Source LLC
Chambersburg PA
CBHW062045220426
43662CB00010B/1663